MASCULINE VIRTUE IN EARLY MODERN SPAIN

New Hispanisms
Cultural and Literary Studies

Series editor: Anne J. Cruz

New Hispanisms: Literary and Cultural Studies presents innovative studies that seek to understand how the cultural production of the Hispanic world is generated, disseminated, and consumed. Ranging from the Spanish Middle Ages to modern Spain and Latin America, this series offers a forum for various critical and disciplinary approaches to cultural texts, including literature and other artifacts of Hispanic culture. Queries and proposals for single author volumes and collections of original essays are welcome.

Medical Cultures of the Early Modern Spanish Empire
Edited by John Slater, Maríaluz López-Terrada, and José Pardo-Tomás

Memory and Spatiality in Post-Millennial Spanish Narrative
Lorraine Ryan

The Formation of the Child in Early Modern Spain
Edited by Grace E. Coolidge

Masculinity and Queer Desire in Spanish Enlightenment Literature
Mehl Allan Penrose

Masculine Virtue in Early Modern Spain

SHIFRA ARMON

ASHGATE

© Shifra Armon 2015

All rights reserved. No part of this publication may be reproduced, stored in a retrieval system or transmitted in any form or by any means, electronic, mechanical, photocopying, recording or otherwise without the prior permission of the publisher.

Shifra Armon has asserted her right under the Copyright, Designs and Patents Act, 1988, to be identified as the author of this work.

Published by
Ashgate Publishing Limited
Wey Court East
Union Road
Farnham
Surrey, GU9 7PT
England

Ashgate Publishing Company
110 Cherry Street
Suite 3-1
Burlington, VT 05401-3818
USA

www.ashgate.com

British Library Cataloguing in Publication Data
A catalogue record for this book is available from the British Library

The Library of Congress has cataloged the printed edition as follows:
Armon, Shifra, 1956–
  Masculine virtue in early modern Spain / by Shifra Armon.
    pages cm. — (New hispanisms: cultural and literary studies)
  Includes bibliographical references and index.
    ISBN 978-1-4724-4189-8 (hardcover : alk. paper) — ISBN 978-1-4724-4190-4 (ebook)— ISBN 978-1-4724-4191-1 (epub) 1. Spanish drama—Classical period, 1500–1700—History and criticism. 2. Masculinity in literature. I. Title.
  PQ6102.A76 2015
  862'.30935211—dc23

2014037443

ISBN: 9781472441898 (hbk)
ISBN: 9781472441904 (ebk – PDF)
ISBN: 9781472441911 (ebk – ePUB)

Printed in the United Kingdom by Henry Ling Limited, at the Dorset Press, Dorchester, DT1 1HD

A mi querido Guille

Contents

List of Figures	*ix*
Acknowledgements	*xi*
Introduction: *Homo Agens*	1
1 Masculinity, Conduct, and Empire	21
2 Fame	41
3 Dissimulation	65
4 Adaptability	95
Epilogue	121
Bibliography	*125*
Index	*139*

List of Figures

I.1 "A Compass for Courtly Conduct." Gabriel de la Gasca y Espinosa, *Manual de avisos para el perfecto cortesano*, 1681, Madrid. General Collection, National Library of Spain.   3

1.1 "Qui a secretis ab omnibus," Empresa 56. Diego Saavedra Fajardo, *Idea de un príncipe politico christiano*, 1675, Valencia. The Harold and Mary Jean Hanson Rare Books Collection, Special & Area Studies Collections, George A. Smathers Libraries, University of Florida.   39

1.2 "Sceptrorum imitatio potentissima," Emblem 29. Juan de Solórzano Pereira, *Emblemata centum regio politica*, 1653, Madrid.   40

3.1 "In Aulicos," Emblem 86. Andrea Alciati, *V.C. Emblemata*, 4 ed., 1591, Leiden. The Harold and Mary Jean Hanson Rare Books Collection, Special & Area Studies Collections, George A. Smathers Libraries, University of Florida.   67

3.2 "Bellum collegit qui discordias seminant," Empresa 75. Diego Saavedra Fajardo, *Idea de un príncipe político christiano*, 1675, Valencia. The Harold and Mary Jean Hanson Rare Books Collection, Special & Area Studies Collections, George A. Smathers Libraries, University of Florida.   82

3.3 "Formosa superne," Empresa 78. Diego Saavedra Fajardo, *Idea de un príncipe político christiano*, 1675, Valencia. The Harold and Mary Jean Hanson Rare Books Collection, Special & Area Studies Collections, George A. Smathers Libraries, University of Florida.   83

3.4 "Siempre el mismo," Empresa 33. Diego Saavedra Fajardo, *Idea de un príncipe político christiano*, 1675, Valencia. The Harold and Mary Jean Hanson Rare Books Collection, Special & Area Studies Collections, George A. Smathers Libraries, University of Florida.   85

3.5 "A deo," Empresa 18. Diego Saavedra Fajardo, *Idea de un príncipe político christiano*, 1675, Valencia. The Harold and Mary Jean Hanson Rare Books Collection, Special & Area Studies Collections, George A. Smathers Libraries, University of Florida.   86

3.6 "Ut sciat regnare," Empresa 43. Diego Saavedra Fajardo, *Idea de un príncipe político christiano*, 1675, Valencia. The Harold and Mary Jean Hanson Rare Books Collection, Special & Area Studies Collections, George A. Smathers Libraries, University of Florida.   87

3.7 "Nec a quo nec ad quem," Empresa 44. Diego Saavedra Fajardo, *Idea de un príncipe político christiano*, 1675, Valencia. The Harold and Mary Jean Hanson Rare Books Collection, Special & Area Studies Collections, George A. Smathers Libraries, University of Florida.   88

3.8 "Non majestate securus," Empresa 45. Diego Saavedra Fajardo, *Idea de un príncipe político christiano*, 1675, Valencia. The Harold and Mary Jean Hanson Rare Books Collection, Special & Area Studies Collections, George A. Smathers Libraries, University of Florida.   89

3.9 "Sub luce lues," Empresa 48. Diego Saavedra Fajardo, *Idea de un príncipe político christiano*, 1675, Valencia. The Harold and Mary Jean Hanson Rare Books Collection, Special & Area Studies Collections, George A. Smathers Libraries, University of Florida.   90

3.10 "Nulli patet," Empresa 62. Diego Saavedra Fajardo, *Idea de un príncipe político christiano*, 1675, Valencia. The Harold and Mary Jean Hanson Rare Books Collection, Special & Area Studies Collections, George A. Smathers Libraries, University of Florida.   91

Acknowledgements

Many hands, eyes, and hearts have helped to bring this book into print. I have received generous institutional support from the University of Florida Office of the Provost, the College of Liberal Arts and Sciences, the UF Center for the Humanities and the Public Sphere, and the Department of Spanish and Portuguese Studies. I have benefitted from sharing my work-in-progress with colleagues across campus through the Center for the Humanities' seminars, the Center for Women's Studies and Gender Research's brown-bag lunches, and my own department's *Entre Nos Colloquia*. Three colleagues in particular who have supported me through thick and thin are my department chair, Gillian Lord, my esteemed colleague in French, William Calin, and Bonnie Effros, Rothman Chair and Director of the UF Center for the Humanities and the Public Sphere. I would also like to thank my graduate and undergraduate seminar students for joining me on this detour from the canon. They deserve extra credit for braving the esoteric world of emblematics; for puzzling over not-so-funny-anymore Renaissance quips; for untangling Baroque plot lines with me; and for tempering indignation over early modern gender codes with a measure of curiosity.

Colleagues around the country and the world have opened doors, extended invitations, hosted conferences, and inspired me with their leadership, scholarship, and guidance. The list begins with Harry Sieber, continues with Edward Baker, and would not be complete without the names of Charles Ganelin, Diane Marting, Joe Schraibman, Emilie Bergmann, Meg Greer, Nieves Romero-Díaz, Laura Bass, Adrienne Martín, Mechthild Albert, Rafael Bonilla Cerezo, Lía Schwartz-Lerner, Jim Parr, and Ed Friedman. I owe a special debt of gratitude to Anne Cruz for her vision and dedication in founding a statewide Cervantes Symposium in Florida. Our annual meetings are an ongoing source of learning and comradery. Regarding emblems and *empresas* in the book, I hasten to thank Samuel Huang, Curator of Rare Books at UF's Smathers Libraries, who took great pains to obtain high resolution reproductions of Diego Saavedra Fajardo's *empresas* from the collection. Dennis Sears, Public Programs Manager of the University of Illinois Urbana Champaign Rare Books and Manuscripts Library kindly expedited digital processing of Juan de Solórzano Pereira's Emblem 29. When the image of Gabriel de la Gasca's wind rose arrived from the Biblioteca Nacional marred by bleed-through from the anverso type, Tom Summerford at the UF Online office volunteered to do a digital clean-up before I even thought to ask. Also, I am grateful to unnamed referees of two journals for their invaluable suggestions: the Universidad Complutense de Madrid's *Ingenium*, which published an earlier iteration of my analysis of dissimulation in the *Galateo español* in 2011, and *Comedia Performance*, which included my initial observations concerning Neostoic constancy in *El perro del hortelano* in its 2013 issue.

The people who have given me new eyes—almost literally—are Dr. George Kornfeld of Rochester, NY, and Dr. Marc Gannon of Ft. Lauderdale, Florida. Madeline Davidson and Mary Ann Hastings of the Florida DOBS have also provided invaluable visual resources and support. I am very grateful to all of the members of my family: Armons, Shimbergs, Freemans, Grays, Sayre-Littles, and their flourishing offshoots. Most of all, I thank my husband, William Little, for his unstinting editorial assistance, encouragement, wisdom, and irrepressible love.

Introduction
Homo Agens

[No] todos los caballeros pueden ser cortesanos, ni todos los cortesanos pueden ni deben ser andantes: de todos ha de haber en el mundo; y aunque todos seamos caballeros, va mucha diferencia de los unos a los otros.[1]

[[Not] all knights can be courtiers, and not all courtiers can or should be knights errant; there has to be some of each in the world; and although we are all knights, there is a vast difference between us.][2]

A Compass for Conduct

Historians generally concur that Spain slipped from preeminence on the world stage some time during the latter half of the seventeenth century.[3] Spain's political decline is likewise thought to have accompanied a parallel muting of cultural vigor. The end of Spain's literary "Golden Age," for example, is said to coincide with the death of playwright Pedro Calderón de la Barca in the year 1681. However, in that year, a slim conduct manual, Gabriel de la Gasca y Espinosa's *Manual de avisos para el perfecto cortesano* [Advice manual for the perfect courtier] was published in Madrid. De la Gasca served as royal secretary to Charles II of Spain. His *Manual de avisos* asserted that even the near-divine person of the king could commit errors. Like contemporaneous skeptical philosophers Baltasar Álamos

---

[1] Don Quixote is explaining to the Housekeeper the difference between courtiers and knights errant (672). All Spanish quotations are from the Spanish edition of *Don Quijote* by the Instituto Cervantes, Editorial Crítica (1998).

[2] II.6, 672; Grossman 492. Translation paginations refer to Edith Grossman's translation of *Don Quixote*. All other translations throughout this volume, except where noted, are my own.

[3] Portugal and Catalonia revolted in 1640. Spain lost Portugal, but managed to maintain control of Catalonia. The Peace of Westphalia treaty of 1648 cut off Spanish access to the Netherlands, while the Peace of the Pyrenees treaty of 1659 obliged Philip IV against his will to wed his eldest daughter, María Teresa, to Louis XIV of France. John Elliott, *España y su mundo*, takes issue with many entrenched details of the decline narrative, but even after "shuffling the deck" of causal factors, he concludes that the economic crisis that Castile suffered from 1590 to 1620 gave rise to the country's political crisis of 1640 (271–98). It should be noted that Kamen denies the decline "myth" on the grounds that Spain never actually "rose" in the first place.

de Barrientos and Antonio López de Vega, Gabriel de la Gasca subjected the monarch's capacity for decision-making to the "disenchanting light of reason."[4]

De la Gasca's guidebook did not presume to correct the monarch directly: it was not a guide to princes, but rather a guide for royal advisors, following in the tradition of Castiglione's *Il libro del cortegiano* [Book of the Courtier] (1528), Antonio de Guevara's *Aviso de privados y despertador de cortesanos* [Advice to favorites and wake-up call to courtiers] (1539), and Francisco de Quevedo's *Discurso de las privanzas* [Discourse on favorites] (1606–08). Moreover, despite its name, the *Manual de avisos* was actually an anti-manual that called for an "end of conduct"; that is, an end of axiomatic approaches to the education of the courtier.[5] De la Gasca recognized the urgency of preparing the man of court to assist the monarch in making decisions of state. As we will see in greater detail in Chapter 4, De la Gasca compared the court secretary (and, by extension, all royal advisors) to the captain of a ship at sea, who must continually adjust his course to accommodate changing winds and currents. No a priori set of rules could be counted upon to anticipate the combinatory factors at play for any given scenario. To illustrate this maritime conceit, De la Gasca indulged in a visual pun familiar to readers at that time of sailing vessels: he inserted a fold-out illustration of a compass dial, or wind rose, into his *Manual*.

Comparing the exercise of choice to piloting a ship was not a new idea in De la Gasca's day. Plato, in Book VI of *The Republic* (c. 380 BCE), had compared the commander of state to a navigator. De la Gasca adapted this well-known metaphor to a technological advance of his day: the mariner's needle. The mariner's needle resting on a round dial evoked for De la Gasca the array of options available to the court secretary when advising on decisions of state or composing court documents.

---

[4] Barrionuevo's *Tácito español* [Spanish Tacitus] of 1614 recommended that leaders of state follow moral precepts only once they had been proven efficacious by prior example. Antonio López de Vega composed an influential dialogue, the *Heráclito y Diógenes de nuestro siglo* (1641), that challenged the unreliability of sense perception and questioned blind acceptance of unproven claims. López de Vega's skeptical protagonist, Democritus, declares that "en el desconsuelo de tan forzosas tinieblas a los humanos ojos, saben acomodarse a creer y a determinar, si muy poco por infalible, algo, por lo menos, por verosímil y probable [wise men compensate for the dispiriting murkiness of the human eye's perception by believing and deciding things that, while not infallible, are at least credible and likely]" (306; qtd in Robbins, "Scepticism" 180). Democritus therefore subjects his view of the world to "la desengañada luz de la razón [disenchanting light of reason]" (9, qtd in Robbins 180). In *Arts of Perception*, Jeremy Robbins argues that Spanish skeptical philosophers, by questioning both received wisdom and sense perceptions, laid the groundwork for the development of an Enlightenment epistemology based on observation and method.

[5] I appropriate the phrase "end of conduct" from Correll, who situates Friedrich Dedekind's *Grobianus*, a German satirical manual of indecent behavior, within the conduct guide tradition. My use of the term refers to De la Gasca's disavowal of fixed paradigms and an end of rules for conduct.

Introduction

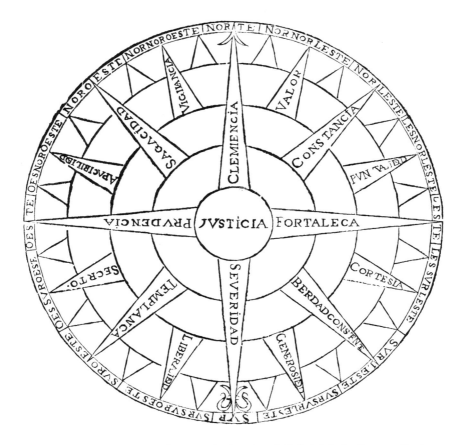

Fig. I.1   "A Compass for Courtly Conduct." Gabriel de la Gasca y Espinosa, *Manual de avisos para el perfecto cortesano*, 1681, Madrid. General Collection, National Library of Spain.

When writing diplomatic correspondence, for example, combining the proper salutation, honorifics, linguistic register, and overall tone began with empirical observation of the situation at hand. Was this a petition? A recommendation for reform? A complaint? A reply? If the document originated with the king, it was necessary to determine whether it was a brief, a grant of favor or reward, a proclamation, a request, etc. Once the secretary had reviewed the repository of choices available to him, a process of rational selection followed. His decisions were extemporaneous, but by no means random, and they were governed by circumstance, not precept. The final document corresponded precisely to the power relationship of sender and recipient, gravity of the matter at hand, and nature of the missive. The only two universal principles that De la Gasca permitted the royal secretary to fall back on were equanimity and generosity:

la mesura se debe templar con la discreción de calidad, que evitando la lisonja necia, por ningún modo se falte de un punto a dar a cada cual la cortesía cumplida que corresponde a su estado, y merecimiento; y caso que haya descuido, es más disculpable el alargarla, que acortarla, porque puede engendrar odio; y d[e] él ¿qué se puede esperar? La total perdición. Y el exceso de la cortesía, que no es declarada lisonja, queda en afabilidad.[6]

[moderation should be tempered with discretion such that, while avoiding foolish flattery, the letter should never depart even one iota from the courtesy owed to the status and attainments of each correspondent. In the event that there is a slip-up, it is more pardonable to defer too much than too little, since the latter can provoke hatred, and what could come of that? Utter failure. An excess of politeness, as long as it is not altogether fatuous, suggests cordiality.] (60)

De la Gasca's *Manual de avisos* functioned as a navigational instrument—a compass for conduct—rather than a book of immutable rules. The ideal courtier that emerges from the pages of De la Gasca's writing manual announces the advent of a reasoning agent, not a masculine subject in crisis or decline. Yet the narrative of Spain's decadence and the monarchy's accompanying eclipse by England and France in the latter half of the seventeenth century have dampened inquiry into currents of intellectual innovation that did prevail under the latter Hapsburgs. De la Gasca merits recognition as a strong proto-Enlightenment voice rather than an obscure retainer at the court of the notoriously rachitic and enfeebled king, Charles II. De la Gasca chose the genre of the conduct manual on which to stake his literary legacy. To appreciate his achievement, it is necessary to link De la Gasca's concern for fashioning a perfect man of court to the literary and historical currents that nourished it. Conduct literature—writings that prompt reflection about the art of social interaction—assembled in print the distinguishing acts that constituted normative masculinity and femininity at the Spanish imperial court. From 1500 to 1700, Spanish presses unleashed a vast outpouring of utopian, prescriptive, and descriptive ideations of noble conduct. But the discourse on noble conduct did not stop at the didactic treatises per se. The search for texts that prompted reflection about the art of sociability reached deep into more popular literary territories as well.

Spain was Europe's first post-Medieval empire. As the royal court in Madrid rose and fell from prominence, Spanish playwrights, poets, novelists, and social theorists vied with one another to envisage the ideal servant of this new state: the Spanish courtier. How could this subject, gendered male under the law, best serve the changing needs of an increasingly centralized, bureaucratized, and globalized polity that had only just begun calling itself Spain?[7] By tracing the circulation of

---

[6] Original spellings have been modernized except in cases where the old spelling is deemed useful.

[7] When the Spanish monarch Charles I was crowned Holy Roman Emperor Charles V in 1519, Spain could truly call itself an empire. But upon Charles V's abdication of the Spanish throne in 1556, the title of Holy Roman Emperor passed to his brother, Ferdinand of

literary responses to this question, I am inaugurating a genealogy of masculine virtue. This discursive framework restores De la Gasca's *Manual de avisos para el perfecto cortesano* to a meaningful place within the history of masculinity in Spain. In addition, it offers a counter-narrative of cultural vigor that places in doubt the standard narrative of Spain's cultural anemia, in particular the notion that there occurred a "crisis" of masculinity in the latter half of the seventeenth century.

Masculinity as Social Performance

Masculinity and femininity have been theorized as regulatory practices (Foucault), signifiers denoting power imbalances (Scott), and performances (Butler, *Gender Trouble*). Gender can be seen to interpellate physical bodies, psyches, social roles, groups, even entire discourses (Dutch). Discussions about gender (and even sex according to Butler, *Bodies that Matter*) can hinge on biology, developmental psychology, anthropology, or philosophy. One starting point for analyzing textual representations of masculinity is the general consensus that gender "itself" does not exist, embodied and unmediated, somewhere beyond language or action. To the contrary, speech and action produce and reproduce gender, and it is in speech and action that gender's recombinations and relocations occur.

A second pillar of contemporary gender studies is the adoption of plurality as a theoretical response to hegemonic beliefs and stereotypes that freeze both men and women into untenable positions. In this vein, Judith Kegan Gardiner writes that masculinity is not one static thing,

> but the confluence of multiple processes and relationships with variable results for differing individuals, groups, institutions and societies. Although dominant or hegemonic forms of masculinity work constantly to maintain an appearance of permanence, stability, and naturalness, the numerous masculinities in every society are contingent, fluid, socially and historically constructed, changeable and constantly changing, variously institutionalized, and recreated through media representations and individual and collective performances. (11)

In order to replace the static sociotypes of "knight," "courtier," "nobleman," "royal advisor," etc. with more nuanced concepts of early modern gender, it is advisable to conceive of masculinity as a repertoire of acts that changes over time. "[G]ender ought not to be construed as a stable identity or locus of agency from which various acts follow," argues Judith Butler in *Gender Trouble*,

---

Austria. Thereafter, the "empire" technically denoted Austrian lands, and Spanish territories became known as the "Spanish Monarchy." As John Elliott explains, "Su Monarca no era un emperador, sino un Rey que gobernaba sobre un aglomerado de territorios conocidos como la *Monarquía Española*, entre los que se contaban la propia España, las posesiones del Rey en Italia y el norte de Europa y sus territorios americanos (llamados por los españoles *las Indias*)" (*España* 27).

rather gender is an identity tenuously constituted in time, instituted in an exterior space through a *stylized repetition of acts*. This formulation moves the conception of gender off the ground of a substantial model of identity to one that requires a conception of gender as a constituted social temporality. (140–41)

Masculinity comes into being as an assemblage of acts or socially signifying gestures. "Gestures are signs," explains Jacques Revel, referencing the rise of conduct literature in Europe, "and as such can be organized into a language, interpreted and read as moral, psychological, and social markers" (170). Conduct literature teaches those distinctive gestures that *tenuously constitute* manliness at a given moment, and such texts make those gestures available for readers to imitate and perform. Viewed diachronically from 1500 to 1700 these texts also exhibit the instability of gender identity over time.

To the extent that the present volume addresses gender in terms of social interactions, performances, and processes, this is a book about *homo agens*, "man the doer." Why *homo agens*? Why not *homo sapiens* [man the knower] or *homo ludens* [man the player]?[8] At first it may appear that this narrowing of the range of inquiry to the external acts that signify masculinity represents a return to the idea that the object of poetic imitation is human action, as Aristotle maintained in the *Poetics*.[9] Evidencing the pervasive influence that Aristotelian poetics exerted on Spanish literary precept, humanist Francisco Cascales wrote in 1606:

> La poética es arte de imitar con palabras. Imitar es representar y pintar el vivo de las acciones de los hombres, naturaleza de las cosas, y diversos géneros de personas de la misma manera que suelen ser y tratarse.
>
> [Poetics is the art of imitating with words. Imitating is representing and painting the liveliness of men's actions, the nature of things, and the diverse kinds of people in the same way that they normally exist and relate to each other.] (*Tablas poéticas* [Poetic tables] Tabla 1, qtd. in Rivas Hernández 84)

Since literature about conduct does "paint the vitality of men's actions" in social relationship, restricting the scope of the word 'masculinity' to figurations of

---

[8] In *Homo ludens* (1949), Huizinga anticipated speech-act theory with the concept of *homo ludens*, man the player. For Huizinga, many kinds of social reciprocity including boasting, war, and gift-giving resemble a competitive game that conforms to certain rules.

[9] In the *Poetics*, Aristotle writes, "It clearly follows that the poet or 'maker' should be the maker of plots rather than of verses; since he is a poet because he imitates, and *what he imitates are actions*. And even if he chances to take a historical subject, he is none the less a poet; for there is no reason why some events that have actually happened should not conform to the law of the probable and possible, and in virtue of that quality in them he is their poet or maker" (Section 1, Part IX). While the *Poetics* was never completely lost in Spain thanks to Averroës's twelfth-century Arabic translation and Mantinus of Tortosa's fourteenth-century Latin translation, it was Robortello's Latin translation with commentary, the *In librum Aristotelis de arte poetica explicationes* (1548) that led to widespread revival of Aristotelian poetics in Spain.

outward behavior might initially appear as an attempt to align with prevailing Renaissance theories of mimesis.

The diffusion of Aristotelian precept in Spain, however, did not preclude contestation. Dramatist Lope de Vega (1562–1635), in his anti-Aristotelian *Arte nuevo de hacer comedias* [New art of writing plays] (1609), defied critics dissatisfied with his radically reception-driven style to return to their Aristotle (see Chapter 4). In the realm of lyric poetry, Luis de Góngora (1561–1627) cultivated an equally anti-Aristotelian poetics of difficulty. For Góngora and his followers, the purpose of art was to beautify rather than to imitate. Jesuit social theorist Baltasar Gracián (1601–58) valorized this aestheticizing impulse in the *Agudeza y arte de ingenio* [*Art of Wit*]:

> El entendimiento, pues, como primera y principal potencia, álzase con la prima del artificio, con lo extremado del primor, en todas sus diferencias de objetos. Destínanse las Artes a estos artificios, que para su composición fueron inventadas, adelantando siempre y facilitando su perfección.
>
> [Understanding, since it is the first and foremost power [of the mind], when augmented by the imposing elegance of artifice, heightens its impact upon all of its multifarious objects. The Arts promote and perfect these artifices, which they were invented to create.] (Discurso 2; 317)

There being no agreement over literary theory or style in Golden Age letters—no single unifying preceptive school—the value of hewing to the organizing principle of *homo agens* does not lie in matching my critical approach to those available to early modern readers (see Rivas Hernández). Instead, conceiving of manliness as a repertoire of face-to-face behaviors provides a bridge that links early modern concepts of agency to modern gender theory.

Inasmuch as Butler situates gender in the realm of action rather than cognition or production, her view of identity fits closely with post-Tridentine doctrine, which defined a person's character before God largely in terms of good works. The Council of Trent (1545–63) repudiated Protestantism, in part, by denying that faith or providence alone sufficed to guarantee salvation. Faith was to be accompanied by pious deeds. Calderón de la Barca's *auto sacramental* (allegorical Corpus Christi pageant) *El gran teatro del mundo* [*The Great Theater of the World*] (c. 1633) forcefully endorsed the primacy of good deeds in manifesting the true self by dramatizing a direct relationship between ultimate identity (everlasting salvation) and good performance in the "theater" of this world. The play revolves around the conceit of life as a stage, with God as judge of the performances of each actor. Calderón's *auto* stages the moments of birth and death as the borrowing and returning of temporary stage props to be used during temporal life. Beauty (a vain and beautiful woman), for instance, receives a bouquet, and the king receives a crown, but all props are relinquished on Judgment Day. "Obrar bien que Dios es Dios [Perform well for God is God]" (61, line 667), exhorts the allegorical figure of Law, as if trying to throw Calderón's characters their lines. Poverty (a beggar) and Discretion (a nun) heed Law's stage-whisper by "acting their parts" well, while Wealth (a rich man) dismisses her prompt and denies alms to Poverty. Driving home the direct causal link between acting well and divine reward, Poverty and Discretion receive eternal glory as a reward for their good performances, but Wealth is punished with damnation.[10]

Counter-Reformation theology shares with Butler's performative formulation of gender the linking of identity with ephemeral performance rather than with essential being or mere bodily appearance. Just as *El gran teatro del mundo* promises salvation to those who obey Divine Law, so too the aristocratic vassal could expect reward only if he rendered obeisance to his earthly king. Social historian Antonio Maravall calls the enactment of obedience to the sovereign "colaboración positiva en el poder [collaborative exercise of power]" (*Teoría del estado* 322):

> Sólo en régimen de sociedad y, consiguientemente, en obediencia a un poder, los hombres pueden *ejercer virtudes* y *realizar con eficacia actos para lograr ciertos bienes* que fuera de aquel estado no son posibles.

> [Only within a social regime, and hence subject to a hierarchy of power, can men *exercise their virtues* and *effectively act to garner certain benefits*. In the absence of this state of obedience to a higher power, such efforts and rewards would not be possible.] (323, emphasis added)

Military service, financial aid to the Crown, diplomatic cooperation, and forging alliances could secure favor from the monarch. However, sociability—that is, the art of pleasing others—also served to publicize the nobleman's collaboration with the powers at court.

Secular conduct literature held out the carrot of admiration, favorable marriage alliances, and social ascent to those who acted in accordance with codes of manly propriety. But fear of public shame acted as a powerful stick that also incentivized compliance with norms of sociability. What nobleman, after all, would care to be thought by Critilo of Baltasar Gracián's *El Criticón* [*The Critic*] (1651–57) to dwell among the uncouth?

> así lo más del mundo no son sino corrales de hombres incultos, de naciones bárbaras y fieras, sin policía, sin cultura, sin artes y sin noticias, provincias habitadas de monstruos de la herejía, de gentes que no se pueden llamar personas sino fieras.

> [well, most of the places in the world are nothing but barnyards filled with uncouth men; barbaric, fierce and lawless nations without culture, without arts, without a clue; backwaters infested with monstrous deviants, with people who cannot be called persons but wild beasts.] (III Crisi 9, "Felisinda descubierta"; 1437)

---

[10] Three characters whose actions are mixed—Laborer, Beauty, and King—are sent to purgatory prior to being saved, while an unbaptized Child, who dies before having the chance to act at all, is sent into everlasting purgatory.

Critilo here establishes a binary opposition between civilized men and animals, whether domesticated or wild. To avoid disgrace, it was necessary to shed one's beastly cluelessness and cultivate the art of manly conduct. However, that art underwent notable changes from 1500 to 1700.

The present volume aims to forge a genealogy of masculine conduct as figured forth in secular print culture during the period from 1500 to 1700. Certainly, books were not the only source for imparting a repertoire of socially signifying acts. Painting comprised another persuasive medium. Print was nonetheless the most novel and effective technology for the diffusion of new social practices during the early modern period, and also one of the most enduring. *Masculine Virtue in Early Modern Spain* flows directly from and, in a sense, may be seen to complement my first book, *Picking Wedlock*. In that volume, I shifted attention away from "Cervantes & Co."[11]—that is, canonical male authors—to consider how and why women wrote recreational fiction in seventeenth-century Spain and Portugal. In the present instance, while it might appear exclusionary to limit the scope of this investigation to manly conduct with only limited reference to contemporary practices of femininity, I believe that this "exclusion" is justified.

Burning brightly at the methodological heart of this book is the question that Joan Gadol Kelly asks in her groundbreaking essay, "Did Women Have a Renaissance?" While much evidence suggests that norms of manly conduct underwent a dynamic series of far-reaching transformations from 1500 to 1700, female norms of sociability developed along a separate temporal axis and therefore demand separate treatment. Support for unhinging the history of women's conduct from that of their male contemporaries comes from several indicators. The first is early modern royal women's domestic segregation from their male counterparts. Spanish queens, according to Jonathan Brown and John Elliott, maintained separate households in separate wings of the royal palace, with their own budget, staff, and rules of etiquette. As Félix Labrador-Arroyo noted at the 2010 meeting of the Renaissance Society of America, men and women of the Spanish court were bound by separate sets of protocol. Men followed Burgundian protocols of etiquette used by Philip the Fair (officially imposed in 1548 by Charles V), while women observed the Castilian protocols utilized a half-century earlier by Isabel I. To fold the genealogy of women's conduct into that of men's would not only elide the unique periodicity of each that Kelly first observed, but would also perpetuate the assumption that gender is constituted exclusively by contrast to an "opposite sex." In fact, as the contrast between man and beast

---

[11] The phrase "Cervantes & Co." offers a convenient shorthand for recalling the masculinist bias in favor of "dead white authors" that characterized nineteenth- and early twentieth-century Golden Age literary criticism. Ironically, the phrase was adopted by Juan de la Cuesta Publishers of Newark, Delaware, to market an imprint that itself vigorously supports the de-masculinization of the Hispanic literary canon. To date, the "Cervantes & Co." series of student editions features such formerly neglected women authors as María de Zayas (*Novelas amorosas y ejemplares* and *La traición en la amistad*) and Ana Caro (*Valor agravio y mujer*).

in the *Criticón* cited above hints, gender in the Renaissance was constituted along many axes—human/animal; hot/cold; wet/dry; strong/weak; normative/deviant—some contrastive, others more graduated. Noted scholar Sister Prudence Allen examines the history of sex identity structures. Allen finds that gendering structures fall into three categories: those that conceive of there being one sex (unifying theories), those that conceive of two sexes that complement one another (complementary theories), and those that conceive of two sexes in conflict with one another (polarizing theories) (4). Until future scholarship determines which of these structures predominated in early modern Spain, I consider it more a matter of caution than exclusivity to avoid qualifying early modern gender as a strictly oppositional structure.

A Crisis of Masculinity?

Masculinity studies authorities Michael Kimmel and Michael Messner write with respect to masculinity that "the meaning of masculinity is neither transhistorical nor culturally universal, but rather varies from culture to culture and within any one culture over time" (xvii). By uprooting gender from the realm of inalterable biological fact, and by resituating it within the realm of historical discourse, gender studies have taken the lead in asking what masculinity meant in early modern Spain. For example, in *Feminizing the Enemy*, Sidney Donnell argues that the perception of gender operative in the seventeenth century was performative rather than physiological; that is, women and men enacted their gender by presenting themselves in accordance with or in defiance of prevailing norms. This non-essentializing approach to gender, Donnell asserts, opened the way for cross-dressing on the Spanish stage. Sherry M. Velasco likewise highlights deviations from the heterosexual norm that circulated despite inquisitorial scrutiny. Her books, *The Lieutenant Nun, Male Delivery*, and *Lesbians in Early Modern Spain*, celebrate a variety of non-normative gendering practices that were fully compatible with prevailing medical, moral, and philosophical schema. Velasco's article, "*Marimachos, hombrunas, barbudas*: The Masculine Woman in Cervantes," shows how Galen's theory of the humors as well as Huarte de San Juan's widely read medical treatise of 1575, *Examen de ingenios para las ciencias* [*The Trial of Wits*], provided a normative framework for understanding the phenomenon of sexual transmutations (from female to male). Velasco also illustrates how awareness of the plasticity of gender posited by the natural sciences produces new readings of canonical texts. Within this context, Velasco finds Don Quixote's unstable perception of reality in Cervantes's novel "to be an accurate reflection of the 'fluid' state of gender identity and sex assignment during the early modern period" (76).

Donnell, Velasco, and others who have recast early modern gender as a motile category owe a debt to the work of American philosopher and gender theorist Judith Butler. In her groundbreaking 1990 volume, *Gender Trouble: Feminism and the Subversion of Identity*, Butler attacked the practice of pegging womanhood to a set of fixed proclivities including heterosexual desire. By positing gender as a dramatic effect produced and reproduced by repetitive acts, Butler dislodges gender from innate sexual traits. Non-traditional or "hybrid" gender identities can be created by varying those acts, as in the case of drag performance. Butler has continued to refine her position on the performance of gender relative to Foucault (*Bodies that Matter*) and Lacan (*Antigone's Claim*).

The theorization of gender as a discursive field marked by variation, hybridity, and flux has facilitated queer readings of Lope, Tirso, Calderón, Cervantes, and others. Nonetheless, there persists a tendency to conflate the presence of polymorphic or changing gender performances in literary texts with Spain's political troubles of the same period. France and England did curtail Spain's expansionist ambitions, and this migration of power away from Madrid may well, at least from the Spanish perspective, be characterized as a "crisis" or "decline." However, it does not necessarily follow that the shrinking prospects of the Spanish imperial project precipitated or were accompanied by a "crisis" of masculinity. Yet, the title of Bernardo Blanco-González's study, *Del cortesano al discreto: Examen de una "decadencia"* [From the courtier to the discreet gentleman: investigation of a "*decadence*"] (emphasis added), announces resistance to the perceived shift from courtier to discreet man of court. The second half of Donnell's book title, *Feminizing the Enemy, Imperial Spain, Transvestite Drama and the* Crisis of Masculinity (emphasis added), seems to implicate transvestite drama in a crisis of gender rather than a political crisis. The language of crisis likewise creeps into María Cristina Quintero's insightful analysis of Calderón's *El médico de su honra* [*The Physician of his Honor*]. Quintero qualifies the principal male character Gutierre's obsession with his wife's suspected unfaithfulness as "a manifestation of a pathological *crisis of masculinity*" (7, emphasis added). Elizabeth Lehfeldt's influential essay on masculinity in early modern Spain, "Ideal Men: Masculinity and *Decline* in Seventeenth-Century Spain" (emphasis added) likewise succumbs to the parallelist fallacy. For Lehfeldt,

> the seventeenth-century discourse of masculinity failed due to nostalgia and a lack of creativity. Contributors to the debate could only imagine solutions rooted in late Medieval and (occasionally) sixteenth-century exemplars, *and failed to envision a new model of masculinity better suited to the circumstances of the seventeenth century* (466, emphasis added).

Against the current tendency to conflate Spain's decline with a decline or crisis of masculinity, I argue that the seventeenth-century discourse on masculine virtue neither failed nor underwent a crisis.

Invocations of the language of decline and panic seem to bespeak a nostalgia for pre-Butlerian certainties regarding gender. In the case of Calderón's uxoricide dramas, there is no doubt that gender inequality and an uncompromising honor code provided the canvas on which Calderón painted these plays. And I agree with Quintero that "the conventions of the *comedia* (in this case, the proverbial happy nuptials at the end) and the belief in the monarch as the ultimate source of justice are ironically deconstructed in the performance of the play" (6).[12] However, at a more symbolic level, I would suggest that Calderón calls upon the female sacrifice trope in *El médico de su honra* not to protest gender disorder but rather to allegorize a political crisis: the despot's active role in perpetuating injustice. To borrow Joan Scott's phraseology, gender (disorder) in Calderón's *El médico de su honra* becomes "a primary way of signifying relationships of power" (1067).

José Cartagena Calderón also frames gender instabilities in the language of crisis. The title of the introductory chapter of his *Masculinidad en obras: El drama de la hombría en la España imperial* [Masculinity under construction: the drama of manliness in imperial Spain] is "Masculinidades en crisis y bajo escrutinio" [Masculinity in crisis and under scrutiny] (9–53). In this case, however, Cartagena Calderón offers compelling insight into the tendency to stigmatize the operation of early modern masculinity in Spain. As he explains, Golden Age writers themselves were the first to blame Spain's political crisis on changing gender norms. Moralists, for example, disparaged the disruption of Medieval gender practices by new standards of courtly refinement. He cites Francisco de Quevedo, María de Zayas, Cristóbal Suárez de Figueroa, and Fray Antonio de Ezcaray among many concerned writers who attributed Spain's political and economic decline to what they regarded as the effeminization of the Spanish (male) character: "La opinión cada vez más extendida era que el imperio se había ido irremediablemente a la ruina por haberse presuntamente desvirilizado [The increasingly dominant view was that the empire had fallen irreparably into ruin as a consequence of its presumed loss of virility]" (9). The prevailing consensus that Spanish masculinity was in crisis even led reformists to try to turn back the clock and reinstate Medieval martial ideals: "[Es] un período en que se pretende restaurar y reformar una masculinidad heroica, militar e imperial que los excesos de la vida cortesana del siglo XVII habían 'erosionado' [[It is] a period of trying to restore and reform an ideal of heroic, military, and imperial masculinity, which the extravagances of seventeenth-century courtly life had 'eroded']" (12).

Anxieties regarding the enactment of masculinity played themselves out on the Spanish stage, where effeminate caricatures and equally overblown portrayals of virility abounded. Playwrights queered not only the effete gentlemen of court, but also Spain's colonial subjects, the Amerindians, perceived to be both primitive and dangerous to Christian hegemony. Cartagena Calderón speculates that pragmatism motivated Lope and his followers to accentuate the virility of their dramatic

---

[12] The trope of the innocent woman whose sacrifice restores social order had been a theatrical staple since Euripides drew inspiration for his two Iphigenia plays from Greek myth. The fact that Spanish (or Greek) law legitimized the unjust expiatory sacrifice of the female responds to one of the few dramatic principles upon which Aristotle and Lope agreed: "guárdese de imposibles [avoid the impossible]" (Lope, *Arte* line 284); that is, the principle of verisimilitude. Pathological gender disparities are a constitutive mimetic element of *El médico de su honra* that piques modern sensibilities just as the news from Dubai that a Norwegian rape victim received a harsher jail sentence than her attacker provoked an international outcry in May of 2013 ("Dubai Rape").

heroes and the effeminacy of their foils: "dicho discurso desvirilizador del 'Otro' tiene más que ver con quienes lo producen que con el sujeto conquistador o desmasculinizado [the aforementioned emasculating discourse of the 'Other' has more to do with those who produce it that with the conquered or emasculated subject]" (186). Golden Age theater was already under siege for creating a class of consumers whose passive receptivity to stage performances was seen to pose yet another threat to Spanish masculinity. By exaggerating the contrast between virile and effeminate characters, playwrights hoped to dispel fears that theater itself was an emasculating institution.

It is perhaps understandable that early modern moralists should bemoan the hyperbolic versions of reality refracted back to them on the Spanish stage, and that a nobility threatened by competition from the ranks of the *letrados* (university-educated bureaucrats) should decry the feminization of Medieval ideals of masculinity. Nonetheless, their panic need not panic us. Feminizing rhetoric belongs to a very long European tradition of debate over the relative merits of arms versus letters. For example, *Elena y María*, a festive poem (c. 1250) which survives only in fragmentary form, debates the merits of loving a warrior or loving a man of letters (cleric). The appearance of an ingrained literary *topos* does not announce, in and of itself, a "crisis." Indeed, it is typical for patriarchal societies to resort to defaming adversaries by recourse to misogynistic taunting. Equating courtiers with women symptomized dread on the part of sectors of society that stood to lose ground to new courtly arrivistes. Reading a "crisis of masculinity" in this familiar symbolic displacement would seem to privilege a defensive rhetorical strategy with greater historical weight than it warrants.

Furthermore, accusations of sexual deviance often arise in response to the challenges of social upheaval. Juvenal, Martial, and Catullus are among the Roman poets for whom sodomy figured as a convenient trope of anti-tyrannical invective. Jason von Ehrenkrook points out that a twelfth-century German chronicle, the *Kaiserchronik*, portrayed the despised Roman Emperor Nero as a monstrous pregnant man who gave birth to a toad through his mouth. Rather than accept the accuracy of this account, von Ehrenkrook cautions that "gendered characters become critical reference points for a particular notion of self and other," whose ultimate function is "to mediate a particular view of the social, cultural, and/or political landscape" (146). He continues:

> However much these literary monsters distort the underlying historical realities of the objects of invective, they nevertheless offer a crucial glimpse into the ideological realities at work within a particular historical context. The pervasive presence of gender deviancy within political invective, not only in antiquity but also today, thus underscores its rhetorical potency, its capacity to map boundaries, be they social, political, cultural, or ethnic. (146)

Von Ehrenbrook's insights into the rhetoric of gender deviancy sheds light on the mincing, effeminate monsters produced by playwrights and moralists of early modern Spain. Such distortion addressed the insecurity of those threatened by competition from this new breed of refined gentlemen. While they point to the perception of a threat to the status quo, they should not in themselves be mistaken for a historical boiling-point, turning point, or "crisis" of masculinity.

As Cartagena Calderón's title, *Masculinidad en obras*, suggests, masculinity in imperial Spain was "en obras [under construction]." However, the incompletion and motion associated with a construction or even a demolition site do not inspire the same level of alarm as, say, a site of earthquake or bomb devastation. In fact, signs of instability and change are as vital to the history of gender as are its repetitions. Moreover, the question of what would constitute the ideal subject of the Spanish imperial project produced new iterations of masculinity not only at the margins of society (Velasco's bearded women, Donnell's transvestites, Garza Carvajal's sodomites) but also at the epicenter of power, the royal court. For this reason, I propose in the following pages to examine models of heterosexual masculinity within the flexible framework of gender change set forth by such pioneers of queer studies as Judith Butler and Eve Kosofsky Sedgwick. In so doing, I am meeting a challenge that Butler herself foresaw in an interview with Robert Shail in 2000. When Shail asked whether Butler's "conception of a hybrid gender identity" was threatened by the return to more restrictive gender identities such as the "men's movement," Butler replied,

> I think that the most useful way to respond to it might be to establish a *critical form of heterosexuality studies*, one that does not take its norms to be established or beyond criticism, one which asks *how sexuality and gender interrelated within heterosexuality*, and how heterosexual definition is, as Sedgwick has taught us, bound up with homo definition. If the reason for the reaction is that heterosexual women want their "place" back, then it probably makes sense to seize the occasion to *rethink heterosexuality itself. My own sense is that it is usually more queer than it is willing to know.* (Sönser Breen 23, emphasis added)

In keeping with Butler's challenge, the present study offers a "critical form of heterosexuality studies" that "asks how sexuality and gender interrelated within heterosexuality" to produce a genealogy of normative masculine identity in early modern Spain.

Methodology

Masculine Virtue draws from three senses of literary conduct. In the first instance, texts that teach the art of masculine self-display are also seen to display themselves so as to compound their appeal. A stunning range of writerly strategies delivers Renaissance conduct literature from the generic dungeon of the didactic treatise and helps to account for the genre's ferocious appeal to early modern readers. Among the rhetorical and narratological resources summoned by these texts: Castiglione rallied the dialogic colloquy to teach the art of urbane conversation; Gracián adopted Martial's aphoristic style; Guevara, for his *Reloj de príncipes* [Dial of princes] composed the pseudo-chronicle of a Roman emperor to advise

Charles V on the art of governance; Gracián Dantisco fashioned his *Galateo español* [*Spanish Gallant*] after the manner of an epistolary treatise; and Salas Barbadillo dispensed advice to the aspiring man of court under the cloak of fictional biography in *El caballero perfecto* [The perfect gentleman].

American literary critic J. Hillis Miller validates the study of literature as a form of conduct in *Literature as Conduct: Speech Acts in Henry James*. He also adds that literary conduct may be understood to include representations *of* human conduct, as well as literature as a force that induces or *conducts* readers to act in new ways: "My title, *Literature as Conduct*, can refer to the way writing literature is a form of conduct, or to the representation of conduct within literary fictions, or, using *conduct* as a verb, to the way literature may conduct its readers to believe or to behave in new ways" (2). Literature *as* conduct for Miller signals the behavior of Henry James's texts, in much the same way that Castiglione, Gracián, and Guevara's works engage distinct rhetorical strategies to capture their respective readers' attention. Conduct *within* literature for Miller points to representation of human action, while the verb *conduct* evokes the power of texts to lead or induce readers to change the ways that they think or act. The present volume seeks to exploit all three of Miller's approaches to the literature of manly self-presentation.

Mariana de Carvajal's novella, "La Venus de Ferrara," which pits one textual performance against another in courtly combat for the hand of an eligible duchess named Venus, illustrates Miller's first usage, that of literature *as* conduct. Published in 1663 in a collection of similar novellas entitled the *Navidades de Madrid y noches entretenidas* [Christmastide in Madrid and entertaining nights], "Venus" would normally be shelved with other Baroque narrative collections, not with guides for manly conduct. But Carvajal's novellas contrast successful courtship strategies with unsuccessful ones, thereby inserting a didactic element into her plots. "La Venus de Ferrara" stages a series of courtship competitions that include jousting, self-presentation, and the composition of clever amorous aphorisms. Venus, her mother, and their advisor serve as judges as each suitor parades before them, presenting at sword-tip a short love poem written on parchment. The quality of the verse metonymically represents the inner virtue of its author. The fact that only one of the poems is metrically complete does not escape the attention of the judges, who single out the superior poet as the best match for Venus. By equating good or bad literary conduct with inner virtue, the conduct *of* Carvajal's text facilitates extraction of its didactic message.

Regarding Miller's second sense, that is, representations of conduct *within* texts, *Masculine Virtue* seeks to answer two questions. First, what were the stylized repetitions of acts required during this period to enact masculinity? And second, how did representations of these repertoires change over time? Returning to "La Venus de Ferrara," the Duke of Módena enacts three stylized behaviors that marked new terrain for masculine virtue in early modern Spain: he distinguishes himself from others (fame); he hides information from adversaries (dissimulation); and he switches from one role to another (adaptability). To defeat his rivals for Venus's hand in marriage, the Duke of Módena excels at calculating when to conceal his identity and when to reveal it. This skill corresponds to the manly virtue of dissimulation explored in Chapter 3 of this volume. By alternating between candor and secretiveness, the Duke practices adaptability, the new conduct strategy that occupies Chapter 4. The Duke of Módena likewise repeats a stylized act that Baltasar Gracián refers to as eminence, but that we will call fame, by triumphing over his rivals at every turn (*Oráculo manual* [*Art of Worldly Wisdom*] Aphorism 61; 224). Chapter 2 traces the growing acceptability of fame, and its shifting semantic resonance in a wide-ranging corpus of Medieval through early modern texts. Miller also observes that "conduct" is a verb that may "conduct its readers to believe or to behave in new ways." Courtly conduct not only determines the outcome of courtship in the *Navidades de Madrid*; it overdetermines it. The most courteous, discriminating, and urbane rival always wins in Carvajal's novellas, which renders them reliable as models of polite conduct. As we have seen in "La Venus de Ferrara," the Duke of Módena surpasses his competitors by executing superior courtship performances. In much the same way that Calderón's *El gran teatro del mundo* rewards those who "perform well," the distributive justice of Carvajal's text invites readers to imitate the Duke of Módena's conduct, with the hope of reaping similar rewards.

Despite professing clearly stated didactic ends, early modern conduct writings must always be suspected of concealing other agendas. This is so because, even as Renaissance and Baroque conduct literature promised to inculcate savvy, to instill wit, to model grace, to transform ignorant newcomers into suave insiders, and to convert boors into Brahmins, the same texts also taught the art of dissembling that permitted the man of court to conceal his ultimate aims. As Gracián advised in Aphorism 98 of the abovementioned *Oráculo manual*: "Cifrar la voluntad [...]. El más práctico saber consiste en disimular; lleva riesgo de perder el que juega a juego descubierto [Encode your intentions [...]. The most practical wisdom consists in dissimulating. He who shows his cards risks losing]" (236). A body of writing that teaches behavioral precepts by example quite likely practices what it preaches. If conduct manuals teach wittiness, they should be witty; if they advocate erudition, they should be erudite. Paradoxically, it follows that if the art of dissimulation forms part of the *desideratum* of courtly performance, those texts that teach courtly conduct are themselves likely to dissemble rather than announce their intentions outright. For instance, courtesy manuals that appear to support newcomers at court may actually aspire to obfuscate or mystify the process of enculturation required to pass as a gentleman. Or they may simply be appropriating the outward form of a conduct manual to impress a potential patron through conspicuous displays of erudition. Yes, conduct literature leads its readers to behave in new ways, but what those new ways are may lie beneath the surface of the text. For this reason, *Masculine Virtue* seeks to tease out the difference between the stated aims and the probable effects of Spanish conduct literature.

Miller's schema provide the methodological basis for analyzing representations of early modern conduct literature in Spain that will inform chapters 2 through 4 of this volume. Each chapter will inquire into 1) the writing of conduct literature as itself a form of conduct; 2) the representation of *homo agens* (man the doer), within Spanish conduct literature; and, 3) the new beliefs or behaviors to which the text *conducts* its readers. Collectively, these observations allow a performative or conduct-based genealogy of masculine conduct in Spain to emerge. Yet they also have broader applications.

Conduct Literature and Social Change

The genealogy of masculine virtue that this volume develops provides a starting point for measuring the relevance for Spain of Norbert Elias's theory of civilizing processes. A pioneer in the field of conduct literature, Elias observed a heightening of self-restraint and impulse management among European noblemen from the sixteenth century onward. Basing his research largely on etiquette manuals and historical records of Ancien Régime France, Elias adduced a series of factors that obliged the French seigniorial estate to relinquish its former defensive function in favor of behaviors better suited to serving the despot at court. Succinctly stated,

> [Norbert Elias] studied how, from the Renaissance onward, overturning the rusticity characteristic of Medieval courtesy, and taking up where exhausted codes of courtly love had left off, there developed a new concept of civility that consists of a series of conduct norms appropriate to new social circumstances and which encompassed attire, table manners, phatic communication and forms of verbal address.[13]

Like Butler, Elias affirmed that, since identity comes into being through repetitive acts, it is unstable and susceptible to transformation (over extended periods of time in Elias's case). When advances in weaponry, the development of a money economy, and increased bureaucratization of the state shifted power from the periphery to the center and from the landed nobility to the king the French aristocracy had to evolve new modes of behavior designed to coax favor from the sovereign. According to Elias,

> when the balance of power within the whole figuration shifts after a series of struggles between the representatives of the estates and the king in the latter's favor, as is the case in France in the seventeenth century, the king has the chance of controlling social mobility in the interests of the royal position or simply his own interests and inclinations [...]. The king's favor is thus one of the most important opportunities open to families of the nobility of the sword to counteract the vicious circle of enforced ostentation at the cost of their capital. It is understandable that people were unwilling to mar this opportunity by behaviour disagreeable to the king. (*Court Society* 71)

---

[13] "[Norbert Elias] estudió cómo, superando la simplicidad característica de la urbanidad Medieval y al margen del caduco formalismo cortesano, madura a partir del Renacimiento un nuevo concepto de civilidad, que consiste en una serie de normas de conducta apropiadas para la nueva situación social, y que se extienden al vestido, los modales en la mesa, y las fórmulas de saludo y tratamiento" (Martínez Torrejón 94).

In *Power and Civility*, Elias compared Versailles to the modern stock exchange (271). The commodity in play at court was not capital, but status, a good guaranteed not only by birth but also by "moderation of spontaneous emotions, the tempering of affects, the extension of mental space beyond the moment into the past and future, the habit of connecting events in terms of chains of cause and effect" (236). The entire *habitus*, or cluster of behaviors that distinguished the aristocracy from other social sectors, proved susceptible to change in response to the need to please the king. As a result, performing the role of noble man or noble woman—that is to say, normative gender itself—underwent profound changes with the emergence of court society.

Elias's theories regarding the European nobility's increasing self-surveillance, first published under the title *Über den Prozess der Zivilisation*, came to be known in English as the "civilizing process." However, the term "civilizing" carries positivist connotations that distort Elias's message. Take the example of early modern Spain, which first developed its court society thanks in part to state-sanctioned violence against the indigenous peoples of the New World. For Elias personally, the supposedly "civilized" high culture of Vienna furnished the breeding ground for Nazism, which forced Elias into exile and precipitated his mother's deportation to Auschwitz. Elias conceived of the civilizing process as reversible, not inevitable: "it would be a serious misreading of the theory of civilizing processes," writes Stephen Mennell, one of Elias's modern exponents, "to see it as a model of progress, much less *inevitable* progress."[14] For this reason, Mennell translates *Über den Prozess der Zivilisation* not as "The Civilizing Process" but as "Processes of Civilisation," implying that social figurations are free to move toward or away from internal pacification and state control.[15]

Another concern to bear in mind when applying Elias's theories to Spain is that he drew his data largely from French sources. As Benet Davetian notes in *Civility: A Cultural History*, "His study of court society is mostly based on the court in France [...]. A cross-cultural study including countries governed by varying political systems would have provided Elias with the opportunity of seeing how different people have adopted different ways of constructing their civility" (349). It is perhaps ironic that Elias relied for his conception of the self-regulating man of court on the French adaptation of a Spanish source. In 1684, Nicolas-Abraham Amelot de la Houssaye (1634–1706) published *L'Homme de cour* [The man of court], a loose translation of Baltasar Gracián's *Oráculo manual y arte de prudencia* [*Art of Worldly Wisdom*] (1647).[16] *L'Homme de cour*

---

[14] Mennell and Goudsblom, Introduction 19 (Mennell's emphasis).

[15] The association of increased self-surveillance with processes of state formation posited by Elias informs the majority of recent accounts of social change in early modern Europe. See, for example, Asch, Bates, Braudy, Burke, Correll, Chartier, Goldsmith, Greenblatt, Gronow, Hazard, Lehfeldt, Mennell, Ogborn, Posner, Revel, Scaglione, Stanton, and Whigham. Bryson and Duindam offer more skeptical readings. Jon R. Snyder criticizes Elias for overlooking the sixteenth-century Italian courtesy tradition.

[16] Amelot de la Houssaye or Houssaie was a historian whose study of Tacitus, the *Tibère: Discours Politique sur Tacite*, was also published in 1684 (see Soll).

enjoyed instant success and was reissued 16 times between 1684 and 1696 (Serra Muñoz 54). However, Amelot's adaptation reveals deep cultural differences between France and Spain. The French concept of *honnêteté* [the appearance of authenticity] that Amelot promulgates in *L'Homme de cour* is more cynical and amoral than Gracián's original. For Inés Serra Muñoz, "In *L'Homme de cour* the code of *honnêteté* is superimposed on Gracián's text, modifying the meaning of the work through (Amelot's interpretation of) words that refer to very different realities and concepts" (54).

Renaissance imitation precept allowed for such liberal reappropriation of existing texts, so there is nothing alarming or "wrong" with Amelot's reworking of Gracián[17] nor with Elias's reliance on Amelot. But the triple prism of a German (later British) critic who made use of a French conduct manual modeled after a Spanish source does make it necessary to proceed cautiously when applying Elias's paradigm of the "processes of civilization" to changes in representations of Spanish court society. For this reason, *Masculine Virtue* works inductively, beginning with the Spanish sources themselves in order to ascertain the ongoing descriptive usefulness that Elias's social thought holds for Spain.

Chapter Organization

Chapter 1 elucidates processes of unification and centralization during the early years of Spanish imperial expansion under Charles V and Philip II, leading to the founding of a sedentary, permanent court in the new capital of Madrid. The urban capital became a nexus of power and a magnet for all who sought social advancement. To tap into the resources of the crown, a nobility that had formerly served the king from the periphery, on its ancestral lands or on the field of battle, required new skills adapted to court society. Chapter 1 foregrounds the burgeoning marketplace of conduct literature produced and consumed by the new men of the Spanish court in their efforts to survive and compete for status.

Chapters 2 through 4 map three social skills or display strategies that grew out of the need to act effectively at court. This trio of strategies—fame, dissimulation, and adaptability—marks a departure from Medieval ideals of masculine virtue. However, it is important to note that post-Medieval conduct strategies seldom converged to form a unitary sociotype. Different texts assemble variant combinations and proportions of each faculty, assigning to them divergent meanings. Such inconsistency follows from sociolinguistic practice, as discourse analyst Jay Lemke notes: "Our identities are always mixed from the point of view of the ideal social types, and they may be relatively more consistent in some settings vs. others, or even may construct different (and from the viewpoint of the culture, conflicting) identities in different activities" (n. pag.). The variability in representations of masculine conduct also accords with Kegan Gardiner's formulation of gender noted above, as being "contingent, fluid, socially and

---

[17] See, for example, Weinberg.

historically constructed, changeable and constantly changing" (11) rather than static or univocal. Indeed, unpacking what Robyn Wiegman has called the "myth of masculine sameness" in early modern palatine culture is a motivating ambition of this book.[18]

Chapter 4 concludes with a close reading of De la Gasca's *Manual de avisos para el perfecto cortesano*. De la Gasca's *Manual de avisos* falls into place as the heir to earlier writings, particularly those of Baltasar Gracián. The *Manual*'s pragmatic skepticism rebuts Lehfeld's contention that the discourse on masculinity in early modern Spain "failed to adapt itself to the circumstances of the seventeenth century" (466). Finally, the Epilogue synthesizes the preceding observations and collates them with Elias's theory of the "processes of civilization" to affirm that Spain pioneered the art of image management that Louis XIV would later perfect at Versailles.

---

[18] *American Anatomies* 180, qtd. in Kegan Gardiner 12.

Chapter 1
Masculinity, Conduct, and Empire

La cortesía es el mayor hechizo político de grandes personajes.

[Courtesy is the most influential spell cast by great statesmen.]

—Baltasar Gracián

As Renaissance states consolidated and became more complex, they came to depend on bureaucrats and ministers to carry out the business of government. "[M]ucho menos se puede regir la nave de una República y de un Reino" wrote Andrés Mendo in 1662, "ni fabricar en él el edificio del gobierno político, si no hay muchos que ayuden y cooperen [scarcely can the ship of state of a Republic and a Realm be governed, nor can the edifice of public administration be erected within it, without the help and collaboration of many men]."[1] The development of the administrative councils, courts, and other organs designed to channel the efforts of those many men into a more or less effective crew has been well documented.[2] Less attention has been paid to the protagonist of palatine activity, the man of court, as the arc of Spain's fortunes rose and fell from 1500 to 1700. This chapter delineates the spatio-temporal matrix within which the Spanish courtier came to represent a new ideal of Spanish masculine conduct.

Historians caution that the multitudes who flocked to court to help steer the giant ship of the Spanish state included at least three very different social profiles: *letrados*, or university-trained functionaries and jurists; rich merchants and other non-nobles recently elevated to the aristocracy; and the old nobility who abandoned their lands for posts in the royal ministries and household (García Marín 45–98). To unify the many into a conceptual whole and to instruct them in the ways of court comprised the ostensible *raison d'être* of the literature of courtly conduct. But conduct literature also offers a glimpse into the contentious process of Spanish identity formation through which a new post-Medieval model of vassalage, the *cortesano* or courtier, was constructed and contested. In order to trace the changing face of Spanish seigniorial masculinity from 1500 to 1700, it will be useful to situate the rise of the Austrian court in Madrid and to understand how the court has been characterized by others. We will start with an overview of the diverse and often competing ends that the history of early modern Spain has been made to serve, and the major historiographic currents that condition the perception

---

[1] *Príncipe perfecto y ministros ajustados* (Lyon, 1662), 320–21 (qtd. in García Marín 53).

[2] See for example Albaladejo; Maravall, *Teoría*; Elliott, *España*; García Marín; and Vicens Vives.

of imperial Spanish culture. The documents on courtly conduct to be examined in this study were printed and published. Therefore, it is also important to see how these products have been organized into categories that shape perception of their production. I argue that the widespread exclusion or occlusion of conduct literature from generic classifications of early modern print culture reflects limitations in these classificatory systems. To restore conduct literature to prominence requires reconnecting with its function within the nexus of court culture. The next task this chapter sets for itself is to place conduct literature at the locus of the royal court. For this purpose it will be useful to review the conditions leading to the rise of palatine culture during the European Renaissance with particular attention to the changing social position of the new gentleman of court. Finally, we will apply the concept of transculturation to the relationship between the monarch and his retinue. Through transculturation, the royal model of magnificence and refinement becomes the courtier's inspiration and ultimate *desideratum*. The man of court will be seen to adopt three regal behavioral strategies: eminence or fame, dissimulation, and adaptability. These "masculine virtues" will come to distinguish the Renaissance nobleman's performance of seigniorial manliness from that of the Medieval knight.

Views of the Court

As the first European monarchy to forge a worldwide empire in the sixteenth century, and the first to lose preeminence in the seventeenth, Spain, like an oldest child, grew up fast, without the benefit of older siblings' examples. Multiple challenges of governance—the administration of far-flung territories, the transformation of Madrid into an international court, and the forging of a new national identity being just three—have elicited an equally heterogeneous historiography. Historians have variably framed the period of approximately 1500 to 1700, during which Spain confronted these questions, as Spain's Golden Age, Age of Decline, or Age of Uncertainty.[3] Each of these schema foregrounds a different aspect of the process of cultural negotiation set in motion by Spain's unexpected expansion and the concomitant centralization of state power. The age was golden in the literal sense that imported precious metals wrested from conquered New World territories constituted Spain's primary source of wealth. Figuratively, too, historians have looked nostalgically back upon a period of imperial splendor when "the sun never set" over the Spanish Empire. During the Spanish Golden Age, Philip II (r. 1527–98) and his son, Philip III (r. 1598–1621), were invested with 32 titles, 13 of which pertained to realms beyond the Iberian Peninsula (García Cárcel 12). Subsequently, the golden mantle of nationalist pride settled over the cultural production of the same period casting such writers such as

---

[3] Américo Castro, in *De la edad conflictiva* (1961), named the period 1500–1700 an "Age of Conflict" in light of the Crown's efforts to create unity by suppressing the practice of Judaism and Islam. Radical in its day, Castro's exposure of ethnic conflict in the "writing of the state" has become a methodological mainstay of culture studies (see Gerli).

Cervantes, Lope de Vega, Calderón de la Barca, and Quevedo, and painters such as El Greco, Velázquez, Murillo, and Zurbarán in the guise of enduring monuments to the ephemeral greatness that was Hapsburg Spain.

Spain's seventeenth century is also widely viewed as an Age of Decline in recognition of a process of contraction on both domestic and foreign fronts. As early as 1600, jurist Martín González de Cellorigo compared Spain's malaise to a sick body. Cellorigo, in his *Memorial de la [...] restauración* [Appeal for the [...] revival], could well point to a "común declinación de estos reinos [general decline of these realms]" (qtd. in Gelabert 206). Troubling symptoms included the sinking of Spain's Armada off the coast of England in 1588, military defeats in the Low Countries, territorial shrinkage, rampant nepotism at the highest levels of Philip III's government, a plague-depleted populace, and unfavorable trade balances. Under Philip IV (r. 1621–65), the ailing patient did not recover from these ills. Portugal's successful revolt against Spanish rule in 1640, unrest in Aragón, and a subdued revolt in Catalonia gave the lie to claims of a unified Iberian Peninsula. Reflecting this sense of loss, satirist Francisco de Quevedo wryly compared Philip IV's sobriquet, "The Great," to a pit: the more ground it loses, the "greater" it gets.[4] Although John Elliott paints an exceptionally favorable portrait of Philip IV and his *valido* [favorite] in *The Count-Duke of Olivares: Statesman in an Age of Decline*, historians in general tend to fall in behind Quevedo, laying the blame for Spain's losses on the shoulders of the latter Hapsburgs (Philip III, Philip IV, and Charles II). The following passage, excerpted from a 1941 Spanish history textbook, summarizes the traditional rise and fall narrative of the Hapsburg dynasty in Spain:

> Examinando el carácter de los Reyes de la Casa de Austria, se encuentran en Carlos I la energía y el valor; en Felipe II, la reflexión y la prudencia; en Felipe III, la irresolución y la incertidumbre; en Felipe IV, la indolencia y el abandono; en Carlos II la imbecilidad y la impotencia.
>
> [Examining the character of the kings of the House of Austria, one finds energy and valor in Charles I, ponderation and prudence in Philip II, indecision and uncertainty in Philip III, indolence and lack of restraint in Philip IV, and in Charles II, imbecility and impotence.] (qtd. in García Cárcel 11)

A glance at any chronology of seventeenth-century Spain reveals the Hapsburgs' steady loss of power. In 1628, Dutch pirate Piet Heyn sank Spain's treasure fleet in Cuba, and France declared war on Spain. In 1640, Catalonia attempted to secede from Spain and join itself to France, and Portugal declared its independence from Madrid. In 1643, the French defeated Spain's army in Flanders, and in 1648 Spain was forced to renounce its sovereignty over the United Provinces. The 1659 Peace of the Pyrenees treaty with France upended Philip IV's plan to wed his eldest daughter María Teresa to her uncle Leopold I of Austria, forcing him to marry

---

[4] "[Grande] lo es el Rey nuestro Señor a manera de los hoyos; más grande cuanta más tierra les quita" (qtd. in Alabrús 379).

her to the King of France instead (Kamen, *Spain* xvii). Even historian Henry Kamen, perhaps the most ardent opponent of the "decline narrative," concedes that Spain underwent a "shrinking of horizons, a major cultural contraction" in the seventeenth century (*Spain* 270).[5]

Jeremy Robbins characterizes the sixteenth and seventeenth centuries in philosophical terms as a skeptical age challenged by uncertainty. The expansions and contractions of Spain's frontiers and fortunes eroded the doxa of Catholic providentialism. Bartolomé de las Casas's disturbing revelations regarding Spanish savagery in the New World in his *Brevísima relación de la destrucción de las Indias* [*A Very Brief Account of the Destruction of the Indies*] (c. 1552) struck a blow against Spain's sense of moral superiority over its European rivals and transatlantic subjects. De las Casas provoked national reflection on the implicit conflict between Spain's commitment to conquest and evangelization on the one hand, and the Christian humanist doctrines of civility and ethics on the other. Miguel de Carvajal's allegorical *Scena XIX* [Scene 19] published by Luis Hurtado de Toledo in 1557 dramatizes the conflict between the indigenous peoples of the New World and their Spanish masters. In Carvajal's play, native chieftains plead for justice in a Tribunal of Death. However, in keeping with Robbins's assertion that "Baroque literature maintains a fraught tension between absolute certainty and radical insecurity," *Scena XIX* does not reach a final verdict on the Indians' complaint ("Renaissance and Baroque Continuity" 145).

The ambivalences and uncertainties that dogged Spain's imperial adventure gave rise to a sense of belatedness and frustration, which is evident in the changing face of Spain's literary heroes. After 1605, Amadís of Gaul—the most famous hero of Spain's popular chivalric romances, fearless warrior, perfect lover, and emblem of Spain's bellicose optimism—lost currency. Instead, amid a mixture of mirth and misgiving, the reading public conceded that honor to a caricature of misplaced chivalry: Cervantes's Don Quixote of La Mancha.[6]

The Information Explosion

Animating all three historiographic schema—Golden Age, Age of Decline, and Age of Uncertainty—is the underlying pulse of discovery: navigational and

---

[5] For Kamen, Spain's apparent "decline" from imperial greatness constitutes little more than a self-justifying myth because Spain's originary triumphs were themselves hollow: "In terms of what really happened, all this was more myth than reality. The Spanish universal monarchy had come into existence through inheritance rather than conquest, and Spain's limited resources had never been capable of an active imperial programme, so that its growing incapacity to fulfil that programme revealed inherent weaknesses rather than provoking a 'decline' from a position of strength" (*Spain* 274).

[6] Francisco Rico argues that Don Quixote's popularity abroad rested largely on foreign readers' willingness to identify Spain's flubbed imperial adventure with Cervantes's hapless hero (see *Tiempos del Quijote* 14–19).

geographic discovery, discoveries in the fields of economics and statecraft, and in natural sciences and cosmography. This investigative impulse derived from sixteenth-century humanism, which optimistically promoted the notion of *dignitas hominis*, the contention that humankind could be molded to live in civic harmony. Marcel Bataillon, who probed the movement's penetration into Spanish letters, wrote that humanists were those who

> entusiasmados con su aprendizaje del latín clásico como medio de expresión más rico que los idiomas vulgares, y luego con sus flamantes estudios de hebreo y griego, lenguas de la Sagrada Escritura, no tardaron en sentirse partícipes de una cultura nueva, y cultivar un sentimiento de superioridad frente a la rancia rutina escolástica [...]. Mientras las disciplinas escolásticas se divorciaban cada vez más de la realidad viva al exigir requintados tecnicismos de lógica formal, pretendían los humanistas [...] asomarse a problemas humanos permanentes de moral y de política.

> [exalted by their training in classical Latin, the richest expressive medium of all of the vulgar languages [such as Spanish], and then by their fabulous studies of Hebrew and Greek, the languages of Holy Scripture, they soon began to feel themselves avatars of a new culture, to cultivate a sense of superiority in the face of stale scholastic routines [...]. While the scholastic disciplines increasingly divorced themselves from real life by demanding exaggerated technical displays of formal logic, the humanists [...] sought to venture into ongoing human problems of morality and politics.] (162)

Erasmus of Rotterdam and other humanists, while not rejecting a Medieval Christian view of humanity as sinful vessels in need of salvation, also extolled the human being as a creature made in the divine image. This made that creature an intrinsically worthy and valid object of inquiry. To this end, humanists applied the grammatical and literary tools of Latin, Greek, and Hebrew to rediscover lost scientific and rhetorical knowledge, reinvigorate the study of doctrinal Christian texts, and unearth forgotten classical models of sociability.

Contact with the New World fueled further humanistic inquiry. The "Discovery" granted Europeans a glimpse into undreamed varieties of habitat, industry, and culture. Printing rapidly channeled this outpouring of raw data into the hands of European readers. Of this information explosion John Elliott remarks, "The sheer quantity of ethnographic information available to the sixteenth-century European reading public continues to be impressive. Print and navigation technologies carried the world to Europe's doorstep" (*España* 69). New sources of knowledge further relativized the universal claims of classical antiquity and led to further advances in medicine, the natural sciences, cartography, and much more. More significantly, they inspired new epistemologies. Francis Bacon's *Novum organum* [The New Organon] of 1620, a treatise that credits the onset of the modern age to the inventions of gunpowder, printing, and the compass, laid the groundwork for replacing scholastic syllogism with a more empirical, open-minded approach to knowledge. However, Elliott's word "information" above may be misleading because the chronicles and natural histories of the New World that so fascinated their European readers reflected many different perspectives and served many causes. For this reason, Jeremy Robbins cautions that the relationship between discovery and literature is "not so much of external influences shaping literary creation as of literature being an integral part of a process of cultural negotiation and national self-definition" ("Renaissance" 138). Conduct literature played a vital part in those processes as Spanish writers such as Guevara, Gracián Dantisco, Quevedo, and others fashioned and refashioned their visions of the ideal servant of the state.

What is Conduct Literature?

Normative literature, that is, books that taught how one ought to act, either before God or man, comprised some of the first texts mass-produced by the printing press. Antonio Fernández-Luzón explains: "Los libros que se editaban eran aquellos que parecían tener una demanda segura: textos normativos y colecciones legislativas, libros litúrgicos, obras escolares y la literatura profesional en sus vertientes jurídica, teológica y médica [The books that were selected for publication were those that seemed to command a ready market: normative texts and law books, liturgical books, textbooks, and professional writings of a juridical, theological, and medical nature]" (576). The Catholic Monarchs, Ferdinand and Isabel, banned from publication "cosas vanas y sin provecho [vain and unprofitable things]" (qtd. in Cruickshank 86), which further incentivized the production of practical guidebooks.[7] While the Church monopolized the market for books related to religious action, the parallel field of secular conduct literature became one of the earliest success stories in the history of Western print culture.

Civility and courtesy were key concepts of the mentality of the elite that implied, to quote Anna Bryson, "not just ways of doing things, like eating or washing, but ways of structuring and interpreting the social world" (20). Rather than merely prescribe ceremonial behavior, courtesy literature conveyed "the logic of relationality" by which similarity and dissimilarity were constructed at court (Arditi 14). Yet they taught this relational logic to different subgroups of readers by highlighting diverse issues and assuming a variety of literary forms. As a result, conduct literature defies conventional generic divisions and can be difficult to "see" as a field of inquiry. Before addressing the challenge of rounding up this heterogeneous cluster of writings under a single definition, let us first contemplate its overall scope in terms of readership, thematic range, and formal diversity.

The implied readership for courtesy guidebooks varied greatly. Erasmus's *De civilitate morum puerilium* [On the education of young boys] (1530), for example, explicates rules of propriety to young boys. Its simple aphoristic style also made it a

---

[7] Godly books were no less susceptible to censorship than worldly ones. Luis de Granada's *Guía de pecadores* and his *Libro de oración y meditación* joined Erasmus on Fernando de Valdés's *Index of Forbidden Books* of 1559.

popular Latin copybook. Gracián Dantisco wrote *El galateo español* [*The Spanish Gallant*] (c. 1586) as if to a younger brother "avisándole lo que debe hacer, y de lo que se debe guardar en la común conversación, para ser bienquisto y amado de las gentes [warning him regarding what he ought to do and what to watch out for in public conversations in order to be well liked and beloved of the people]" (105). Baltasar Castiglione's *Il libro del Cortegiano* [*The Book of the Courtier*] (1528) initiated a more exclusive adult milieu into the art and mystique of aristocratic self-presentation at court. Antonio de Guevara directed his *Aviso de privados y despertador de cortesanos* [Warning to favorites and wake-up call to courtiers] (1539) simultaneously to aspiring courtiers and to the royal favorites that they hoped one day to unseat. Antonio de Liñán y Verdugo penned his satirical *Guía y aviso de forasteros que vienen a la corte* [Guide and warning for newcomers at court] (1620) to warn *bisoños* [newcomers] of the dangers awaiting them at court in Madrid.

A prime concern of conduct literature is image management: propriety of attire, manners, and speech at court. Corollary issues include the moral dangers of palatine life, the nature versus nurture (birth versus upbringing) debate, questions of sex and gender, the difference between human beings and other creatures, and the rights and duties of vassalage. Humanistic in their quest to delimit the outer bounds of human potential, moral-political in their pursuit of public good, and pragmatic in their response to the centripetal flow of political power, conduct guidebooks took part in the discourse of national self-definition even as they delineated the proper use of handkerchiefs or satirized those who blew their noses into them too noisily.

An emphasis on form at the expense of function has blurred these commonalities and resulted in the generic atomization of courtesy literature. The hieroglyphs of Diego Saavedra Fajardo's *Idea de un príncipe político cristiano en cien empresas* [*Royal Politician*] (1640), also known as the *Empresas políticas*, and the narrative intrigues of Alonso Jerónimo de Salas Barbadillo's didactic novel, *El caballero perfecto* [The perfect gentleman] (1620), share their commitment to entertain the reader while imparting principles of decorum. Yet this similarity is lost to view when Saavedra Fajardo is cast in the company of moralists, emblem-compilers, or treatise-writers, while Salas Barbadillo is shelved with authors of prose-fiction.[8]

---

[8] It is interesting to observe the different taxonomic strategies that historians of Spanish literature have adopted in attempting to grapple with the hybrid discursive field of conduct literature. Del Río, Alborg, Ticknor, and Díaz-Plaja situate literature of conduct within the domain of didactic prose, but they disagree as to which authors or works should be included in that domain and they do not distinguish the literature of conduct from other treatises. Chandler and Schwartz include a generous smattering of early humanist conduct writers—Erasmus, Vives, Guevara, Pérez de Oliva, Juan de Valdés, Antonio Pérez—under the rubric of *nonfiction prose of the sixteenth century*, but, again, they do not acknowledge the commonality among conduct writers, nor do they set them apart from other nonfictional prosists. The classificatory system that Menéndez Peláez and Arrellano Ayuso mobilize scatters conduct treatises among various separate headings including "Francisco de

In his survey of the contents of 65 Spanish library inventories from 1600 to 1650, José María Díez-Borque found a fairly high incidence of Gracián Dantisco's courtesy guide, *El galateo español*: six copies. But since Gracián Dantisco's little book cannot be made to fit into any canonized genre, Díez-Borque simply sets it apart as "a curious courtesy manual that incorporates novellas, stories, and anecdotes" (190).[9] For his history of Spanish literature, García Cárcel cautiously assigns Castiglione and his followers to a unit entitled "Prosa ensayística" [Essay-like prose], while in his account, R.O. Jones appears to mention Boscán's translation of Castiglione's *Il libro del Cortegiano* only because the renowned lyric poet Garcilaso de la Vega composed its preface.

How might this generic confusion be resolved in order to bring the dispersed field of conduct literature into higher relief? Northrop Frye and John Snyder offer two alternatives. Frye acknowledges the real-world applicability of conduct writings but regards the fictional worlds that many such texts create as a useful starting point for systematizing them. Because conduct literature "deals less with people as such than with mental attitudes," much of this body of work can be gathered into Frye's generic order of Menippean satire (9). Menippean satire is dialogic, imaginative, tragicomic, and socially observant, less concerned with mimesis than with conceptual analysis, and it is endlessly polymorphic. Among its many forms, Frye cites the imaginary journey, as in Swift's *Gulliver's Travels*; dream, as in Scrooge's nocturnal flight in Dickens's *A Christmas Carol*; framed collections of narratives; and colloquy (9). In fact, Frye points to the refined colloquy that structures *Il Cortegiano* to illustrate this point.[10] As we have seen, conduct guides adopt multiple forms—festive gathering, epistle to a son, "found"

Quevedo," "Baltasar Gracián," "diálogos y misceláneas [dialogues and miscellanies]," and the even more miscellaneous category, "arbitristas, tratadistas políticos y la literatura de emblemas [utopian theorists, political essayists, and emblem literature]." For Nieves Romero-Díaz, María de Guevara's anti-aulic treatise, the *Desengaños de la corte* (1663), combines the thematic preoccupation with Reason of State, as exemplified by Machiavelli's *The Prince* (1513) or Erasmus's *De Institutio Principis Christiani* (1516), with a current of writings that express concern for moral decay at court, both of which she tucks into the political essay genre (see Guevara).

[9] As awkward as Díez-Borque's single-item classification may sound, it is preferable to the fate that befell María de Guevara. One of only a few women known to have enriched the discourse on conduct with the *Desengaños de la corte* (1663) and *Tratado y advertencias hechas por una mujer* (1664), her works have only recently been made available to modern readers thanks to Nieves Romero-Díaz's critical edition of 2007.

[10] *Il Cortegiano* unfolds in the guise of a conversation at which the Duchess of Urbino and her guests fancifully, and at times philosophically, play at constructing a portrait of the ideal man and woman of court. The Duchess's guests agree that self-display occurs principally via the medium of verbal exchange, so their colloquy not only succeeds at delineating the features of an ideal man or woman of court; it simultaneously exemplifies the practice of witty conversation that distinguishes such a person. Castiglione's characters are real historical figures, but his claim to "remember" their conversations is widely understood to be a rhetorical convention.

manuscript, etc. However, the inclusivity of a class of books dealing "less with people as such than with mental attitudes" diminishes its usefulness for delineating the field of courtesy.

John Snyder moves even farther away from the formal taxonomies of the past in the attempt to grasp the heterogeneity of all literary genres. Genre for Snyder is the method by which texts engage their figural power to act upon readers: "all genres must be understood for the ways they deploy figural power" (21). He approaches texts by asking what they *do* to the reader. This privileging of the text's rhetorical force is especially relevant to a body of texts whose commonality is not structural but pragmatic. Snyder elucidates three broad generic categories differentiated by their figural power: tragedy imitates actions in order to awaken its public to (political) action; satire mobilizes rhetoric and gesture to provoke rational thought; and essay awakens self-discovery by means of philosophical experimentation. Of the three, satire is the most formally protean, "unstable," or "shape-shifting" (15–17) and at the same time the most apt descriptor for conduct literature.

For the purposes of this book, conduct literature will be understood to consist of a formally heterogeneous sub-field of satire, a genre which, for Snyder, induces rational reflection rather than political action or self-discovery. Conduct literature deploys its figurative power to prompt the reader to think about courtesy—the art or discipline of pleasing others at court. Explicitly didactic, courtesy guidebooks provided instruction for managing one's public face in urbane conversation, proper table etiquette, and ceremonial gestures. Following De Certeau, such politeness displays might be called "tactics" because, like tricks, they are "limited by the possibilities of the moment" (38) rather than launched systematically from a position of strength.[11] Once the courtier secures a toehold at court, conduct literature also professes to assist him or her in consolidating power; that is, returning to De Certeau, it teaches "strategies" for exhibiting, augmenting, and safeguarding one's place on the social pyramid.[12] Unlike the tactics listed above, such strategies presuppose the stable spatial field of the palatine environs. Chapters 2 through 4 below will trace three courtly strategies—cultivation of renown (fame), premeditated suppression of facts (dissimulation), and accommodation to unforeseen circumstances (adaptability)—that gradually altered, and were altered by, the changing profile of masculine virtue at the Spanish court.

Court and Monarchy

As the spatio-temporal field of the Spanish royal court settled in Madrid (initially in 1561; definitively after 1606), new opportunities for social ascent opened.

---

[11] "A tactic is a calculated action determined by the absence of a proper locus" (De Certeau 36–7).

[12] "Strategies pin their hopes on the resistance that the *establishment of a place* offers to the erosion of time" (38).

However, attaining an office at court required a set of competencies distinct from skill-sets cultivated by the Medieval nobleman. The Medieval lord had defended his lands from within a castle, joining forces with the then-ambulatory royal court only when summoned. To better understand the changing demands that palatine life would place upon the men and women who served at court, it is helpful to recall how the new imperial capital in Madrid differed from its Medieval predecessors. A legal definition of the Medieval court is found in Part Two of the *Siete Partidas*:[13]

> Corte es llamado el lugar donde está el rey y sus vasallos y sus oficiales con él, que le han continuamente de aconsejar y servir, y los otros del reino que se llegan allá o por honra de él, por alcanzar derecho, o por hacer recaudar las otras cosas que han de ver con él. Y tuvo este nombre de una palabra del latín que dice *cobors*, que muestra tanto como ayuntamiento de compañías, que allí se allegan todos aquellos que han de honrar y de guardar al rey y al reino.

> [The place where the King and his vassals and the officials who continually advise and serve him, and the men of the realm who are found there either in order to honor him or to acquire privileges or to stock up on the things that it supplies, is called a Court. And it got this name from the Latin word *Cohors*, which shows how the military companies all amass there, since everyone comes there to honor and guard the king and the realm.] (Part 2 Title 9 Law 27. Qtd. in Núñez de Castro 5)

This formulation makes evident that the Medieval court was a physical place [*lugar*] defined by the presence of a king, surrounded by two kinds of subjects: permanent and transient. The permanent *vasallos y oficiales* [vassals and officials] are designated as those who continually serve and advise the monarch. The transient subjects "who are found there" [*que se hallan allí*] arrive at one time or another to pay homage, sue for privileges, or obtain arms and other supplies. In addition, a strong military inflection adheres to the notion of the court through its Latin root *cohors* because the cohorts or troops of the realm, whose duty consisted in protecting the king and the kingdom, were marshaled at court.

The first quality required of a court, according to the *Partidas*, was the presence of a king. As supreme judge and military leader, the Medieval monarch convened his court in successive locations throughout the realm: where the king moved, the court accompanied him. As long as it retained its mobile character the royal court would remain, for logistical reasons, a relatively modest affair. Even Holy Roman Emperor and Spanish King Charles V continued to govern in this manner, but his Spanish successor, Philip II, converted the court from an ambulatory improvisational tribunal into an orchestrated, sedentary capital.[14] For his seat of governance, Philip selected the geographic center of the Iberian

---

[13] Literally, "Seven Entries," an influential compilation of law, custom, and social codes redacted under the supervision of Alfonso X of Castile (1251–65).

[14] The Catholic Monarchs' grandson, Charles I of Spain, became known as Charles V when he was elected Holy Roman Emperor in 1519. He was crowned emperor by Pope Clement VII in 1530.

Peninsula, Madrid. This choice earned him renown, particularly among Castilians, who benefited from having the capital seated within their borders. "[L]a mayor gloria de Felipe II [The greatest glory of Philip II]," wrote the President of the Council of Castile in 1629, "fue desde su silla, con la pluma en la mano gotosa, tener el mundo sujeto a sus resoluciones [was, from his seat, with dripping pen in hand, to have the world subject to his decisions].[15]

This change from a peripatetic to a fixed court responded to a centralizing of political power under increasingly autocratic governments, a process observed throughout Renaissance Europe, and evident in the unification of crowns under the Catholic Monarchs.[16] In fact, the ostensibly "united" Spain remained two kingdoms: jointly ruled, ethnically and religiously heterogeneous, and deeply divided. To reinforce their contested hold on this fractious aggregate, the Catholic Monarchs imposed a series of social engineering policies. They diminished the powers of the local judiciary and the aristocracy,[17] expelled the Jews in 1492, and conquered Muslim-held Granada the same year.[18] The Crown also supplanted the Church as the ultimate source for dispensing favor, or, to use Jorge Arditi's term, "grace" (107). In 1478 Pope Sixtus IV authorized the Monarchs to open a royal council of the Inquisition, known as the "Holy Office," subject to the Spanish Crown instead of to Rome. The Catholic Monarchs also obtained the papal concession known as *Patronato Regio* that granted Spanish kings the right to name archbishops, bishops, and even parish priests (Soria 443–4). To cite but a minor example of the utility of this privilege, it empowered Charles V to name royal preacher and chronicler Antonio de Guevara to the posts of Bishop of Guadix and Mondoñedo in 1527 and 1537 respectively.

---

[15] Archivo Histórico Nacional, Estado, Bk. 856, fol. 118. Qtd. in Elliott, "Máquina" 51.

[16] Ferdinand of Aragon and Isabel of Castile secretly wed in 1469 and fought to unite their hereditary realms into one kingdom. In 1479, following a five-year war of succession, their sovereignty was acknowledged throughout Spain.

[17] See Weissberger. Kamen (*Spain: 1469–1714: A Society in Conflict*) on the other hand argues that the aristocracy acceded to centralization because this preserved its own prestige. He supports this view by citing the increasing numbers of titles granted: "The political function of the aristocracy, then, had changed but not decreased. *Letrados* were prominent at all levels of government—in the councils, as *corregidores*, in the municipalities—but the great nobles still dominated the Council of State in the centre and political power in the countryside" (259–60).

[18] Nonetheless, true unification remained elusive. As late as 1625, the Count-Duke of Olivares observed in a letter to Philip IV: "quiero decir, Señor, que no se contente V[uestra] M[erced] con ser Rey de Portugal, de Aragón, de Valencia, Conde de Barcelona sino que trabaje y piense con consejo mudado y secreto, por reducir estos reinos de que se compone España al estilo y leyes de Castilla sin ninguna diferencia [I mean, Sir, that Your Majesty not content himself with being King of Portugal, of Aragon, of Valencia, Count of Barcelona; rather that, with altered and secret resolve, you labor and consider how to reduce these realms that comprise Spain to the style and laws of Castile without any difference]" (Marañón, *El Conde-Duque* 429; qtd. in Díaz-Plaja 111).

Continuing on this path of transferring power from crosier to scepter, Philip II refused to found his capital in Toledo, seat of the Archbishopric Palace; yet, as the state absorbed former Church privileges it also absorbed the mores and customs of the ecclesiastical courts. In *Knights at Court*, Aldo Scaglione traces this three-stage process of cultural borrowing from the curial courts to the chivalric courtly love tradition, to the great courts of Renaissance Europe: "there was a logical as well as factual connection among curiality/courtliness, courtesy (including courtly love) and speculation on civilized manners—all the qualities, that is, of the knightly character and chivalric gentleman, later to be generalized into the civilized gentleman" (66).

With the unprecedented expansion of the Spanish empire came expansion of the Crown's powers as well, a development that historians today see as both "impressive" and "alarming."[19] European political theorists, including Niccolò Machiavelli (1469–1527), who sought to justify strengthening royal authority, turned to Thomas Aquinas's disciple, Guido Colonna (1247–1316), later named Archbishop of Bourges, for inspiration. Colonna's *De regimine principum* first printed at Augsburg in 1473 was translated into Spanish in 1494. Colonna claimed that the prince was anointed by God; his will embodied divine will.[20] According to this doctrine of divine right, the prince functioned as a superior judge who created law but remained immune to its decrees: "He is the one who creates law, who is above it, who should govern with realism but is also obliged, as supreme judge, to govern with justice so as not to fall into tyranny."[21]

The relationship between king and kingdom was considered to be co-extensive, the realm being viewed as the body and the king as its head (or soul). Clearly the head in this conceit dominates the body, but the corporal comparison also permits a degree of reciprocity to slip into the equation, particularly in Spain. As renowned Jesuit diplomat and author Pedro de Rivadeneira (1526–1611) wrote in his anti-Machiavellian treatise on kingship, *Tratado de la religión* [Treatise on religion] (1595):

> Above all, the Prince should understand that the honors and wealth that he possesses belong more to the republic than to himself, and that he ought not distribute them according to his whim and fancy [...] because, just as prince and republic and king and kingdom make up one body, all of the service that is done for the King—as lord and head of the realm—redounds to the benefit of the whole realm, and all of the weal of the realm, as his body is the king's, and he

---

[19] For John Elliott in *La Europa dividida (1559–98)*, the monarch's powers had become "impresionante y alarmante [impressive and alarming]" (303, qtd. in García Marín 306).

[20] Guido Colonna's *De regimine principum* (1473, 1517) was known in Spain as the *Regimiento de príncipes*. It was translated into French as *Le Miroire Exemplaire et tres Fructueuse* in 1520 (qtd. in García Marín 286).

[21] "[É]l es quien crea la ley, quien está por encima de la misma, quien debe gobernar con realismo, pero también el que está obligado, como juez supremo, a gobernar con justicia para no caer en la tiranía" (García Marín 286).

should consider it as his own and grant boons accordingly with the goods of the realm, whose administration the Sovereign King of Heaven entrusted to him.[22]

As Rivadeneira sees it, to preserve himself, the king must serve and nurture the state. This mutuality would theoretically temper the king's absolute power.

Most historians agree that the Hapsburg regimes did not attain an absolutist monopoly over the reins of state. Early modern political theorists raised their voices against the unlimited royal power implicit in the doctrine of divine right. Spanish political historian J.A. Fernández-Santamaría cites three "liberal" theorists of the period who argued against absolute monarchical authority: Bartolomé de las Casas, Alonso de Castrillo, and Juan de Mariana (*La formación* 255). Countermanding pressures of Church, regional courts, and aristocratic interests prevented true absolutism from taking root in Spain (see García Marín 308–9). Humanist theologian and poet Arias Montano (1527–98) emphasized the king's duty to educate his people rather than dominate them in his *Aforismos* of 1609: "El príncipe para gobernar bien téngase por tutor y no señor de sus vasallos [To govern well, the prince should consider himself the tutor rather than the lord of his vassals]" (qtd. in García Marín 301). In practice, too, Antonio Maravall affirms that the apparatus of government under the Hapsburgs resembled a "monarchical-seigniorial complex" in which the king, the military, the upper nobility, and royal chanceries formed a sort of oligarchy rather than a purely absolutist monarchy (*Poder* 185–97).

Common to all stakeholders was the need for access to one another and especially to the monarch. The Catholic Monarchs (1479–1504) are credited with the political unification of the Iberian Peninsula. However, the physical consolidation of the Spanish court did not begin in earnest until 1561. In that year, Philip II established a permanent royal court at the Alcázar of Madrid,[23] thereby distancing the seat of government from Toledo, home to the Spanish Archbishopric, and the former capital of Visigoth Spain. Deficient in infrastructure, plagued by burning summers and freezing winters, Madrid at this time was distinguished solely by its position at the geographic midpoint of the Iberian Peninsula. The city's transformation from a town of 2,500 households into an imperial seat represented, in Jonathan Brown and John Elliott's estimation, "a triumph of policy over plausibility" (vii). However, Madrid grew quickly; by 1623, its population had swollen to 150,000.[24] Simultaneously, the monarch's retinue increased in size and splendor. Improvements were made to the austere Alcázar but Phillip IV,

---

[22] *Biblioteca de Autores Españoles* Vol. 60 (1952), 458 (qtd. in García Marín 301). Other sixteenth-century theorists included Alonso de Castrillo, Alfonso de Valdés, Juan Luis Vives, Francisco de Vitoria, Erasmus, and Juan Ginés de Sepúlveda.

[23] The Alcázar, a ninth-century Muslim fortress, was expanded in 1537. A new façade was added in 1636. It was destroyed by fire in 1734. The current Royal Palace of Madrid was built to replace the Alcázar on the same site between 1738 and 1755.

[24] Madrid remained the capital until 1601 when Phillip III yielded to pressure from his favorite, Francisco Gómez de Sandoval y Rojas, the first Duke of Lerma, to relocate his court to Valladolid, closer to the Duke's ancestral lands in Tordesillas. However, by 1606, the court returned permanently to Madrid.

urged on by his *privado*, the Count-Duke of Olivares, would supplant the fortress of the Alcázar with the more ambitious Palacio del Buen Retiro in 1633.[25]

Just as the Count-Duke envisaged the Buen Retiro palace as a physical symbol of the king's magnificence, the men and women of court were charged with inspiring awe on the world stage. The magnitude and splendor of the king's entourage metonymically represented his vassalage, and therefore, his power. By the year 1623 the royal household numbered 1,700 with each member inhabiting a rigorously choreographed orbit that revolved around the royal bodies of the king and queen (Elliott, *España* 188). In addition to the exhaustive list of ceremonial attendants and staff, the royal councils swarmed with jurists, lawyers, chroniclers, secretaries, notaries, and scribes.[26] Visiting foreign dignitaries and Spanish nobility seeking to protect and better their social status also crowded the patios and halls of the royal palace.

The movements of these intersecting social strata were highly controlled. As mentioned in the Introduction, Emperor Charles V had imposed Burgundian protocol on the men of court in 1548, which was subsequently refined and explicated in a series of decrees known as the "etiquetas de palacio [palace protocols]" (Brown and Elliott 31). But beyond the hairsplitting degrees of deference pertaining to each rung of the pyramid of power, a need arose to theorize the overall art of self-display required for advancement at court. If the doctrine of divine right theoretically invested the monarch with demagogic stature, the office of accompanying and serving the king assumed a semi-sacral air. In 1640, Saavedra Fajardo compared the privilege of counseling the king to Moses hearing the Divine Word on Mount Sinai: "Clear the brow of the glow of royal favor, as Moses did when he came down from God's presence to speak with the People, without showing magisterial ambition or flaunting your special relationship."[27] Conduct literature, beginning with Castiglione's *Il libro del Cortegiano*, aimed to teach this new urban priesthood how to defend its cause and to help it steer the monarch through one unprecedented situation after the next.[28]

---

[25] The Retiro Park in Madrid today occupies sections of the Buen Retiro palace grounds. The Baroque *estanque*, an artificial pond in the middle of the park, was also part of the palace grounds.

[26] These included majordomos, chamberlains and chambermaids, ladies and gentlemen in waiting, those in charge of the royal table, stables, grounds and wardrobe, chaplains, confessors, preachers, royal guards, court musicians, dramatists and painters, dwarves, buffoons, and the lower service staff required by the separate households of the king and queen.

[27] "Despeje de la frente los resplandores de la privanza, como hacía Moisén para hablar al pueblo cuando bajaba de privar con Dios, sin que en él se conozcan motivos de majestad ni ostentación del valimiento" (Empresa 50, 601)

[28] Although Castiglione's text is fundamentally Italian, its debt to Spanish letters merits acknowledgement. From 1525 until his death in 1529, Castiglione served in Madrid as papal nuncio to Charles V, who admired him greatly. Castiglione was buried in Toledo just days before he was to have been named Bishop of Ávila. Castiglione wrote that he

Sociability and Social Ascent

Three interwoven forces converged to bring about changes in Medieval ideals of seigniorial conduct. First, the geopolitical reunification of the Iberian Peninsula coincided with Spain's sudden emergence as a global empire. Centralization and expansion created the second factor: a burgeoning government bureaucracy that opened up new opportunities to serve the Crown in the domain of letters. Third, but also contributing to the expansionist project noted above, new military technologies called for a different style of warfare that eroded the traditional defensive function of the nobility. To meet the needs of administering Spain's vast territories in Europe, Asia, and the New World, post-Medieval universities began turning out graduates trained in rhetoric and civil law, as well as canon law. These *letrados*, as they were known, enjoyed a period of spectacular social ascent, as illustrated by Diego de Riaño Gamboa, a Salamanca-educated judge who rose to become President of the *Consejo de Castilla* and was named Count and Lord of Villariezo.[29] The prospect of social advancement attracted unprecedented numbers of both noble and non-noble families to send their sons to train at the universities (Fernández-Luzón 585–7).

At the same time, the advent of gunpowder in the West was transforming the character of early modern warfare. Military strategists came to rely less on cavalry units drawn from the noble warrior caste, the *caballero* (chevalier or knight) skilled in the arts of fighting, turning instead to large armies of harquebus- and pike-wielding infantrymen conscripted from the non-noble classes.[30] Now the sovereign looked to the landed nobility not for direct military assistance but rather to raise

---

considered himself no less a Spaniard than Italian, and his text shows a high regard for Spanish language, literature, religious fervor, military prowess, and culture (see Mades 9–32). The first translation of *Il libro del Cortegiano* into any language was Boscán's Spanish translation of 1534.

[29] The University of Salamanca was the most famous and well attended of the Spanish universities, boasting a student enrollment in the sixteenth century of 7,000, compared with 3,000 at Cambridge or the new humanist campus of Alcalá de Henares, east of Madrid (see Enrique Soria 450–51).

[30] Blanco-González avers that the Medieval class of *ricoshombres*, literally "rich men," rather than the *caballero* gave rise to the early modern courtier: "En la Edad media castellana se necesitaban tres palabras para agotar [el campo semántico] que la Edad moderna reunía en el 'cortesano': 'caballero', 'hidalgo' y 'ricohombre'; la menos rigurosa es la de 'caballero'; la intermedia, la segunda; los grandes palaciegos modernos hallaron sus antecesores en los *ricoshombres* [In Medieval Castilian, three words stood for what 'courtier' would come to represent in modern parlance: 'knight,' 'gentleman-squire,' and 'rich man.' 'Knight' is the least demanding; the second term [was] the middle one; the palace grandees descend from the 'rich men']" (30). Partida IV of the *Siete Partidas* defines *ricoshombres* as nobility of title, "aquellos que en otras tierras dicen Condes o Barones [those who in other lands are called Counts or Barons]" (qtd. in Blanco-González 95). Ramón Llull and Alonso de Cartagena require that *caballeros* be chosen from the *hidalguía* (lowest rung of the nobility), without respect to whether or not they were considered *ricoshombres* (see Cartagena 24n88). Because of their similar defensive function, I do not find it useful to maintain Blanco-González's distinctions.

and outfit private armies (Kamen, *Spain* 259–60) and to underwrite the Crown's expenses. In order to preserve their ancestral privileges, the Spanish nobility began a process of transformation from men of arms to men of arms and letters. The new services that they performed—bureaucratic, diplomatic, juridical, cultural, ecclesiastical, ceremonial, financial, and political—increasingly demanded their physical presence at the royal court in Madrid.

Whereas the right to wield a sword and mount a horse had conferred instantaneous recognition and "distinction"[31] upon the Medieval knight, the new "knights at court," as Aldo Scaglione has dubbed these urban paladins, sought distinction by refining their social skills in accordance with prevailing tastes. Norbert Elias included the development of such group-defining social codes within his theory of *civilizing processes*.[32] As Daniel Javitch explains,

> For what the courtier marks historically is the transformation of the late feudal warrior aristocrat into the polite courtier (the "civilizing process" as Elias called it) that occurred as first princely courts and then the absolutist state forced the nobility to give up its belligerence and other feudal entitlements and assume a new role as model of *politesse* and social refinement. (viii)

The new "civilized" codes of behavior that supplanted the self-evident status symbols of sword and mount were meant to demonstrate a removal from the gross material plane inhabited by soldiers, merchants, and tax-paying peasantry or *pecheros*. The *habitus*, or distinctive pattern of self-presentation of the courtier, differed from that of the Medieval *defensor*, defender or knight, who had been prized above all for military valor. At court, vulgar words were to be avoided; bodily fluids hidden; corporeal functions privatized. Conversation, too, became a competitive display of self-control.

Deference and display rituals at court became the post-Medieval battlefield on which status was negotiated. "The assertion of superiority," writes Domna Stanton with regard to the emergence of the *honnête homme*, or French gentleman of court of the seventeenth century, "always entails a component of aggression" (63). Stanton, following Nietzsche's *Genealogy of Morals*, argues that the art of courtesy appropriated the bellicose vocabulary of war in such phrases as capturing or seizing attention, dominating a discussion, vanquishing a (conversational) foe, etc. (61–105). Antonio de Guevara drew a similar parallel in his *Aviso de privados y despertador de cortesanos*, admonishing the sovereign's secretary to behave as assiduously at court as he would on the battlefield: "[E]n palacio tanto vale a las veces señalarse uno en la crianza como fuera de palacio señalarse otro en la guerra [At court, it is just as crucial to excel at civility as outside the court it is to excel at war]" (214; IX).

---

[31] Pierre Bourdieu proposes that social groups self-identify by engaging in acts of "distinction," patterns of consumption, and modes of conduct that set them apart from other groups.

[32] Elias posited a link between the separation of public behavior from private bodily functions and the gradual replacement of displays of physical prowess with displays of sociability.

This battle for recognition at court recalls Bourdieu's concept of modern class "distinction" whereby different strata of society assert their identity through distinctive patterns of consumption and taste. Regulatory technologies ranging from cod-pieces to hoop skirts—the notorious farthingales or *guardainfantes* that hid unwanted pregnancies beneath their broad flounce—sprang into prominence. The honeycombed lace collar, or *golilla*, another courtly extravagance, symbolized wealth and self-styling while separating the head from the body below. For Stephen Mennell, the court was a prison-house of fashion which turned men into "specialists in the art of consumption, entrapped in a system of fine distinctions, status battles, and competitive expenditure from which they could not escape because their whole identity depended upon it ("On the Civilizing" 389–90).

In addition to consumerism, the urban elite asserted itself sociolinguistically, in non-material status displays involving speech and gesture. "A status, a position, a social place," observes Erving Goffman,

> is not a material thing, to be possessed and then displayed; it is a pattern of appropriate conduct, coherent, embellished, and well articulated. Performed with ease or clumsiness, awareness or not, guile or good faith, it is none the less something that must be enacted and portrayed, something that must be realized. (75)

Goffman defines face-to-face interaction as the sum of all the verbal and non-verbal interaction which produces "reciprocal influence of individuals upon one another's actions when in one another's immediate physical presence" (15). It is important to distinguish these impromptu contestations from the more formalized ceremonial protocols or *etiquetas de palacio* mentioned above. Such protocols specified rights, privileges, and obligations for every cast-member in the theater of royal spectacle. However, they did not govern the spontaneous status competitions or "agonistic play," to borrow Huizinga's phrase (55–62), by which courtiers jockeyed for favor and renown.

Artificial language, artful self-presentation, and artifice itself became prized marks of sophistication and status among a nobility whose *raison d'être* had shifted from one of defense to one of display. What was to be gained by submitting to this "civilizing process"? Clearly the spectacular function of courtiership was by no means a trivial matter: the plumed and prancing men and women of court were the power brokers of their day. Frank Whigham describes the court of Elizabeth I of England as a pyramid of power. The sovereign occupied its peak. She dispensed honor, patronage, and privilege to those closest to her, and these powerful courtiers in turn furnished those below them with patronage and protection, and so on down the pyramid.

Antonio Feros observes of the Spanish court from 1580 to 1640: "Nadie podía valer algo si no era apoyado por un patrón, por un favorito real, o por el favorito del favorito [No one was worth anything without the backing of a patron, a royal favorite, or a favorite of the favorite]" (74). The intense clientelism of the court began at the apex of the pyramid of power with the king and his *privado*.

Privanza probably existed as long as the institution of monarchy itself.[33] But with the ascent to power under Philip III of Francisco Gómez de Sandoval Rojas y Borja, the first Duke of Lerma, *valimiento* attained a semi-official status it had not hitherto enjoyed.[34] Francisco de Quevedo, a contemporary of Lerma, wrote an anti-Machiavellian treatise on the subject of *privanza* in which he defined the institution as "un amor o afición entre muchos sujetos determinado a uno [A love or affection of one from among many subjects]" (107).[35] For Jesuit theologian and royal preacher Andrés Mendo (1608–84), *privanza* consisted of a more intense form of friendship: "[Although] everyone loves their prince, to the point of giving their lives for him, friendship verges on *valimiento* with he who most delights him and who best accords with his temperament" (*Príncipe perfecto* 322, qtd. in Díaz Martínez 41). Personal secretary, advisor, and confidant, the *privado* served, again in Quevedo's words, as "intermediary between the king and the people: the man on whose shoulders rest the will of the king and the weight of the republic" (211).[36] Empresa 56 of Diego Saavedra Fajardo's *Idea de un príncipe político cristiano en cien empresas* [*The Royal Politician*], "Qui a secretis ab omnibus" [He who guards the secrets of everyone], credits the secretary with being the closest confidant of the monarch, the "stomach" of the realm: "Estómago es donde se digieren los negocios y si salieren d[e] él mal cocidos será achacosa y breve la vida del gobierno [He is the stomach wherein matters of state are digested, and if he leaves them half-cooked, the life of the government will be agonizing and short]" (660).

The same combination of astuteness and opportunism that propelled a courtier to *valimiento* also made him vulnerable to corruption and influence-peddling.[37] The dangers to which the office was susceptible inspired a subgenre of moral-political treatises parallel to those devoted to kingship. Fadrique Furió Ceriol's *El concejo y consejeros del príncipe* [The prince's advice and advisory council] (1559) and Guevara's and Quevedo's abovementioned works typify a genre which imitated the traditional "mirrors of princes" treatise, only with reference to the royal favorite.[38]

---

[33] The execution of King Juan II's *privado*, Don Álvaro de Luna, Condestable de Castilla, by order of the king in 1453, served as a reminder of the risks that such privilege entailed. In 1539, the dedicatory poem preceding Antonio de Guevara's *Aviso de privados y despertador de cortesanos* speaks as if from the grave of the dead Condestable to warn future favorites to learn from his errors.

[34] The terms *privado* and *valido* refer interchangeably to the king's favorite, who was apt to receive titles and privileges and to exercise great influence over both the monarch and the royal councils. Unlike the posts of secretary or prime minister, however, *privado* and *valido* are unofficial offices. *Valimiento* is the practice of retaining a favorite.

[35] Eva María Díaz Martínez dates Quevedo's *Discurso de las privanzas* between 1606 and 1608 (see 51–8).

[36] Díaz Martínez's introduction to Quevedo's *Discurso de las privanzas* traces the history of the Spanish *privado* from the fourteenth century.

[37] Manuel Peña notes that what may look corrupt to the modern eye may be seen more objectively as merely a social network based on personal and family loyalty (251).

[38] See Díaz Martínez 39–49.

Fig. 1.1   "Qui a secretis ab omnibus," Empresa 56. Diego Saavedra Fajardo, *Idea de un príncipe politico christiano*, 1675, Valencia. The Harold and Mary Jean Hanson Rare Books Collection, Special & Area Studies Collections, George A. Smathers Libraries, University of Florida.

As noted above, despotic kingship in early modern Europe legitimized itself by recourse to a number of conceits. The republic was likened to a body with the king as head, while the monarch was compared to an actor on a world stage with the court serving as backdrop, supporting cast, and audience. But a process of transculturation contaminated the backdrop and invaded the body from the head downward. Like the hall of mirrors at Versailles, the king's retinue simultaneously exalted and reflected the supreme object of its adoration and desire. In his *Emblemata centum regio politica*, Spanish jurist Juan de Solórzano Pereira (1575–1655) praised the emulative principle whereby vassals strove to imitate their prince in an emblem dedicated in 1653 to Philip IV. Emblem 29, entitled "Sceptrorum imitatio potentissima" [The imitation of the scepter is very powerful], alludes to the biblical story of the sheep and the rods recounted in Gen. 30.31–70.[39] Solórzano's emblem depicts a herd of sheep looking into a stream in which they see reflected a thicket of scepters.

The gloss explains that royal subjects, contemplating the king's majesty, become "impregnated" by his example:

> Como la vara contemplada de distinto color bajo las aguas por el rebaño consigue que el retoño produzca un vellón de diverso color. Así la plebe considerando el ejemplo del Soberano se impregnará de los colores con los que imbuyeres la Majestad Real.

---

[39]   Jacob coaxed his father-in-law Laban's flocks into producing mixed-color offspring by displaying polychrome tree branches as they procreated.

Fig. 1.2   "Sceptrorum imitatio potentissima," Emblem 29. Juan de Solórzano Pereira, *Emblemata centum regio politica*, 1653, Madrid.

[Just as the flock viewing the reflected underwater rod which appears to have a color distinct from the original produces kids that grow fleece of a different color, so too the people looking upon the sovereign are impregnated by the colors with which the royal majesty is imbued.] (Elliott, *Lengua* 65–6)

As courtiers strove to imitate all that set the king apart, the appearance of eminence or greatness came to be considered an indispensable courtly stratagem leading to real and lasting renown.[40] Chapter 2 of this book, Fame," explicates the growing recognition that a lofty monarch required eminent men to clothe him in everlasting fame.

Following this revaluation of the functionality of acquiring fame, chapters 3 and 4 delineate parallel reappraisals of dissimulation and adaptability respectively. The ambitious subject of the Spanish court could not reveal the enmity that he felt for rivals that threatened his bid for power. To the contrary, he was obliged to display a mild and affable disposition in order to optimize his relationships with potential patrons. Chapter 3 explicates the discourse on simulation and dissimulation as the latter became an increasingly accepted tool of statecraft and self-presentation at court. Likewise, as Spain slipped from its dominant position on the world stage, the Neostoic virtue of constancy became less relevant. Nimbleness or adaptability proved to be a more effective mode of operation than rote adherence to past assumptions. Chapter 4, then, traces the re-appropriation of inconstancy—formerly a negative female gender marker—as adaptability, which became a respectable manly course of action.

---

[40] At the same time that the cultivated man endeavored to emulate royal magnificence, he also fled from the appearance of vulgarity. In the *De civilitate*, for example, Erasmus continually exhorts young boys to avoid behaving like peasants or animals. For this reason, Ronald Asch describes the process of social distinction as one of aversion to negative stereotypes rather than attraction to positive ones: "In fact, the ideals which determined noble self-perception and self-fashioning were and remained to a considerable extent dependent on a set of contrasting images which embodied everything that was vulgar and ignoble and therefore to be rejected" (151).

Chapter 2
Fame

¿Quién arrimaría a los muros las escalas, quién subiría el primero por ellos no esperando la gloria del premio?

[Who would place the ladders against the battlements; who would climb up first if not lured by the glory of the prize?]
—Juan de Lucena (1430–c. 1506)[1]

Aquí yace un hombre
que vivo dejó su nombre

[Here lies a man survived by his name]
—Epitaph for Rodrigo Manrique Lara (d. 1476)

I sometimes wonder how many address books I am in.
—Edward Zuckerman, *New York Times* contributor

Fame's Many Faces

The first time that Sansón Carrasco tries to provoke his neighbor Alonso Quijano into abandoning his knightly adventure as "Don Quixote," he poses as the Caballero del Bosque [Knight of the Woods] (II.12–15). In that guise, Sansón boasts that the greatest feat of his career had been to defeat the famous knight Don Quixote in combat: "But what gratifies me the most and makes me proudest is having conquered in single combat the most famous knight, Don Quixote of La Mancha [...]; and since I conquered him, his glory, fame, and honor have passed and been transferred to my person."[2] An astute reader of Part I of the novel (1605), Sansón Carrasco understands that Don Quixote's madness feeds on his appetite for fame. To extract from Don Quixote a pledge to return home, Sansón had decided that the easiest course of action would be to goad him into defending his fame in a mounted duel, and then topple him from Rocinante. At lance-point, he would then

---

[1] Lapesa, *Collected Studies in Honor of A. Castro's 80th Year* (Oxford, 1965), 285–6; qtd. in Rico, ed., *Lazarillo de Tormes* 6n4.

[2] Grossman 539. "Pero de lo que más me precio y ufano es de haber vencido en singular batalla a aquel tan famoso caballero don Quijote de la Mancha [...]; y habiéndole yo vencido a él, su gloria, su fama y su honra se ha trasferido y pasado a mi persona" (II.14, 735).

spare Don Quixote's life in return for promising to desist from knight errantry. But when Don Quixote unexpectedly emerges victorious from the skirmish, Sansón must retreat until he can provoke a second face-off, this time as the Caballero de la Blanca Luna [Knight of the White Moon] in chapter 64 of Part II. Carrasco's botched challenge as the Knight of the Woods frees Don Quixote to pursue his headlong quest for glory for 48 additional chapters.

Initially, the reader shares Don Quixote's ignorance of the Knight of the Woods' true identity, but the mysterious (and spurious) knight's hyperbolic speech and far-fetched claims arouse suspicion that all may not be as it appears to be with the braggadocious knight or his disguised squire. Cervantes's comedic treatment of Don Quixote's zest for *fama* in the Caballero del Bosque episodes parodies the vaunting pretense of the chivalric novel genre which reached its zenith in the sixteenth century.[3] But it also reveals that without the engine of *fama* there would be no Don Quixote and no Part I or Part II of the novel.[4] It had been *fama* that drove Don Quixote out of his hamlet and onto the plains of La Mancha, as he rhapsodizes at the outset of his first sally: "Fortunate the time and blessed the age when my famous deeds will come to light, worthy of being carved in bronze, sculpted in marble, and painted on tablets as a remembrance in the future."[5] Don Quixote's fantasy of sharing the collective glory of the Doce pares de Francia [Twelve Peers of France] and the Nueve de la Fama [Nine Worthies] also numbs him to the humiliation of his defeat at the hands of a lowly muleteer at the close of his first sally (I.5, 73).[6] Indeed, as *Don Quixote*'s putative narrator, Cide Hamete Benengeli, hangs up his quill at novel's end he apostrophizes his writing instrument, saying that it too is destined to enjoy everlasting fame (unless later historians profane it) (II.74, 1222). The quest for fame, then, is both the fertile soil that nurtures Cervantes's narrative as well as the target of its mockery. This equivocation—the text's refusal to say for sure whether fame makes or breaks its

---

[3] For Eduardo Urbina, their encounter epitomizes Cervantes's ironizing technique (137).

[4] In "La singularidad de la fama de *Don Quijote*," E.C. Riley examines *fama* in the novel as well as the singularity of the novel's fame for posterity. He reflects upon the interdependence between the themes of heroism and commemoration because "no hay fama sin publicidad [there is no fame without publicity]" (30). He also traces the theme of celebrity in Part II when Don Quixote discovers that his exploits have become known to all. Riley further acknowledges the "autonomy" of Don Quixote and Sancho, who become folkloric or legendary characters in their own right in Part II, as well as for posterity.

[5] Grossman 25. "Dichosa edad y siglo dichoso aquel adonde saldrán a luz las famosas hazañas mías, dignas de entallarse en bronce, esculpirse en mármoles y pintarse en tablas para memoria en lo futuro" (I.2, 47).

[6] The Twelve Peers were Charlemagne's knights. The Nine Worthies comprised an agglutination of three pagan, three Christian, and three Jewish heroes: Hector, Alexander the Great, and Julius Caesar; Joshua, King David, and Judah Maccabee; and King Arthur, Charlemagne, and Godfrey of Bouillon. For more on the concept of collective fame, see Van Anrooj 11, 12.

hero—invites closer scrutiny. Is it unusual for its time and place? Does it stake a new claim? The purpose of the present chapter is to reconstruct the discourse on fame in early modern Spain the better to situate the ambiguous operations of *fama* observed in *Don Quixote* either within or beyond prevailing paradigms.

The discourse on fame addresses primal anxieties concerning human mortality, the debates over corporate versus individual identity, the ethics of humility and distinction, and the polemic on ascribed versus achieved social status. The politics of reputation or *fama* set in motion sociological, religious, and psychological polemics that helped to reshape the image of masculine virtue in early modern Spain. This reshaping process was complicated by the wide semantic range that derivations of the Latin word *fama* have acquired. As Thelma Fenster observes in *Fama: The Politics of Talk and Reputation in Medieval Europe*:

> [Fame] is "rumor" and "idle talk," "the things people say." It is "reputation" and "memory" or "memories," "the things people know." It is "fame," or perhaps "glory," as well as their opposites, "infamy" and "defamation." Across its semantic range *fama* intersected with a number of other terms, such as honor, shame, status, and witnessing, and it glossed the essential nexus of performance, talk, reputation, and speech regulation [...]. It retained and incorporated meanings that had been active in Latin-speaking cultures. [Both] a good name and a bad one were called *fama*; and while *fama* denoted information or news, at the same time it meant the image formed of a person by that information. (2)

The discourse on fame from the twelfth century onward inscribes itself in texts concerned with shaping and judging men's actions and prescribing social order: in moral-political treatises, conduct guides, and funerary orations, as well as in their more consciously literary counterparts: poetry, fiction, and drama. Although the renowned Spanish critic Américo Castro (1885–1972) equated Spanish honor with fame, the implications of fame are broader and more nuanced than this equation would suggest ("Algunas observaciones" 3). In the following pages we will trace the Medieval roots of the Renaissance discourse on fame, bringing into higher relief those tensions that Cervantes's novel elaborates and transforms.

For the poet, artist, or Renaissance politician, the answer to the question of whether or not to stand out, to seek temporal fame, or to remain unrecognized begins with Dante. In the *Divine Comedy*, Dante boldly claimed for himself as poet the privilege of conferring fame and infamy on great personages of the past. In addition, as Leo Braudy observes, Dante projected himself as the figure of a lost wayfarer into the heart of the text, transforming his own search for truth into the principal dramatic action of the poem:

> Dante's decision to cast his great spiritual epic in terms of the names and careers of men and women who deserve to be remembered with honor or loathing makes a decisive break with the Medieval use of a few emblematic figures. His double role as voyager through the after-life and creator of the poem mimes his own implication in the history he attempts at once to celebrate, to judge, and to transcend. (237)

Boccaccio, Chaucer, and Petrarch would affirm Dante's vision of the author as arbiter of historical greatness.[7] Their voices joined the Christian humanist project, which shifted the ultimate purpose of life away from the afterlife and toward achievement on the earthly plane. Instead of belittling human accomplishment, humanists exalted great deeds and aspired to win recognition from others. Fame, the winning of praise, not just ephemerally, by a single act, but so thoroughly that one's name would be enshrined in the hearts of future generations became a Christian humanist virtue. However, fame's Medieval associations with infamy, vanity, gossip, and pridefulness continued to challenge emergent revalorizations of worldly accomplishment in the sixteenth and seventeenth centuries in an ongoing dialectic.

Medieval Fame

The prospect of cultivating a lasting reputation began shedding its Medieval stigma of vanity to emerge in early modern Spain as the ultimate *desideratum* of a noble life. Renown offered a kind of secular immortality, which, while less secure than everlasting salvation, could console survivors, inspire future generations, and grant a measure of satisfaction on the temporal scale of human history. The promise of ennoblement held out by Spain's eight-centuries-long *Reconquista* lends a unique Spanish spin to the discourse on renown. The Berber chief Tarik Ibn Ziyad entered Visigoth Spain to claim most of the peninsula for Islam in 711. From 756 to 1212, the Umayyad Caliphate of Córdoba and its successors maintained control over much of the peninsula, extracting tributes from the formerly Christian kingdoms in exchange for relative religious and economic autonomy. The balance of power started tipping back toward the Christians around 1212, but both before and after that date, knights who fought against the domestic "infidels" (known as the "Moors") stood to win lands, wealth, and ennoblement for themselves and their descendants. In this manner, many noble bloodlines arose from non-noble origins during the *Reconquista*.[8] It is telling for example that while France's Medieval epic hero, Roland, was of royal blood, his rough equivalent in Spain, El Cid Campeador [El Cid the Champion], based on the exploits of Rodrigo Díaz de Vivar (1043–99), belonged to the ranks of *infanzones* or minor nobility. As Colin Smith notes, Rodrigo's middling origins did not prevent him from marrying King Sancho II's niece, Ximena, or, in turn, wedding his daughters to titled noblemen (35).

El Cid wins fame in *El cantar del mío Cid* [*The song of the Cid*] (c. 1240) through social ascent, but care must be taken to distinguish the semantic variations

---

[7] Braudy cites other classical precedents as well. For example, Petrarch (1304–74), who detailed the outstanding deeds of military and political figures of antiquity in his *De viris illustribus* [On famous men], written in 1347, took as his model the Roman historian Livy.

[8] "El fácil acceso a la hidalguía desde los siglos de la Reconquista, había hecho inmenso el número de los privilegiados [Easy access to the lowest rung of the nobility ever since the centuries of the Reconquest had swelled the numbers of the privileged]" (Rico, ed., *Lazarillo de Tormes* xxxii).

that *fama* continued to exhibit throughout the Medieval and early modern periods. *Fama* in *El cantar del mío Cid* does not refer to terrestrial glory but rather to the annulment of *infamia* [infamy]. In his last triumphal discourse, El Cid thanks God for the restoration of his daughters' honor (they had been abused and disgraced by their first husbands), without a word regarding the heroic exploits he had undertaken to make them whole again:

> ¡Grado al rey del cielo, mis fijas vengadas son!
> ¡Ahora las hayan quitas heredades de Carrión!
> Sin vergüenza las casaré a qui[en] pese o a qui[en] no.
>
> [I thank the Sovereign of Heaven that my daughters are avenged.
> Let them now be rid of the Carrión estates.
> Without shame I shall marry them off as I see fit.] (269)

Fama, here signifying good reputation, accords with the Cid's humility before God, and his lack of boastfulness regarding his military feats. However, other usages would associate *fama* with the sin of vanity.

The *Libro de la Orden de Caballería* [*Book of the Order of Chivalry*] written by Catalonian mathematician and mystic Ramón Llull (c. 1232–1313) rehearses the theological argument against aspiring to fame. Llull's ideal knight would defend his king's territories and his own, while adhering to the Christian principle of humbleness. Two passages from the *Libro* especially denounce the thirst for personal glory:

> If the squire is prideful about his deeds, he is not a good candidate for knighthood, as pridefulness is a vice that destroys the virtues and honors that are Chivalry's rewards. (III, sec. 19)
>
> [[…] if you, prideful knight, wish to overcome your pride, gather in your heart humility and fortitude.] (VI, sec. 13)

Llull binds the urge for renown to the sin of pridefulness. For him, the lure of fame represents a mortal temptation. In an appendix to the *Libro de la Orden de Caballería* called the *Libro de contemplación* [Book of contemplation], Llull explains that the knight who sacrifices his life for the sake of glory or riches forfeits heaven because fame and wealth are false gods that cannot offer their adherents salvation from death (Appendix, sec. 8). Analogously, to cite cultural anthropologist Ernst Becker's analysis of the cruel joke that capital plays on its worshippers, "the new god Money that we pursue so dedicatedly is not a god that gives expiation! It is perverse" (89).[9]

---

[9] In 1974 Becker was posthumously awarded the Pulitzer Prize for *The Denial of Death* (1973), which argues that identity springs from the individual's ability to face his or her mortality.

Against Llull's condemnation of the idolatry of riches and fame, the secular defense of fame appeared in Spain as early as the fourteenth century. Guarding one's *buena fama* or "good name" and combating *mala fama*, "bad name" or infamy was a matter of legal consequence in Medieval Spain. According to Alfonso X's Castilian legal code, the *Siete Partidas* [Seven Entries] (1261–65): "Reputation (*fama*) is the good state of a man who lives justly according to law and good customs, having no defect or mark. Defamation means an attack made *contra la fama* of a person called in Latin *infamia*" (VII.6.2, qtd. in Bowman 103). *Infamia* disqualified the accused from serving at the royal court or in Church offices, and rescinded certain legal prerogatives such as the right to draw up a will or testify in court. Because idle gossip could spread *infamia* without the benefit of a trial, it became essential to take proactive measures to safeguard one's valuable—and volatile—reputation.

Castilian warrior-prince and author Don Juan Manuel (1282–1348) staged a full-throated apology for *fama*. Don Juan Manuel anticipates three facets of *fama* that would gain visibility with the rise of humanism: good reputation, renown, and individuality. His *Conde Lucanor* [*Count Lucanor*], an anthology of prudential conduct *exempla* [examples] gleaned from oriental and Latin sources, opens with a prologue explaining Juan Manuel's method for shielding his reputation as an author. It is his custom to deposit an original manuscript of each of his works at his castle in Peñafiel in order to defend the purity of his work against distortions caused by scribal error:

> E porque don Juan vio e sabe que en los libros [a]contecen muchos yerros en los trasladar [...] e los que después fallan aquello escrito ponen la culpa al que hizo el libro; e porque don Juan se receló de [e]sto, ruega a los que leyeren cualquier libro que fuere trasladado del que él compuso, o de los libros que él hizo, que si fallaren alguna palabra mal puesta que no pongan culpa en él hasta que vean el libro mismo que don Juan hizo [...].
>
> [And because Don Juan realizes that many errors arise in the process of copying books [...] and that those who later find those writings place the blame for those errors on the author, and because Juan Manuel feared this, he implores that whoever might read a copy of a book that he composed or that he created, should he find any misplaced words, that he not blame the author until he has seen the original that Juan Manuel himself made [...].] (70)

Like Dante, Juan Manuel projected himself into the fictional universe of *El Conde Lucanor* in order to gain renown, not as a pilgrim, but as a judicious editor and critic. At the end of each tale, an omniscient narrator states that he, Juan Manuel, deemed the preceding example worthy of inclusion in his book. Whereupon "Juan Manuel" seizes upon this metalepsis to insert a couplet of his own that summarizes the moral lesson just recounted. For instance, at the end of perhaps the most widely anthologized of the *Conde Lucanor*'s 51 examples, Example 11, entitled "De lo que [a]conteció a un Deán de Santiago con don Yllán, el Gran Maestro de Toledo" [What happened to a Deacon of Santiago with Don Illán, the Great Master of Toledo], the narrator informs the reader:

Y porque entendió don Juan que era éste muy buen consejo, hízolo poner en este libro e hizo estos avisos que dicen así:
Al que mucho ayudare y no te lo conociere,
menos ayuda habrás d[e] él des[de] que en gran honra subiere.

[And because Don Juan understood that this was very good advice, he had it put in this book, and he composed these wise words that say the following:
From him whom you've helped to win fame / Do not expect help once he's earned a name.] (124)[10]

Furthermore, in his prologues, Juan Manuel takes the opportunity to publicize his other works.[11] He also promotes his image as a literary dynamo by not mentioning that most of his *exempla* borrow from extant sources (Manuel 53).

Juan Manuel, in his *Libro de los estados* [*Book of the Estates*] (c. 1326–30), generally considered the best extant portrait of fourteenth-century Spanish seigniorial society, not only promotes his own reputation; he urges readers to cultivate theirs as well. Like Plato, Juan Manuel divides society into three estates: *oradores* [clerics], *defensores* [knights], and *labradores* [laborers]. In the *Libro de los estados*, Juan Manuel urges his readers not to hide behind these corporate identities, but rather to earn renown for themselves. However, as Villacañas Berlanga cautions, the prospect of competition for glory does not threaten the social order because the *Libro de los estados* only encourages achievement within the bounds of each estate:

> Man, each man, should earn renown through his deeds and not hide behind those of his lineage. But, even taking family extraction into account, not just anyone can work his way up to functions assigned to a different estate. To the contrary, estate-based society applies the test of birth to all social functions. It is birth that determines access to any given office (4–5).

Implicit in Juan Manuel's call for renown is the notion of individuality. This becomes more explicit in the second prologue to the *Conde Lucanor*, in which the author develops an authentic theory of subjectivity to account for the phenomenon of differential reader response. After adducing the fact that no two human faces are alike, he observes that no two men share the same desires or motives: "menor marabilla es que aya departimiento en las voluntades y en las entenciones de los omnes [it is even less surprising that there be deviations in the aspirations and intentions of people]" (71). These deviations from person to person account for the

---

[10] The theme of the ungrateful disciple informs Juan Ruiz de Alarcón's *La prueba de las promesas* (1634) (see Sotelo 117n11, as well as Salas Barbadillo's *El caballero perfecto*). Translator's note: I opted for a looser translation of Juan Manuel's couplet here in order to convey the pleasing mnemotechnical rhythm and rhyme of the original.

[11] He lists only the *Crónica abreviada*, *Libro de los sabios*, *Libro de la caballería*, *Libro del infante*, *Libro del caballero y del escudero*, *Libro del Conde*, *Libro de la caza*, *Libro de los engaños*, and *Libro de los cantares*. The *Libro de la caballería* has been lost, but he is known to have composed numerous other works (see Sotelo 24–5).

author's decision to write all of his works in *romance* (i.e., early Spanish): "que los hizo para los legos, e de non muy grand saber como lo él es [he wrote them for the unlettered, and for those lacking in the vast wisdom that he possessed]" (70). Likewise, given the different abilities of his target audience, Juan Manuel sweetens his moral medicine to make sure that as many readers as possible will "digest" it properly (72–3).[12]

Juan Manuel's *Conde Lucanor* and *Libro de los estados* foreground three distinct yet related oppositional pairs that would continue to mark the discourse on *fama* for the next 400 years: fame/infamy, humility/celebrity, and achievement/pedigree. In the fifteenth and sixteenth centuries, epideictic oratory, that is, speeches whose purpose was to fix the memory of the dead in the minds of the living, began incorporating men's accomplishments into the summation of their worth. The old nobility's concept of merit relied strictly on pedigree, without regard to actions. According to Carrasco Martínez: "For the nobility, part of their definition as nobles was tied to dead ancestors, for it was genealogy that certified their integrity and superiority."[13] Yet a growing number of Spanish subjects who lacked noble ancestry sought distinction through other means. Not least among those determined to scale the social ladder were thousands of "New Christians," Jews who had converted to Christianity to escape the massive pogroms of 1391.[14] For New Christians, as well as other functionaries, merchants, bankers, explorers, conquerors, and men of science and letters who lacked pedigree, distinction lay in each man's unique ability to contribute to society. As the ethos of individual achievement gained adherents, Carrasco Martínez notes, orations commemorating the dead began venturing to praise the departed's actions and traits as well as lineage: "Some [sermons for the dead] already showed signs of not being entirely comfortable with opting for the certainty of family honor at the expense of celebrating the deceased's individual traits."[15]

Perhaps the most well-known funerary poem of the fifteenth century is the *Coplas por la muerte de su padre*, which Jorge Manrique (1440–79) penned upon the death of his father, Rodrigo Marique de Lara, Grand Master of the Military Order of Santiago (1406–76), elegantly rendered into English by Henry Wadsworth Longfellow as "Ode to the Death of his Father" (Crow 22–31). The

---

[12] While the author's insistence on his superiority to his target audience might strike modern readers as condescending, it is noteworthy for its frank treatment of the challenge posed by different cultural literacy levels. To the extent that he prides himself on his literary superiority and believes that his writings augment his honor, Juan Manuel anticipates the democratizing impulse of humanism that would place arms and letters on at least an equal footing.

[13] "Para los nobles, la referencia a los muertos del linaje era parte de su definición como tales nobles, pues era la sangre familiar la que acreditaba las virtudes y la superioridad" (Carrasco Martínez 31).

[14] Estimates vary greatly. Jane Gerber estimates 100,000 Spanish Jews converted after 1391, with another 50,000 converting by 1415 (Gerber 115–17).

[15] "En algunos casos ya no resultaba tan claro que fuese tan confortable convivir con las certezas de la excelencia si anulaban los rasgos de lo individual" (Carrasco Martínez 32).

40-stanza poem measures the sum of Rodrigo's life in transcendent Christian terms. As a slayer of infidel Moslems, as loyal vassal, and as benevolent lord of his lands, the poem argues that Rodrigo merits divine redemption. The *Coplas*'s reiterative allusions to the soul, salvation, and afterlife lend it a solemn, doctrinal air, while elegiac *topoi—ubi sunt* [where have they gone?] and *tempus fugit* [time flees], etc.—impart a patina of cultural refinement. The poetic and philosophical impact of the *Coplas* is further intensified by its accessible yet powerful imagery, which compares life to a road (line 49) and to a tributary flowing into a great river of humanity toward the sea of death (lines 25–36).

While the *Coplas* tells us that the purpose of Rodrigo's life had been to merit salvation, Manrique's verses also show signs, in Carrasco Martínez's words, of "not being entirely comfortable with opting for the certainty of family honor at the expense of celebrating the deceased's individual traits" (32). Almost a quarter of the poem (lines 289–390) pays tribute to Rodrigo's worldly fame, earned through military, political, and social achievements. As if catching himself, however, the poetic voice inserts a parenthetical caveat recalling that earthly glories count little compared to the rewards of eternal life:

> (aunque esta vida de honor
> tampoco no es eternal
> ni verdadera);
> mas, con todo, es muy mejor
> que la otra temporal
> perecedera)

[A life of honor and of worth / Has no eternity on earth, / 'T is but a name; / And yet its glory far exceeds / That base and sensual life, which leads / To want and shame] (lines 415–20, Crow 30).

The caveat-within-a-caveat that constitutes the last three lines of this stanza assembles a hierarchy of perdurability. Celestial glory guarantees the most enduring afterlife, followed by the more perishable glory of earthly honor, followed in last place by the tenuous flash of earthly renown. Nonetheless, Manrique's ode ends most earthily, shifting focus from its metaphysical and historical treatment of Manrique's life to the psychological impact that his death will have on heirs and survivors. The poem admits that abstract knowledge of Rodrigo's eternal and even terrestrial glory—matters that had taken up the preceding 39 stanzas of the poem—cannot comfort those who mourn his loss. Only the memory of Rodrigo's life can ease the survivors' grief:

> que aunque la vida perdió
> dejónos harto consuelo
> su memoria.

[And, though the warrior's sun has set, / Its light shall linger round us yet, / Bright, radiant, blest.] (lines 475–80, Crow 31)

Although the *Coplas* initially appear to ratify doctrinal Christian mistrust of fame, they perform an act of homage that undercuts their own homiletic pretenses. By lavishing attention on Rodrigo's military feats, by conceding that fame offers a lesser form of eternal glory, and by celebrating the consoling power of human memory, the *Coplas* ultimately shine with the "bright, radiant" light of Rodrigo's worldly fame. Furthermore, the poem reflects hallowing light on its author, making Manrique look superior to his literary peers. The unadorned poetic voice of the *Coplas* recalls the simplicity of biblical parable. Rather than compete with the heavy Latinate style of his contemporaries, Manrique draws a subtle parallel between his father's exemplary life and that of a character from the New Testament, and ties his own legacy to that of a sacred text. In Kristin Kennedy's words, "the writer ennobles his subject and the subject ennobles the writer" (115).

El Cantar del mío Cid, Llull's *Llibre de l'ordre de cavalleria*, Juan Manuel's didactic writings, and Manrique's *Coplas* do not obey Manrique's conceit of tributaries flowing toward the sea. Rather than a swelling river that inexorably engulfs the Renaissance in its "frenzy of renown,"[16] these Medieval texts sound different, often discordant notes regarding fame that recur in varying combinations with scant regard for chronological progress. Recall for example that *El Cantar del mío Cid* celebrated Ruy Díaz's dizzying social ascent, a feat more reminiscent of Horatio Alger or Jay-Z than of traditional models of feudal stratification. Conversely, the concept of "eternal glory" trumpeted by Llull and echoed two centuries later by Manrique retains suasive potency into the twenty-first century. President Obama in his speech to residents of Newtown, Connecticut following the massacre of 20 kindergarteners in December 2012 invoked the ancient New Testament promise of life everlasting: "For our light and momentary troubles are achieving for us an eternal glory that far outweighs them all."[17] Instead of charting an evolutionary trend, this cluster of Medieval texts foregrounds three recurring issues associated with fame—the problem of avoiding infamy by cultivating a good name or *fama*; the choice of seeking acclaim on earth or seeking God's reward in Heaven; and the question of whether man's worth derives from ascribed (inherited) virtue, individual achievements, or a combination of the two. As we shall see, these tensions continue to energize the Renaissance discourse on the manly virtue of fame.

Early Modern Fame

Leo Braudy has documented the "frenzy of renown" that swept Elizabethan and Jacobean England, converting arts and letters into cultural forces potentially rivaling those of Church and State. The printing press, the centralization of power in the hands of a diminishing number of semi-autocratic monarchs, the advent of secular humanism, and the economic opportunities offered by international trade

---

[16] See the discussion of Leo Braudy's *The Frenzy of Renown* below.
[17] 2 Cor. 4.17.

and commerce can be cited as factors contributing to this shift. Without ignoring Spain altogether, Braudy's interest lies in the cult of fame in Reformation Europe. Regarding Spain, he notes that the Jesuits promoted art "that would glorify the Church and the Catholic reformers" (315), and he counts Velázquez among those painters who wrested art from servile instrumentality to grant it expressive agency in its own right, thus opening the door to *fama* for artists. Braudy's canny analysis of the paintings-within-a-painting of *Las Meninas* [The maids of honor], as well as the pose that the figure of Velázquez assumes within that composition, expose both the tension between the court painter's aspiration to rise above the level of a journeyman to claim humanist eminence in his own right and his awareness that striving for fame entails high-stakes risks (326–30). The paintings that Velázquez shows lining the studio where he paints himself in the act of painting the royal family in *Las Meninas*, depict several Ovidian allegories that warn of the dangers of overreaching; for example, the castigation by Apollo of Marsyas and Minerva's revenge on Arachne. As Braudy states, "By invoking the Marsyas analogy made by Raphael, Titian, Michelangelo and others, Velázquez combines motifs of artistic assertion with motifs that stress the limits of what an artist can be" (327).

In addition to allegorizing the conflicts raised by self-referential art and committing the defiant act of placing himself within his painting, Velázquez imposed his presence on his canvas through his *colorido* [coloring] painting style. The *dibujo/diseño* [draw/design] style practiced by Velázquez's master, Francisco de Pacheco, required the painter to create many preliminary drawings prior to filling in his canvas, a procedure resulting in a polished, finished product. By contrast, Velázquez's *colorido* style drew attention to the process of brushing pigment directly on the canvas. Thickly textured strokes permitted the artist to redo his work along the way and obliged observers to adjust their gaze to the point at which the resulting swishes of color merged into an intelligible whole (Robbins, *Arts* 82–3).

Like Velázquez, Spanish Renaissance and Baroque authors sought to chart a safe passage between the Scylla of self-effacement and the Charybdis of ambition and vanity. In the age of print, Renaissance writers courted renown through publishing. Yet they prefaced their books with professions of humility to their patron and readers. Moralists bent on dissuading readers from pursuing worldly fame faced a similar paradox. They could scarcely be said to practice what they preached if they gained renown by publishing their sermons on Christian humility. As fame edged toward acceptance as a humanist virtue, the debate on eminence as both an aspiration and a measure of courtly accomplishment intensified.

Fernando de Rojas's dialogized novel of 1499–1501, *La tragicomedia de Calixto y Melibea* [*The Tragicomedy of Calixto and Melibea*], more commonly known as *La Celestina*, wrestles with questions of fame, achievement, and immortality from the perspective of Pleberio, a self-made magnate. Pleberio's Lament in Act 21 articulates the anguish of a father, Pleberio, who witnesses the suicide of his only daughter and heir, Melibea. Melibea leaped to her death from a tower on Pleberio's estate after learning that her secret lover, Calixto, had fallen to his death after their recent tryst. Ironically, by choosing the tower as her means of suicide, Melibea confronts Pleberio with the futility of erecting a lasting legacy on earth. Peter Russell notes that Pleberio's name derives from the Latin word *plebeius*, or 'commoner' (81), implying that Pleberio had managed to achieve success despite non-noble lineage. As Pleberio wrestles with the implications of Melibea's death, he cries out to his wife with a mixture of anguish, belligerence, and self-concern:

> PLEB: ¡Ay! ¡Ay! ¡Noble mujer! Nuestro gozo en el pozo. Nuestro bien todo es perdido. No queramos más vivir [...]. Que ya quedas sin tu amada heredera. ¿Para quién edifiqué torres? ¿Para quién adquirí honras? ¿Para quién planté árboles? ¿Para quién fabriqué navíos? [...] Del mundo me quejo, porque en sí me crió: porque no me dando vida, no engendrara en él a Melibea. No nascida, no amara. No amando, cesara mi quejosa y desconsolada postrimería. ¡O mi compañera buena, oh mi hija despedazada! [...] ¿por qué me dejaste penado?
>
> [PLEB: Ay! Ay! Noble wife! Our joy in the void! All our fortune is lost; what more is there to live for? [...] For you are bereft of your beloved heir. Why did I build towers? For whom did I win honor? For whom did I plant trees? For whom fabricate ships? [...] I blame the world for I was raised in it, since, had it not given me life, I would not have given birth in it to Melibea. Had she not been born, she would not have loved, and not having loved, this final inconsolable wail would cease. Oh my good companion, o my shattered daughter! [...] why did you leave me in grief?] (337–47)

The fame that eludes Pleberio consists of a kind of immortality imparted by what the early twentieth-century psychologist Otto Rank called "time-defying monuments." For Rank, father-son competition results in the son's drive to build a more impressive, more monumental legacy than that of the father, a legacy which will earn the son lasting recognition in the eyes of future generations (18, qtd. in Becker 74). Pleberio did not reckon that the race to build a "time-defying monument" could jeopardize the more modest legacy promised by his daughter's fertility. However, once Calixto's go-between, the bawd Celestina, had overcome Melibea's scruples, the maiden's only hope for avoiding disgrace would have been keen parental oversight. Tragically, however, her affair with Calixto unfolded undetected while Pleberio sought fame and erected towers. By overlooking Melibea's biological clock and permitting her to remain unwed for too long, Pleberio sacrificed the claim on the future that her offspring would have granted him.

Melibea's death-by-tower betrays Pleberio's failure to treat his daughter as something other than a receptacle for his wealth. Compounding the text's condemnation of the proposition that "accumulated things are a visible testimonial to power" (Becker 89) is the conspicuous absence in his plaint of any thought for the state of Melibea's soul. Surely, according to Spanish Catholic dogma, Melibea must be damned for dying by suicide without confession following an illicit affair. Yet, as Alan Deyermond notes, "He does not think about Melibea's fate in eternity; only of the consequences for himself, in this world: emotional emptiness; a wasted investment" (174).

Melibea's death mocks Pleberio's ambition to fashion his daughter into an enduring monument to his achievements. Self-pity at his failure so engulfs Pleberio that his final recitation of the Catholic "Salve, Regina" hymn, "¿por qué me dejaste triste y solo? *in hac lachrimarum valle*? [Why did you leave me sorrowful and alone in this vale of tears?]" (347) equates his suffering with that of Jesus martyred on the cross. Rojas leaves it to his reader to penetrate Pleberio's "veil" of tears. Self-made Pleberio is no martyr and his suffering does not promise deliverance. He brings about his own demise through the double error of seeking to immortalize his name through "filthy lucre" and, thereby, forfeiting the biological imperative of the species.

Pleberio's abortive mercantile venture marks a divergence between the gender orders of Northern Atlantic Europe and the countries of the Mediterranean. The mercantilist "captain of commerce" ideal toward which Pleberio strove, like Protestantism itself, would be "strangled at birth" in Spain (Kamen, *Spain* 127).[18] Counter-Reformation polities tended to perform worse economically than Protestant ones because Catholicism provided fewer incentives and more stumbling blocks for acquiring and capitalizing wealth (Weber).[19] From the sixteenth century onward, Catholicism retained its Medieval proscription on usury, remained wary of material gain, and maintained that heaven was open to rich and poor alike, while North Atlantic Protestantism, and especially where Calvinist dogma prevailed, made wealth a sign of election by God, reserved for a chosen few, but highly prized by all. While the masculine ideal of the self-made patrician would eventually flourish in Geneva and Holland, mercantile magnates did not succeed in forming a strong merchant class in Rojas's Castile.[20]

The anonymous picaresque novel, *La vida de Lazarillo de Tormes y de sus fortunas y adversidades* [*The Life of Lazarillo de Tormes and his Fortunes and Adversities*] (1554) paints a more robust but equally ambivalent portrait of manly ambition for fame than Rojas's *Tragicomedia*. Although its low-born protagonist, Lázaro, never approaches Pleberio's commercial success, he does manage to

---

[18] The suppression of Protestantism in Spain took many forms. The Spanish Inquisition began targeting suspected followers of Martin Luther in 1528. By 1559, the first Spanish Index forbad books penned by suspected heretics such as Erasmus. *Autos da fe* carried out against convicted Protestants from 1559 to 1562 terrorized the populations of Valladolid and Seville. In 1559 Philip II ordered Castilians studying at most foreign universities to return home (see Kamen, *Spain* 121–7).

[19] In a 2009 study published in the *Quarterly Journal of Economics*, Professor Sascha Becker demonstrated a statistical linkage between the distribution of Catholics or Protestants in European countries, higher education levels, and economic performance. He found that predominantly Protestant countries tended to display both a more highly educated population and superior economic performance (see Arnot).

[20] Nonetheless, a cadre of Dominican, Franciscan, and Jesuit canon lawyers at the University of Salamanca between 1536 and 1605 can be credited with laying the theoretical ground for modern capitalist economics within a Catholic framework. Key members of the "Salamanca School" include its founder, Francisco de Vitoria, Domingo de Soto, Martín de Azpilcueta, and Luis Molina, among others (see Grice-Hutchinson, and Grice-Hutchinson and Moss).

escape the mean streets of Salamanca and Toledo, secure a royal office, marry, and establish a permanent home. Narrating in the first person, Lázaro prides himself on having attained respectability through his own talent and effort: "because consider how unremarkable are the achievements of those who, with Fortune on their side, inherited their titles, compared to the achievements of those who braved the tides of adversity, and by sheer perseverance and cleverness reached a safe harbor."[21] Forty-one years later, Jesuit theologian Pedro de Rivadeneira (1526–1611) would lend support to *Lazarillo de Tormes*'s defense of the self-made man. In his anti-Machiavellian *Tratado de la Religión* [*Treatise on Religion*], Rivadeneira argued that individual achievement deserves greater recognition than lineage because "everyone is the son of his own works."[22] Nobility for writers like Rivadeneira in the sixteenth century and for Juan de Baños de Velasco and Juan de Lancina in the seventeenth made it easier to prove one's worth, but, in the end, high birth provided only "una ventaja de colocación [a placement advantage]" (Maravall, *Teoría* 333) in the race for fame.[23]

Lázaro's birth was anything but auspicious. His father was a thief and his mother bore Lázaro a half-brother with a Morisco stable-hand.[24] Losing this dual stigma alone would have significantly improved Lázaro's social standing, but he did not rest with recounting his escape from *infamia*; he actually hoped that his narrative would launch him to the heights of *fama*. Why else would he—or the anonymous author of this pseudo-autobiography—take the trouble to write down his story if not to win acclaim? Lázaro admits that, like the soldier who fights for fame and glory, the writer writes in hopes that his efforts will bear "algún fructo [some kind of fruit]." As Cicero long ago observed, "honor nurtures the arts" (6).

Both Pleberio and Lázaro crave a kind of secular immortality that had not yet gained widespread legitimacy in early modern Spain. Pleberio fails to project himself into the future because there is no one left standing at the end of the *Tragicomedia* to whom to bequeath his wealth.[25] Lázaro seeks renown by

---

[21] "[P]orque consideren que los que heredaron nobles estados cuán poco se les debe, pues Fortuna fue con ellos parcial, y cuánto más hicieron los que, siéndoles contraria, con fuerza y maña remando, salieron a buen puerto." (7). Navigational metaphors commonly evoked the improvisational skills required for statecraft and social ascent (see Chapter 4 below.)

[22] *Tratado de la Religión y virtudes que debe tener el Príncipe cristiano para gobernar y conservar sus Estados. Contra lo que Nicolás de Maquiavelo y los políticos de este tiempo enseñan* (Madrid, P. Madrigal, 1595), 528–9. In *Boletín de A.A.E.E.*, Vol. 60 (qtd. in Maravall, *Teoría del estado* 332).

[23] See Juan Baños de Velasco, *Discurso de la verdadera y jurídica razón de Estado, formados sobre la vida y acciones del Rey Don Juan* II (Coimbra, 1629); Juan Alfonso Rodríguez de Lancina, *Comentarios políticos a los Anales de Cayo Vero Cornelio Tácito* (Madrid, 1687), qtd. in Maravall, *Teoría del estado* 332–3.

[24] Morisco refers to Moslems converted to Christianity. Although not all Moriscos were dark-skinned, the term implied impurity and dark-hued skin.

[25] Cervantes's exemplary novel, "El celoso extremeño" [The jealous Exremaduran], likewise emblemizes the "sterility" of seeking self-perpetuation through wealth by recourse to the poetics of the unreproductive female body (see Armon, "The Paper Key").

displaying his own ignominy on a printed page that, ironically, symbolizes his entrance into educated circles. But does trading on his defects for the sake of fame produce the desired effect? Extratextually, the novel's anonymity undercuts its claim to fame. But the internal logic of the text is more nuanced. On the one hand, *Lazarillo de Tormes* was a publishing sensation both within Spain and internationally and can be credited with initiating the new genre of the picaresque novel.[26] On the other hand, the character Lázaro pays a high price to obtain the modicum of respectability that a wife, a home, and a livelihood represent. The devil's bargain that he strikes consists of sharing his wife with the Archpriest of San Salvador, who arranges Lázaro's marriage to cover his own affair with the lass in question. This compromise suits Lázaro until it becomes fodder for gossip, or *infamia*. Although the text shrouds this aspect of Lázaro's life in ambiguity, it would appear that the unidentified dignitary who has commanded Lázaro to record his life-story and whom Lázaro addresses as "Vuesa Merced [Your Grace]," is investigating rumors concerning Lázaro's wife's frequent visits to the Archpriest's house. Presumably, Lázaro's amusing account of his peripatetic childhood aims to impress this personage with his resourcefulness at having arrived "en mi prosperidad y en la cumbre de toda buena fortuna [at my prosperity and the height of all good fortune]" (80). But enterprise and initiative did not enjoy the prestige in sixteenth-century Spain that they do today; to the contrary, idleness and unproductivity distinguished the nobility, while toil and effort denoted low birth. When Lázaro's mother, Antoña, releases her son into the care of his first *amo* [master], a blind charlatan, she blesses him with the words, "válete por ti [make do on your own]" (13). Her advice to "make do" becomes the watchword for Lázaro's subsequent struggle for survival and the yardstick by which he comes to measure his own success. Her parting words also explain why Lázaro is willing to place his honor in jeopardy by sharing his wife with the Archpriest in exchange for protection. Self-preservation comes first; honor second.

Lázaro's third master, an impecunious squire, serves as a foil to Lázaro's pragmatism, for he places honor above self-preservation, exile above indignity, and even starvation above accepting charity. Having eaten nothing all day Lázaro's third master ostentatiously picks his teeth with a straw to create the impression that he has dined well. Lacking any money, connections, or means of self-support, this caricature of aristocratic entitlement allows his servant Lázaro to beg for him, on condition that he keep secret their arrangement. The pompous squire abandons his home over a non-existent slight to his honor and brags that, if only they weren't in ruins, his property and dove-cote would make him rich (60–63). He disdains to serve in a noble house yet admits that no one has offered him a position. The squire's elitist "fantasía [empty pomp]" (54) contrasts starkly with Lázaro's effort

---

[26] Four editions are known to have appeared in 1554 (Antwerp, Burgos, Medina del Campo, and Alcalá de Henares), probably following an earlier lost original. A year later, an anonymous sequel came out in Antwerp. In 1559, *Lazarillo* was placed on the Index of Forbidden Books and only reappeared, expurgated, in 1573. It was widely translated and enjoyed a resurgence of interest in Spain following the publication of Mateo Alemán's two-volume picaresque novel, *Guzmán de Alfarache* in 1599 and 1604.

to make do on his own, a contrast that begins to justify Lázaro's willingness to tolerate a ménage à trois. The squire's hollow adherence to a conduct code that he can no longer sustain also underscores the old nobility's growing irrelevance in an increasingly capital-driven economy.

Lázaro parades the charlatan blind man, the pretentious squire, and many other unscrupulous masters before the eyes of Vuesa Merced for two effects. First, to make himself look better by comparison, and second, to heighten the impact of his self-made success. However, fearing that his tale of self-improvement would not suffice to save his name, Lázaro also makes an old-fashioned appeal to nepotism. Vuesa Merced and the Archpriest are good friends. To fault, prosecute, or punish Lázaro for his complicity in the Archpriest's affair, Vuesa Merced would have to betray the Archpriest as well. Given that the narrative ends without revealing whether Lázaro succeeds at clearing his name before Vuesa Merced's inquiring (or perhaps Inquisitorial) gaze, it falls to the reader to form his or her own opinion on the matter. Either Lázaro's *fama* remains intact on the surface despite the rottenness it hides, or Vuesa Merced determines that Lázaro is but a knave and a cuckold, undeserving of the royal office that he holds. Both conjectural scenarios call into doubt the proposition that "those who brave the tides of adversity can expect to reach a safe port."

Although the outcome of Vuesa Merced's interrogation remains unknown, the defendant's account of a *pícaro*'s modest rise to fame would have resonated with *Lazarillo de Tormes*'s readers. The novel's lively anecdotes, bold social satire (as noted above, it was placed on the Index of Forbidden Books in 1559), self-ironic style, and chiaroscuro characterizations of Lázaro and his cruel masters blunt the reader's misgivings concerning its protagonist's shifty past and fishy present. Lázaro's likeability disarms the reader, subverting the desire to see him chastised. As Gregorio Marañón remarks of picaresque anti-heroes in general, "the knave is more compelling than a pleasant rascal: invariably the protagonist is intelligent, competent, clever, before whom all obstacles evaporate; in sum, the hero" (13–14). In this manner, the illogical rhetoric (or in Juan Manuel's formulation, the "sweetness") of the novel thrusts an anti-hero, whose confessed *infamia* would otherwise doom him to universal opprobrium, into unlikely social and literary celebrity.[27]

Lazarillo de Tormes celebrates an equivocal new kind of reputation earned through the exercise of *fuerza y maña* [perseverance and cleverness] against a hostile world.[28] But another facet of Lazarillo's *fama* deserves attention as well.

---

[27] According to Spanish philologist Julio Cejador (1864–1927), the anonymous novel *Lazarillo de Tormes* was as popular as *La Celestina* (1499, 1502) before it, and Mateo Alemán's *Guzmán de Alfarache* (1599, 1604) and Miguel de Cervantes's *Quixote* (1605, 1615) afterward. He calls it the most famous work of genius during the imperial period, and he emphasizes that its popularity reached all strata of society from street urchins to titled nobility to court functionaries (see Marañón 15).

[28] Similar apologies for the self-made man would appear throughout the next century. The entire picaresque genre beginning with Mateo Alemán's *Guzmán de Alfarache* of 1599 and 1604 defends the validity of social ascent through tooth-and-nail perseverance.

As Hans-Joaquim Neubauer notes in *The Rumour: A Cultural History*, the word *fama* acquired during the late Middle Ages the sense of "information or news, at the same time that it meant the image formed of a person by that information."[29] Lazarillo "made news" by embracing two very public roles: that of autobiographer and that of *pregonero de vinos*, a sort of town crier. This type of notoriety recalls Don Quixote's obsession not only with committing great deeds, but also with having them chronicled and publicized. It is noteworthy within a genealogy of masculinity that, despite his thirst for fame, Don Quixote avoids the epicenter of news and information of his day, the court. Unlike Lázaro, who exposes himself to public view by narrating his life story, and by hawking water and wine in the town square, Don Quixote spends all of Part I and much of Part II far from the public eye. The fact that Cervantes sets his narrative of a provincial squire's search for fame against the arid backdrop of La Mancha accentuates the ludicrousness of Don Quixote's quest for fame and highlights the sharp divide between periphery and capital, as the latter was swept up in the craze for celebrity.

Appearing at court was the first step in gaining recognition, favor, and fame as the historical examples of Christopher Columbus, Hernán Cortés, and Francisco Pizarro attest. However, proximity to power did not suffice for becoming newsworthy, nor was it always advisable to draw undue attention to oneself at court. Antonio de Guevara (c. 1480–1545) analyzed the problem of discerning when the man of court should act unobtrusively and when he should flaunt his talents. Guevara served Charles V as preacher, chronicler, and bishop, and his guidebooks counted among the best-sellers of his day. Three of his works, the *Reloj de príncipes* [*Dial of Princes*] (1529), *Menosprecio de corte y alabanza de aldea* [Scorn for court and tribute to village life] (1539) and the *Aviso de privados y despertador de cortesanos* [Warning to favorites and wake-up call to courtiers] showcase the pitfalls awaiting those who seek fame at court. On the one hand, Guevara urges aspirants at court to gain recognition from the king, but he also warns never to annoy or distract the monarch. The first *aporía* facing the ambitious man of court, Mercedes Blanco concedes with reference to Guevara, is that, while winning the king's confidence depends upon impressing him, in his day-to-day affairs the king

---

Cervantes's Basilio, in the Bodas de Camacho [Camacho's wedding] episode of *Don Quixote* (1615), likewise heralds a new paradigm of masculine virtue grounded in the exercise of individual talent. Chapters 19–21 of the Second Part relate the tale of rich Camacho, betrothed to Quiteria, who since childhood had loved her neighbor, Basilio. Although Basilio exhibited many manly traits, he lacked Camacho's wealth, so Quiteria's parents betrothed her to the richer man. When Basilio appears at Camacho and Quiteria's wedding, the heartsick suitor falls on his sword and begs her to grant him her hand in marriage so he may die fulfilled. She and Camacho agree to his macabre request, and the priest weds them, but instead of dying, Basilio jumps up to reveal that he had faked his suicide. Their marriage holds, and Camacho allows the wedding feast to continue, figuring that he will find a better bride. Basilio's *industria*, or "enterprise," like Lazarillo's *fuerza y maña*, manages to out-maneuver Camacho's wealth.

[29] Trans. Christian Braun (London: Free Association Books, 1999), 37 (qtd. in Fenster and Smail 2).

requires unobtrusive obedience: "although the aspiring courtier must take care to disturb the king as infrequently as possible, any topic or pretext he might offer for talking to him already presupposes the goodwill that it is his goal to win" (118–19).

Guevara dedicated his satirical treatise, the *Aviso de privados y despertador de cortesanos*, to Francisco de los Cobos, one of Charles V's closest advisors. As its bipartite title suggests, Guevara devotes the first 10 chapters of the volume to coaching those men of court who wished to unseat the king's *privado* [favorite], and the second half to training the *privado* to defend himself from courtly rivals.[30] Guevara recommends that the favorite guard his eminent position by minimizing his public profile. He should strive to keep his household under control (chapter 12), avoid the appearance of haughtiness (chapter 13), and refrain from throwing lavish banquets (chapter 18).

Future Spanish writers would echo Guevara's injunction to the powerful that they carry themselves with rigorous modesty. Alonso Jerónimo de Salas Barbadillo's didactic conduct novel, *El caballero perfecto* [The perfect gentleman] (1620), sought to provide "un ejemplo imitable a la juventud de estos reinos [an example for the youth of these realms]" (4). *El caballero perfecto* charts the rise of the king of Naples' favorite, Don Alonso de Pimentel, whom it contrasts with the example of a bad *privado*.[31] Once Don Alonso rises to favor, he intentionally maintains a low profile—"Servíase en su casa con menos aparato y ostentación que si no fuera privado [he set up his household with less fanfare and pomp than if he hadn't been the king's favorite]" (53)—in order to avoid the perception that his power rivaled that of the king. By contrast, in one of the novel's four interpolated narratives, another character, César Floro, recounts the ambitious career of a Roman courtier named Aurelio. Aurelio's insatiable thirst for fame culminates in his being crowned Emperor of Rome, yet even then he remains insecure and unhappy. Only by heeding his father's advice to withdraw from public service and find peace in disdain of worldly fame does Aurelio discover "descanso en el desprecio [repose in disdain]." This is the path that Salas de Barbadilo's *caballero perfecto* follows at novel's end. After Alonso completes his mission in Naples, the King of England offers him so many honors and inducements to move to London that, as the narrator marvels, "only this gentleman's spirit, more inclined to bury himself in his present duties than to squander his credit on fresh ambitions, could have found the strength to decline."[32] Like Aurelio of "Descanso en el desprecio,"

---

[30] Guevara was qualified to speak to both sides of the question. As Viceroy of Naples under Ferdinand II of Aragon in 1508, he experienced life near the apex of power, and as a member of Charles V's court he lived the life of a seeker of favors and privileges.

[31] Pauline Marshall adduces convincing evidence that Salas Barbadillo's model for his *caballero perfecto* was Juan Alonso Pimentel de Herrera, Count Duke of Benavente, who served as Viceroy of Naples from 1603 to 1611. Admired by Henry IV of France, he was famed for his just rule. Marshall finds it "certainly significant" that Salas gives his Don Alonso the patronymics of Pimentel and that both their names are Alonso (Salas Barbadillo xlvi, xlvii).

[32] "[S]ólo el ánimo de este caballero, más amigo de acudir al reconocimiento de las obligaciones que de empeñarse por la ambición en otras nuevas, hallara resistencia" (77).

Don Alonso returns home to find "descanso para el espíritu y el cuerpo [repose for body and soul]" (78) with his wife and daughter.[33]

Eminence

Guevara, Salas Barbadillo, and Cervantes—who makes Don Quixote's crusade for glory appear foolish or even mad—evidence a marked mistrust of worldly fame. But a growing appreciation for fame began to mount during the same period. A case in point is Juan de Silva's letter to his son Diego written in 1592 to prepare Diego for service in the court of Philip II.[34] Known as the *Comentarios* [Commentaries], De Silva's letter glosses and updates an unpublished letter of 1548 composed by Juan de Vega, the *Instrucciones* [Instructions] to prepare his son, Hernando, for meeting Emperor Charles V in Flanders.[35] De Silva's commentaries on Juan de Vega's letter bear witness to the rapidly changing demands made on men of court. While De Silva agrees with the substance of De Vega's advice, 50 years later he must update certain passages for Diego. For example, where De Vega urges Hernando to get plenty of rest and not over-exert himself, De Silva dryly inserts, "Más os ha de costar a vos esto que al hijo de Juan de Vega [This is going to be harder for you than it was for Juan de Vega's son]" (qtd. in Bouza 222). With respect to the question of proper decor, dress, and table service at court, De Silva warns that fashion consciousness now runs rampant at Philip's court: "since this instruction was written, the court has become so much more fashionable that what was then judged to be effeminate would now seem uncouth."[36]

Diego must take extra care to avoid bragging since "los portugueses corren más peligro que nación alguna de celebrar singularidades [we Portuguese, more than any other nation, run the risk of bragging about ourselves]" (qtd. in Bouza 222). Nonetheless, De Silva concedes that many powerful Castilians at court use the same tactic for climbing the social ladder:

> Mas porque también sería condenar a bulto los que han caminado por estas sendas menos usadas, pues por ellas se han salvado grandes cortesanos, advertid que, aunque seguirlas no sería seguro, reprobarlos y dejarlos de conversar sería de hombres de mal gusto.

---

[33] While Marshall discerns no link between the "Descanso en el desprecio" episode and the thematic structure of the novel (Salas Barbadillo xlvii), I detect in Aurelio's retreat to a simpler life not only a foreshadowing and justification for Don Alonso's abrupt departure from public life, but a concise summation of the novel's moral lesson.

[34] Juan de Silva (1528–1601) became Count of Portalegre through marriage to Filipa da Silva, the fourth Countess of Portalegre, Portugal. Their son, Diego (1579–1640), became the fifth Count.

[35] Juan de Vega y Enríquez de Acuña, former Viceroy of Sicily, would later serve as President of the Council of Castile under Philip II.

[36] "[D]espués que se escribió esta instrucción han crecido las delicias tanto y de manera que los que entonces juzgábamos por afeminados parecieran ahora rústicos" (qtd. in Bouza 222).

[But since it would also mean condemning wholesale all those high-ranking courtiers who have availed themselves of this less-travelled path, take heed that, although imitating them would not be safe, only a boor would reproach them and avoid conversing with them.] (Bouza 222)

De Silva, while uncomfortable with the shift toward self-glorification that occurred at court between 1548 and 1592, recognizes it as a logical consequence of the competitive hierarchy of power. Described in Chapter 1 as a pyramid, that hierarchy offered aspirants a diminishing number of increasingly powerful positions the higher they rose at court. As noted earlier, the most coveted position was that of *privado*, favorite or advisor to the monarch. Yet, as Fray Juan de Santa María observed in 1615, amity implies a relationship of equality, a claim that no vassal can make with respect to his lord, much less a subject with respect to his prince. For this reason, the monarch only bestows the special status of "friend" or *privado* upon that exceptional man whose singular talents make him a leader among his peers and earn him the sovereign's affection and respect.[37] Here, the problem for those who aspired to *privanza* lay in proving their singularity without offending the king by appearing to rival or threaten him.

The astonishing ascent of Philip II's favorite, Ruy Gómez de Silva (1516–73), to be discussed at further length in Chapter 4, made the metamorphosis from servile courtier to royal favorite into an object of public fascination and political concern. This fascination continued with the era of Philip III's *privado*, the Marquis of Denia, Francisco Gómez de Sandoval y Rojas (1553–1625), whom Philip dignified with the title of Duke of Lerma. In 1618, just as the Duke's political prospects under Philip III were faltering, Pope Paul V made him a cardinal. *Privanza* under Philip IV passed into the hands of the young king's former tutor, Gaspar de Guzmán (1587–1645), whom the king elevated to Count-Duke of Olivares. Philip III and Philip IV deposited so much authority in their "friends" Lerma and Olivares respectively that they became unofficial prime ministers, virtually ruling in the name of the king. The Count-Duke of Olivares's sway over Philip IV was perceived to be so blinding that for Spanish Baroque scholar and critic Frederick de Armas, such plays as Calderón's *Los tres mayores prodigios* [The three greatest marvels] (1636) represented the Count-Duke as a sort of "Circe" or "Medea" who bewitched the king and the public with his magic (De Armas 10). Eventually, the limitless power that these *privados* wielded incited so much fear, jealousy, and mistrust that their respective monarchs were forced to distance themselves from them. But pressure to stake a claim to extraordinariness did not disappear with the fall of the *privados*. Their upward trajectories called into question the Castiglionian virtue of moderation, giving impetus to the new manly ideal of eminence.

---

[37] *República y policía* XXXI, folio 206r–207r (qtd. in Díaz Martínez 45). Fray Juan de Santa María served as royal chaplain to Phillip III and confessor to his daughter, the Infanta Margarita. A Franciscan, Fray Santa María criticized the excessive powers that Philip III entrusted to his *privado*, the Duke of Lerma.

Jesuit social theorist, novelist, and theologian Baltasar Gracián (1601–58) began guiding readers on the "way to eminence"[38] in 1637, while the Count-Duke of Olivares still enjoyed Philip IV's favor. Fame for Gracián meant singularity, domination over inferior rivals, and eternal recognition in the annals of humanity. In *El héroe* [The hero], Gracián elucidates 20 "excellences" or *primores* required of what he calls in his preface the "varón máximo [optimal man]" (3): "Here you shall have a reason for governing not a political nor even an economic state, but rather a reason of state for yourself; a compass pointing toward excellence, an art of being exceptional with minimal rules of etiquette."[39] Although the heroic man may receive certain attributes at birth, Gracián stresses that self-cultivation can make up for hereditary defects. The sixth *primor*, "Eminencia en lo mejor" [Eminence in that which is best], calls to mind Lazarillo's defense of individual effort as opposed to breeding:

> De las prendas, unas da el Cielo, otras libra la industria; una ni dos no bastan a realzar un sujeto. Cuanto destituyó el cielo de las naturales, supla la diligencia en las adquisitas. Aquellas son hijas del favor; estas, de la loable industria, y no suelen ser las menos nobles.
>
> [Heaven confers some gifts, effort yields others; just one or two do not make the grade. Where Heaven withheld inborn gifts, diligence compensates with acquired ones. The first are born of grace; the second, of commendable effort, and these are often not the lowliest.] (17)

Following *El héroe*, Gracián published *El político don Fernando el Católico* [Ferdinand the Catholic: the politician] (1640) and *El discreto* [The discreet man of court] (1646), which advised, "Los varones cuerdos aspiran antes a ser grandes que a parecerlo [Sane men, rather than appear great, aspire to be great]" (Aphorism 21; 179). Gracián's *Oráculo manual y arte de prudencia* [*Art of Worldly Wisdom*] of 1647 condensed his teachings on achieving worldly success into 300 maxims. Fame or eminence rather than mediocrity is both the means to, and the purpose of masculine display at court for Gracián. For example, he contrasts the chimera of fortune to the security of fame:

> Lo que tiene de inconstante la una, tiene de firme la otra. La primera para vivir, la segunda para después; aquélla contra la envidia, ésta contra el olvido. La fortuna se desea y tal vez se ayuda, la fama se diligencia; deseo de reputación nace de la virtud. Fue, y es hermana de Gigantes la Fama; anda siempre por estremos, o monstros, o prodigios, de abominación, de aplauso.

---

[38] In 1652 John Skeffington translated the title of Gracián's *El héroe* as "The heroe of Lorenzo: The Way to Eminence."

[39] "Aquí tendrás una no política ni aun económica, sino una razón de estado de ti mismo, una brújula de marear a la excelencia, una arte de ser ínclito con pocas reglas de discreción" (4).

[Unpredictable the one; firm the other. The first for living; the second for afterwards; that one against envy; this one against oblivion. While you may dream of fortune, sometimes pushing it forward, you cultivate fame. The desire for reputation springs from virtue. Fame was and is the sister of Titans; she always goes to extremes: either massive applause or colossal abhorrence.] (Aphorism 10; 207)

Gracián's advice for gaining fame is to do well at all things, but to excel at one: "Una gran singularidad entre la pluralidad de perfecciones [A great singularity among the plurality of perfections]" (Aphorism 61; 224). Although he preaches prudence, he also recognizes the advantage of enterprise, that is, capitalizing on opportunities ahead of rivals:

Excelencia de primero. Y si con eminencia, doblada. Gran ventaja jugar de mano, que gana en igualdad. Hubieran muchos sido Fénix en los empleos a no irles otros delante. Álzanse los primeros con el mayorazgo de la fama, y quedan para los segundos pleiteados alimentos; por más que suden, no pueden purgar el vulgar achaque de imitación.

[*To move first: excellence.* To do so with eminence, doubly so. He who plays his hand first has an edge; he can defeat his equals. Many would have risen like Phoenixes had they not let others go first. Leaders are entitled to fame which raises them above those hungry beggars who follow. For all of their sweat, they still look like cheap copycats.] (Aphorism 63; 224)

In Aphorism 75 Gracián proposes that men choose a heroic ideal to stoke their ambitions, for "No hay cosa que así solicite ambiciones en el ánimo como el clarín de la Fama ajena [Nothing appeals to a soul's ambitions like the clarion call of another man's glory]" (229). Likewise, Discourse 30 of Gracián's *Agudeza y arte de ingenio* [*Art of Wit*] (1641–48) celebrates the capacity of heroic maxims to inspire emulation:

Consiste la eminencia de [e]stos apotegmas en exprimir el aprecio de alguna majestosa virtud, y cuanto más excelencia ésta, más merecedor el dicho de una inmortal estimación.

[The superiority of these maxims consists in encapsulating the appeal of some majestic virtue, and the more excellent it is, the more worthy the aphorism of everlasting esteem.] (574–5)

The *Oráculo manual* closes with a final word of wisdom: "En una palabra: santo [In a word: saintly]" (300–302). As a moralist, theologian, and anti-Machiavellian, Gracián furnishes his "optimal man" with virtue, because "La virtud es el Sol del mundo menor [Virtue is the sun of the lesser world]." But within this lesser world, a correspondingly lesser form of immortality exists: eternal fame in human history. As Gracián writes in the final *crisi* [chapter] of his allegorical novel, *El criticón* [*The Critic*] (1651, 1653, 1657), the "Island of Immortality" rises from a black sea of the ink spilled by great writers: "ese color proviene de la preciosa tinta de los famosos escritores que en ella bañan sus plumas [that color derives from the precious ink of the famous writers who bathe their quills in it]" (1486). Here Merit guards the gates to immortality, hurling a final anti-Machiavellian malediction against those who would confuse infamy with fame. To the villains and scoundrels clamoring for admission to the Island of Immortality, Merit retorts:

> ¡aquí no entran sino los varones eminentes cuyos hechos se apoyan en la virtud porque en el vicio no cabe cosa grande ni digna de eterno aplauso! ¡Venga todo jayán! ¡Fuera todo pigmeo! No hay aquí mediocristas: todo va por extremos.
>
> [only eminent men enter here, those whose exploits are sustained by columns of virtue, because nothing immense or worthy of eternal applause ever fit into vice's hovel. Calling all giants! Away with pygmies! Here there are no mediocrats; superlatives rule.] (*El Criticón* 1504)

Without specifically referring to Cervantes, Gracián exhorts his *héroe* to replace what we have called Don Quixote's fantasy of military glory with a will to superlative eminence deployed within the nexus of Christian humanism.[40]

Ironically, perhaps, the prime repository for Gracián's heroic vision would not be Spain, but France. Amelot de la Houssaye's adaptation of the *Oráculo Manual*, which he titled *L'Homme de cour* [The man of court] (1684) underwent 16 editions from 1684 to 1696, and 13 from 1701 to 1808 (Serra Muñoz 53). Louis XIV would perfect Philip III's and Philip IV's practice of consolidating power through spectacles of magnificence celebrated at a central court. Luis XIV, too, would rely upon favorites to rule his expanding territories. As France's prospects rose and Spain's diminished in the latter decades of the seventeenth century, France became the testing ground for a more cynical, amoral version of Gracián's *varón máximo*: the *honnête homme*.

Conclusion

This chapter has assembled a corpus of Medieval and early modern conduct literature concerned with valorizing the concept of fame. Questions of reputation, self-reliance, and renown find voice in texts as diverse as the Medieval epic poem the *Cantar del mío Cid*, Jorge Manrique's *Coplas por la muerte de su padre*, Fernando de Rojas's tragicomedy *La Celestina*, and Baltasar Gracián's aphoristic *Oráculo manual*. Diego de Velázquez's *Las Meninas* serves as a pointed reminder that the multifaceted concept of fame continued to generate anxiety well into the seventeenth century. On the one hand, according to Leo Braudy, Velázquez dared to place himself in a more conspicuous spot on his canvas than that of the monarchs he was ostensibly summoned to commemorate. On the other hand, the

---

[40] French historian of ideas Paul Hazard calls Gracián's superlative hero the "First and Only One" (52).

chamber that sets the scene for this self-vaunting spectacle abounds in allegorical warning about the dangers of overreaching.

Norbert Elias also addressed the tensions evident in Velázquez's *Las Meninas*. Unlike Braudy, who calibrates the painting's ambivalence toward renown, or Michel Foucault, who identifies it with the dawn of Modernity, Elias situates *Las Meninas* on a continuum of self-regulatory practices.[41] For Elias, Velázquez's painting performs the delicate function of displaying the painter's place at court, or, more accurately, records how the painter "repositioned" those around him to his own advantage. The domestic setting illustrates Velázquez's inclusion within the exclusive circle of the royal household. Although Velázquez's full-length self-portrait takes up more space than that of the royal couple, his figure remains in shadow while the Infanta and her maids are in the foreground, and Philip IV and Queen Mariana in the background occupy brightly lit areas of the canvas.[42] Elias applies the term "detachment" to Velázquez's acute perspectivism; his ability to view himself as others view him. For Elias, it is not Velázquez's mastery over brush and pigment that earns him pride of place among the royals; it is his capacity to detach himself from the busy scene around him and identify his place within it:

> This shift toward an increased consciousness of the autonomy of what is experienced in relation to the person who experiences, toward a greater autonomy of "objects" in the experience of "subjects," is closely related to the thickening armour that is being interposed between affective impulses and the objects at which they are directed in the form of ingrained self-control. (*Court Society* 252, qtd. in Ogborn 68)

For Elias, this distancing capacity increases as societies afford greater security to their members through processes of state monopolization of violence leading to internal pacification.

In the same vein, Don Quixote's obsession with the image of himself that his chroniclers would (fictionally) someday project in their annals represents a tentative step toward a more detached subject position. At this early stage, however, the knight's ambition outstrips his capacity; his flimsy armor has not yet thickened; he aspires to eminence, but falls flat in the attempt. Gracián's promise of a "reason of state for yourself [...] an art of being exceptional" (*El héroe* 4) arrives too late for Don Quixote, who nonetheless remains a standard-bearer for the process of valorizing personal fame.

---

[41] *Las Meninas* appeared on the flyleaf of the French edition of Foucault's *The Order of Things* first published in 1966 as *Les Mots et les choses* (Paris: Editions Gallimard). *Las Meninas* also served as the cover illustration for Norbert Elias's *Involvement and Detachment*, which originally appeared as *Engagement und Distanzierung* (Frankfurt am Main: Suhrkamp Verlag, 1983). See Ogborn 58.

[42] *Involvement and Detachment* lxi–lxiii (see Ogborn 66–8).

Chapter 3
Dissimulation

Qui nescit dissimulare, nescit regnare.[1]

[He who knows not how to dissimulate, knows not how to rule.]

For the ideal courtier, revealing is robbery; self-regard is concealed as naturalized deception that constructs the perfect courtier.[2]

As we saw in Chapter 2, Gracián's eminent hero does not stumble into fame; he painstakingly crafts himself in a kind of theatrical performance into a spectacular monument.[3] This lesson in self-control anchors Gracián's allegorical novel *El criticón* [*The Critic*], published in three volumes between 1651 and 1657. In *El criticón*, the seasoned courtier Critilo teaches his neophyte pupil Andrenio that sailing to the Island of Immortality is no pleasure cruise. During their journey from obscurity to renown Andrenio learns that the price of admission to the Island of Immortality is to adopt a total lockdown mode in interpersonal relations. By cultivating self-restraint in word and action, the aspirant to fame wins glory and surpasses less disciplined rivals. Norbert Elias chose the word "detachment" to describe the rational capacity that he observed in Renaissance men of court as they fashioned themselves into attractive public personae in their search for fame.

Just as detachment allowed Velázquez in *Las Meninas* to see himself in the visual realm as others saw him, and to reposition himself accordingly, one might equally expect the exercise of detachment in the realm of verbal interaction to allow the courtier to script his speech so as to present himself to his listeners in the most flattering light possible. But the word "script" is troubling here. It implies self-scrutiny and premeditation rather than spontaneous talk. Indeed, in the following pages we will find that authentic speech, a hallmark of Medieval masculine virtue, appears in early modern conduct writings less and less in the guise of a moral imperative and increasingly represented as a personal and political liability.

---

[1] As we shall see below, Diego Saavedra Fajardo adopted a variant of this dictum as the motto for Empresa 43 of his *Idea de un príncipe político cristiano* [*The Royal Politician*], 524, also known as the *Empresas políticas* (see Figure 3.6 below).

[2] Correll 38.

[3] Stephen Greenblatt offers many examples of rational, self-conscious theatricality in *Renaissance Self-Fashioning: From More to Shakespeare*. Especially relevant to the present discussion of dissimulation is his chapter 4, "To Fashion a Gentleman: Spenser and the Destruction of the Bower of Bliss" (157–92).

Simulation and Dissimulation

In *El criticón*, Andrenio learns not only that he must police his every action, but also that whenever he strays beyond the court or its sphere of influence, he loses his bearings. For all of their wanderings, Critilo and Andrenio only progress when they interact with other "civilized" beings. As cultural historian Peter Burke trenchantly observes, "Courtesy has as much to do with courts as chivalry with horses."[4] Europe's first emblemist, Andrea Alciati meditated on the interdependence of court and courtier, performer and audience more than a century prior to the publication of Gracián's *El criticón*.[5] Alciati's Emblem 86, "In Aulicos," translated by Bernadino Daza in 1548 as "Los cortesanos" [The courtiers], reads,

> La Corte vana y pomposa,
> Es cárcel de oro labrada,
> Que en ser prisión es pesada,
> Y por ser de oro es sabrosa
>
> [The vain and pompous court is a gilded jail despised for its bars yet adored for its gold.] (178)

The accompanying hieroglyph depicts an elegant gentleman locked in a pillory, symbolizing that his function, that of serving the monarch, tethers him to the monarchical capital.

Noted Castiglione scholar Daniel Javitch also regards the vertical power structure of court as a subjugator of men. For Javitch,

> The deference, the moderation, the indirection, the tact that were part of the code of courtesy the courtier had to observe did not just affirm his superior breeding but also indicated the much more limited freedom, indeed the subjugation that aristocrats had to accept when they became dependent on princes for their status and privilege. (viii)

Men of court, whether involved in sensitive matters of state or merely anxious to scale the social pyramid, were obliged to surrender the autonomy of their legs and of their tongues to the pillory of self-restraint. In *Pasiones frías* [Cold passions], Fernando R. de la Flor characterizes the "art of pleasing others" as the courtier's obsessive duty: "The fraught, tyrannical construction of an art of pleasing and gratifying definitively inscribes itself as the primary task of a subject hypersensitive to social pressure."[6] The spread of a "pedagogy of fear" that French

---

[4] *The Fortunes of the Courtier*, 14. In *Fortunes*, Burke investigates the European reception of *Il Cortegiano*.

[5] Alciati inaugurated the popular humanist genre of the emblem book about which more will be said below. First published in Latin in 1531, Alciati's collection of emblems was translated by Bernardino Daza into Spanish rhyme in 1548.

[6] "La tiránica, tensa, construcción de un 'arte de agradar y complacer' se inscribe determinantemente como la tarea esencial del sujeto social extremadamente sensible a las coacciones" (29).

Fig. 3.1   "In Aulicos," Emblem 86. Andrea Alciati, *V.C. Emblemata*, 4 ed., 1591, Leiden. The Harold and Mary Jean Hanson Rare Books Collection, Special & Area Studies Collections, George A. Smathers Libraries, University of Florida.

historian Bartolomé Bennassar has attributed to the Spanish Inquisition further bound vassals' and masters' tongues alike.

Under these inhibiting conditions, authenticity took cover behind a carefully cultivated mask of affability. Self-control gained prestige, and stricter protocols of public conduct provided refuge from the danger posed by spontaneous speech and gesture. Dissimulation gained favor as the speech act (or speech-suppressing act) designated to negotiate the increasing segregation of public and private spheres. "Early modern dissimulation," notes Jon Snyder, "involved first and foremost the exercise of strict self-control over the expression of thoughts, emotions, or passions" (6). Dissimulation ensured privacy without crossing the line into uttering untruths. Snyder links dissimulation to a "culture of secrecy" that pervaded the great Renaissance power hubs. Within the precincts of this culture, self-concealment came to be regarded not as a vice but as an indispensable resource for the courtier: a new masculine virtue. The following pages explore a range of linguistic and ethical difficulties associated with this transformation of the apparent vice of hiding truth into a praiseworthy stratagem. These issues are then seen to inform three texts that helped to ensconce dissimulation within the pantheon of courtly virtues at the Spanish court: Lucas Gracián Dantisco's *Galateo español* [*The Spanish Gallant*] (c. 1586), Francisco de Quevedo's *Discurso de las privanzas* [Discourse on favorites] (1606–08), and Diego Saavedra Fajardo's *Idea de un príncipe político cristiano* [*The Royal Politician*] (1640), also known as the *Empresas políticas* [Political empresas].

Aristotle, St. Augustine, and classical skeptical philosophers contributed substantively to exploring the ethical dimensions of dissimulating speech. However, St. Thomas Aquinas's massive *Summa Theologica* of 1265–74 systematized many of the distinctions, paradoxes, and ambiguities that would continue to govern usage of and attitudes toward dissimulation in the early modern period. "It seems that lying is not always opposed to truth," Aquinas wrote in opening the *Summa*'s inquiry "Of the Vices Opposed to Truth, and First of Lying."[7] Ultimately, Aquinas deemed all falsehood sinful, but that negative judgment did not prevent him from discriminating among differing classes of false speech. For example, he was willing to forgive "jocose" lies such as boasting that merely exceed the truth as well as lying by omitting to tell all of the truth. In addition, he looked less severely upon "officious" or helpful lies. For Aquinas, only malicious lies, that is, lies intended to injure others, constituted unpardonable mortal (rather than venal) sins.

Early modern Castilian dictionary entries for the word *disimular* [to dissimulate] and its derivations retained Aquinas's distinction between helpful lies, partial truths, and malicious untruth. These entries ambiguate as much as they disambiguate, due to their polysemous literary examples. Sebastián de Covarrubias's seminal 1611 *Tesoro de la lengua* [Treasury of the language] links dissimulating to Aquinas's concept of partial truth: "Disimular. No darse por entendido de alguna cosa; [...] Bellaco disimulado, el que encubre su malicia [Dissimulate. Not to let on that you understand something; [...] Dissimulating scoundrel, he who conceals his cunning]." While the phrase "Not to let on that you understand something" is merely a normative self-presentation strategy, the *Tesoro*'s second definition cited above ("Dissimulating scoundrel, he who conceals his cunning") clearly associates dissimulation with moral laxness.

The semantic elasticity of dissimulation becomes even more pronounced in the *Diccionario de autoridades* [Dictionary of authorities], published between 1726 and 1739, but relying heavily on sixteenth- and seventeenth-century sources. In one entry, *Autoridades* blandly defines dissimulation as a "Modo artificioso de encubrir la intención u dar a entender otra de la que se tiene [Artificial way of hiding one's purpose or implying that it is other than what one intends]." However, "artificioso" itself was a notoriously ambiguous word, meaning, again according to *Autoridades*, alternately "inventive" and "clever or deceptive." So

---

[7] Part ii of Part II, Treatise on Prudence and Justice, Question 110: "Of the Vices Opposed to Truth, and First of Lying."

even here dissimulation might be taken either as a morally neutral or intentionally deceptive feint.

To demonstrate the use of the verb *disimular*, *Autoridades* cites Góngora's burlesque "Fábula de Píramo y Tisbe" [Fable of Pyramus and Thisbe], which paradoxically attributes artifice to the natural order itself: "Olmo que en jóvenes hojas / disimula años adultos [An elm belying its age / dressed up in youthful foliage]" (lines 300–301, 223).[8] Taken alone, these octosyllabic lines appear to attenuate the elderly elm's moral responsibility for garbing itself in deceptively youthful leaves. After all, isn't this what all trees do every spring? Surely the word "dissimulation" here is free of all malicious intent, for how is a tree be to be blamed for putting out leaves? But in Góngora's sardonic re-rendering of the Ovidian myth, the old elm succeeds by this ruse in attracting the affections of a clinging vine. After a bolt of lightning sunders the entwined pair's "marriage bed," the ashen remains of this illicit botanical union witness Pyramus and Thisbe's analogously abortive tryst:

> An elm belying its age / dressed up in youthful foliage / was wrapped in the loving coils / of a vine already flowering // when a bolt from the blue unsquired / by attendant light or thunder / destroyed its noble crown / and blasted the loving union.[9]

The blasted elm and vine prefigure the fates of Góngora's lusty but ill-fated lovers, Pyramus and Thisbe, and through this mirroring assume human attributes. Like Góngora's Pyramus, who conceals his lecherous intentions from Thisbe, the elm seduces the flowering vine by artfully concealing his true age. Góngora, unlike Ovid, for whom Pyramus and Thisbe's death represented the tragedy of unfulfilled passion, "jumps with a kind of Alice in Wonderland logic" on the chance to transform sprouting leaves into an irreverently premeditated seductive ploy verging on the malicious (Dent-Young xvi).

Etymologically, dissimulation is related to simulation. *Autoridades* defines the Spanish verb *simular* as "Representar alguna cosa, fingiendo o imitando lo que no es [Represent something by acting as if or imitating something that it is not]." In like manner, Spanish humanist Juan Pablo Mártir Rizo (1593–1642) condemned simulation but considered dissimulation to be an indispensable tool of statecraft:

> La disimulación es muchas veces no sólo conveniente, pero forzosa. Ella y la simulación difieren en que la disimulación es no manifestar lo que uno ha sabido o sospechado y la simulación es decir o prometer una cosa y pensar hacer otra, que es engañar, cualidad indigna de un príncipe, y aun de los hombres inferiores.

---

[8] This and subsequent translations from Góngora are by John Dent-Young.

[9] "Olmo, que en jóvenes hojas / disimula años adultos, / de su vid florida entonces / en los más lascivos nudos, // un rayo sin escuderos / o de luz o de tumulto / le desvaneció la pompa / y el tálamo descompuso" (lines 300–307, 323).

[Dissimulating is often not only appropriate, but necessary. It differs from simulation in that dissimulation is not to give out what one knows or suspects and simulation is to say or promise one thing and intend another, which is to deceive, a quality unworthy of a prince, and even of lesser men.] (Chapter 21, 199)[10]

The act of simulation rigs the rhetorical contest by absenting truth. As American author and critic William Kennedy has written, "In writing as in speech the audience participates in a rhetorical contest with the producing agent" (228). The speaker or "producing agent" who simulates displaces truth altogether, making it irrecoverable. But dissimulation, by merely covering up, overstating, or omitting certain facts, allows a fair rhetorical contest between audience and producing agent to take place. The truth remains present and available to be disclosed, uncovered, or discerned. Góngora's elm, for example, did not claim outright to be young; he merely hid his age beneath a green mantle. Had the clinging vine probed further, she might have unmasked him.

Góngora's "Fábula" tells twin tales of doomed romance. But, as in the English-language maxim, "All's fair in love and war," no distinction was made between dissimulation carried out for personal gain in the private sphere and deliberate concealment on behalf of the state. The following verses, composed by Francisco de Borja (1581–1658) and cited in *Autoridades*'s entry for "Dissimular," argue that dissimulation is equally necessary for both private and public success:[11] "Quien de disimular ignora el arte / Ni amar pretenda, ni reinar espere [Whoever knows not the art of dissimulation / let him neither aspire to love nor hope to rule]."[12] By drawing a parallel between private ambition (love) and public ambition (rule), Borja flattens the distinction between personal and civic action.

Does Borja endorse dissimulating in public and private life, or is the art of concealment merely a necessary evil? To answer this question, it will be helpful to return the verses cited above to the sonnet from which they were extracted. Francisco de Borja's Sonnet 68 praises dissimulation as a form of dispassionate Stoicism:

> Whoever knows not the art of dissimulation let him neither aspire to love nor hope to rule, since unarmed Time with cunning will acquire more trophies than Mars [will acquire] by force. And Heaven and Ingenuity will divide up the spoils that blind Violence desires, discovering her hiding place even as her fury grows. He who speaks not conceals his innermost hope. He kills without arms

---

[10] French historian Jean-Pierre Cavaillé, in a recent study on simulation and dissimulation in early modern France, maintains a similar dissociation between the two. "It is one thing to keep a secret," Cavaillé contends, "and another thing to lie." Jean-Pierre Cavaillé, *Dis/simulations* (Honoré Champion, 2002), 31 (qtd. in Snyder xvi, trans. Snyder 180n13).

[11] Great-grandson of the eponymous saint and Superior General of the Jesuit Order, Don Francisco de Borja was also known as the Príncipe de Esquilache [Prince of Esquilache]. Borja served as Viceroy of Perú from 1615 to 1621. He dedicated two editions of his *Rrimas* (1648, 1654) to Philip IV.

[12] *Rrimas* [Complete poems], Sonnet 68.

and waits for fortune to deliver the choicest plunder to suit his pleasure. The will to conquest is not his because, for the man who overcomes his own anger, avenging others is a lesser victory.[13]

Strategic concealment offers greater rewards than those acquired by violence. Unarmed, the person who hides his innermost hope can vanquish the "blind" force of war. As patently political as this message may appear, it is nonetheless delivered simultaneously to the poem's general readers, and to Philip IV to whom Borja had dedicated his volume of collected poems. The "choicest plunder" that the general reader might gain through dissimulation might differ from the trophies that Philip IV might hope to gain by adopting a policy of secrecy, but within the patron-client economy of court, Sonnet 68 affirms the efficacy of dissimulation at both private and macro-political levels.

As we have seen, most definitions of the word "dissimulate" and its derivations assigned to it a meaning akin to that of masking or concealing. But even given this consensus, the connotations of dissimulation for envisaging the ideal subject of Spanish court society would continue to provoke debate. Gracián Dantisco's *Galateo español* of c. 1586, Quevedo's *Discurso de las privanzas* of 1606–08, and Saavedra Fajardo's *Idea de un príncipe politico cristiano* of 1640 represent three nodes in the discourse on dissimulation in sixteenth- and seventeenth-century Spain. The three texts ask the same question posed by all works of normative ethics, "How should one live?"—in this case asking it on behalf of the Spanish man of court. Gracián Dantisco, Quevedo, and Saavedra Fajardo reproduce many of Aquinas's distinctions, but their texts are marked by a willingness to blur the line between personal and public action that contrasts with Aquinas's exclusive concern for the well-being of the individual soul.

Courtesy as Social Lubricant

Dissimulation makes its appearance in the popular sixteenth-century Spanish courtesy manual, Lucas Gracián Dantisco's *Galateo español*, with a mixed range of valuations.[14] Gracián Dantisco was a notary later charged with cataloguing the vast inventory of Philip II's library at the Escorial palace. His *Galateo español*

---

[13] "Quien de disimular ignora el arte, / ni amar pretenda, ni reinar espere; / pues más trofeos desarmado adquiere / con maña el tiempo, que con fuerzas Marte. // Y el cielo atento con la industria parte, / el bien, que ciega la violencia quiere; / y cuanto más en el furor creciere, / la busca más en escondida parte. // Quien calla, encubre su animoso intento, / sin armas mata, y del mayor despojo / la suerte aguarda, que a gozar convenga. // Ni estima la ambición del vencimiento, / porque es en quien venció su propio enojo, / menor victoria, que a los otros venga" (*Rrimas*, Sonnet 68).

[14] Margherita Morreale searched in vain for an edition corresponding to the date of the dedication to Argote de Molina (more properly "Argeto," according to Morreale) of 1582. The earliest she found were those of Tarragona and Zaragoza, both published in 1593 (68–71). However, four copies of a volume referred to as *Galateas españolas* were authorized by the Inquisition to be sent to Peru on September 30, 1586 (see Morreale 5).

adapts for Spanish readers Monsignior Giovanni Della Casa's *Il Galateo* [The gallant], published posthumously in 1558.[15] At first glance, Gracián Dantisco seems an unlikely purveyor of a humanist treatise on courtly manners. Renowned philologist Margherita Morreale characterizes the author as being more practical than erudite; certainly less learned than an earlier but less successful translator of Della Casa's conduct guide, Dr. Domingo Becerro (18–19).[16] Despite these handicaps, Morreale documents 16 extant editions of Gracián Dantisco's *Galateo español* published between 1593 and 1699, noting the omnipresence of the text in bibliographies of early printed Spanish texts.

The *Galateo español*, as a code of amiability aimed at winning allies at court, shows more concern for what sociolinguists call "positive face," or enhancing one's own prestige before others than for avoiding "negative face" or embarrassing social encounters. The treatise's preoccupation with positive face leaves less room for cautionary criticism of untruth than one finds, for example, in Castiglione's *Book of the Courtier* (1528).[17] Nonetheless, chapter 6, "De los mentirosos" [On liars], and chapter 9, "De las ceremonias" [On ceremonies], grapple with the problem of authentic speech.

It is perhaps ironic in light of the popularity of his courtesy guide that Gracián Dantisco showed little patience for excessive displays of courtesy: "one should avoid excessive displays of courtesy, which were less in vogue among the Ancients than they are now, and this insincere custom […] we improperly call ceremonies."[18] Gracián Dantisco finds most deference displays to be inappropriate and hollow. For him, bowing and ceremony belong in the sacred context of Church ritual, not on street-corners and in palace halls:

> Las ceremonias se tomaban por aquella solemnidad que los sacerdotes usaban alrededor de los altares y en los divinos oficios, acerca de Dios y de las cosas sagradas. Y hase usurpado este nombre después acá que los hombres se comenzaron a reverenciar unos con otros con artificiosos modos, inclinándose y torciéndose de lado con reverencias, en señal de acatamiento, descubriendo sus cabezas y llamándose señores y otros títulos extraordinarios besándose las manos como si las tuvieran sagradas, o fueran sacerdotes.

---

[15] For Aldo Scaglione, Della Casa's *Il Galateo* was "one of the most important exemplars of the subgenre of etiquette or courtesy books" (253).

[16] Gracián Dantisco at times translates, but often simplifies and summarizes. He suppresses passages that moralize or dwell on theological distinctions and drops most of Della Casa's literary allusions as well (Morreale 19–53). In the introduction to her critical edition of the *Galateo español* Morreale conducts an admirable comparison between Gracián Dantisco's lexicon and those of Della Casa and Castiglione.

[17] For Harry Berger Jr., the practice of *sprezzatura* laid out by Castiglione's *Book of the Courtier* created a "mordant and defensive" culture of suspicion at court (298). For Jon Snyder, *sprezzatura* was a way of "not letting things be seen as they are" (75). Both critics read *sprezzatura* as a defensive trope of dissimulation.

[18] "[L]as ceremonias superfluas se deben evitar, las cuales fueron de los antiguos menos usadas que no ahora, y a este vano uso […] llamamos impropiamente ceremonias" (130).

[Ceremonies were taken from the rites that priests used to practice at their altars and divine offices with respect to God and sacred objects. And the name was usurped when men began bowing to one another in a pompous manner, reverently lowering their head and tilting to one side to show respect, uncovering their heads and calling themselves lord and other exaggerated titles, kissing each other's hands as if they had been blessed, or they were priests.][19]

In Gracián Dantisco's view, transculturation had produced a ridiculous parody of curial protocol with little intrinsic worth. Such vain gestures necessarily hide authentic feelings of indifference behind a facade of obligatory sociability. Were it not for the pressures of social conformity, Gracián Dantisco's narrator would dispense with tiresome ceremonies. But social pressure obliges the man of court to hide the dictates of his heart beneath a veneer of civility.

Civility rather than morality is also the yardstick against which the *Galateo español* measures lying. In chapter 6, "De los mentirosos" [On liars], Gracián Dantisco reproves two types of liars for violating the core value of pleasing others. The first type, not unlike Mártir Rizo's "simulators," mentioned above, exaggerate mercilessly. Even if their falsehoods are uttered for the sole purpose of entertaining others, they can backfire by boring listeners or insulting their credulity. To illustrate this point, Gracián Dantisco recounts the story of a man who boasted that in order to quench his thirst one day he shot an arrow at a pitcher of water high above on a window ledge, drank his fill from the flow, and then shot a second arrow right into the first hole, completely staunching the leak. But instead of pleasing his listeners, the braggart only angered them:

Y aunque fue bien reída la mentira, uno de los que allí estaban, conocióle el humor tan jactancioso, enfadado de [e]llo, le dijo: "Señor, V[uestra] M[erced] gasta su tiempo en balde y nos cansa a todos, y quien esto nos quiere persuadir, o nos tiene por inocentes o por enemigos."

[And although the lie got a lot of laughs, one of those who was there was irritated by his bragging, and said to him: "My dear sir you waste your time on trifles and weary all of us, and whoever wishes to persuade us of this either takes us for dupes or enemies."] (Chapter 6, 125)

Lying, as this anecdote illustrates, damages credibility, so that people no longer believe anything liars say unless they bring a witness to confirm the veracity of their story. To the case of sheer lying or simulation, Gracián Dantisco adds dissimulation: "Puédese mentir también callando [One can also lie in silence]" (126). The *Galateo español* compares those posturers who drape themselves with medals and jewelry to monkeys who merely ape the powerful. Such fools misrepresent themselves through their deeds without actually uttering falsehoods. The narrator condemns displays of pomp as the symptom of an undiagnosed illness: that of vanity (126).

---

[19] *Galateo español*, chapter 9, 131. Here Gracián Dantisco anticipates the theory of Ernst Curtius (1814–96), more recently endorsed by Aldo Scaglione, that European courtliness evolved out of the Medieval curial courts (*Knights* 47–67).

Gracián Dantisco lists three reasons for suffering the hypocrisy and inconvenience of courtesy rituals: "por utilidad [for reasons of expedience]," "por vanidad [for self-promotion]," and "por obligación [for the sake of custom]." At one extreme, he condemns expedient courtesy as dishonest and immoral: "By expedient we mean any lie pronounced for the sake of the personal benefit and gain of the speaker; and this kind is a fraudulent and sinful thing because one cannot lie honestly."[20] Among those who resort to this ruse, Gracián Dantisco counts false friends, flatterers, and chameleons who change color wherever they go. Self-promoting courtesies "por vanidad" consist of inflationary excess in the display of deference to others so as to oblige them to reciprocate. These the *Galateo español* dispatches quickly as "enojosas y desapacibles por ser tan contra lo que es verdad [irritating and unpleasant because they are so contrary to that which is true]" (132). Gracián Dantisco devotes greater attention to courtesy "por obligación" than "por utilidad" or "por vanidad." The Spanish court was notorious for its punctiliousness. Paradoxically, unavoidable niceties could actually cause harm in the breach by displeasing, insulting, or offending others. Gracián Dantisco warns that obligatory or dutiful ceremony can easily get out of hand, but when practiced in moderation it is merely a sin of the times: "no es pecado nuestro sino del siglo en que estamos" (131).

Pleasing others becomes a complicated business when regional custom, special honorifics, age, rank, and status are taken into account. The *Galateo español*'s introduction foreshadows these concerns. The author frames his treatise in the guise of a letter of instruction to his younger brother, a device not found in Della Casa's text. To reassure his younger sibling that he does not expect him to adopt all of the advice contained in his manual right away, the author tucks a curious anecdote about youth and old age into the epistolary introduction. The authorial voice recounts that while Seneca was still a child living in Córdoba, a delegation of Roman ambassadors paid him a visit to witness the future philosopher's already legendary wisdom. The dignitaries were astonished to find young Seneca playing soldiers with the other children, so they asked him, "'What are you doing little boy?' To which he responded, 'Here I am, giving time its due.' They looked at one another in a daze and dared not ask him anything else."[21] The moral that Gracián Dantisco's epistolary narrator extracts from this vignette is that each age has a purpose; one should not expect more from an individual than his years allow: "En cada edad se dé y se guarde su punto [Each age should realize itself in accordance with its own true condition]" (106). The baby Seneca anecdote prefigures a major preoccupation of Gracián Dantisco's volume: rules of courtesy are not universal, but rather demand constant recalibration depending

---

[20] "Por utilidad se entiende toda mentira que se dice por interés y provecho propio del que la dice; y esta tal es fraude o pecado y deshonesta cosa, pues jamás se puede mentir honestamente" (132).

[21] "'¿Qué haces niño?' Séneca alzó la cabeza y respondióles: 'Aquí estoy dando al tiempo lo que es suyo.' Ellos quedaron confundidos mirándose el uno al otro, y no le osaron preguntar más" (106).

on circumstances. Gracián Dantisco's treatise advises the old, the young, the nobility, and even the commoner who wish to make a good impression on others to modulate their conduct in accordance with their interlocutor's social position, age, etc. By acknowledging variability within the social landscape and recommending accommodation to those variables, Gracián Dantisco evokes Juan Manuel's theory of unique learning styles, discussed in Chapter 2. He also nods at the principle of adaptability that will be addressed more fully in Chapter 4. If Gracián Dantisco has any rule of thumb at all, he recommends imitating the tailor who, in cutting fabric for making clothing, does well to err on the generous side rather than skimp. Likewise, for him, in matters of social form, an excess of civility is preferable to any hint of incivility. Such usage Gracián Dantisco calls "burlas o mentiras lícitas [tricks or acceptable lies]" (138) imposed by society even though in the end they are unnecessary and vain.

The concepts of simulation and dissimulation dominate much of Gracián Dantisco's critique of courtly ritual, yet variants of the word *disimular* appear infrequently. In chapter 11, "De los encarecimientos" [On praise], the author cautions that, although humor pleases others, joking around too much can lead to misunderstanding. If victims of an innocent joke should take offense, they might dissimulate by smiling but continue to nurse their perceived grievance in secret because "what happens if they are stubborn and don't get over their pique even the next day, and they purposely dissemble with hurt feelings and a happy face?"[22] To avoid becoming vulnerable to dissimulating enemies, the narrator recommends minimizing teasing, jokes, and name-calling.

One of Gracián Dantisco's innovations (with respect to Della Casa) is to insert an entire novella, "La novela del gran soldán" [Novella of the Great Sultan] in the middle of his treatise. Just as earlier chapters had both explained and illustrated the arts of quipping and relating brief anecdotes, "La novela del gran soldán" shows by example the art of extended narration. Although this pleasing digression conforms to the Horatian dictum of combining teaching with entertainment, the interpolated novella far exceeds in length the anecdotes, jokes, and legends with which Castiglione and Della Casa enlivened their handbooks. As Gracián Dantisco notes in his prologue to the reader, this procedure makes his "pills" of advice less onerous to swallow.

The "Novela del gran soldán" is a Byzantine romance in miniature which, true to its generic roots, brims with secrecy, deceit, and disguise.[23] The novella

---

[22] "¿[Q]ué sería si son cabezudos y no se les pase el enojo, aunque duerman sobre ello y disimulan, con la intención y ánimo dañado y el apariencia alegre?" (145).

[23] The Renaissance genre of Byzantine romance took its impetus from the rediscovery in Hungary in 1534 of Heliodorus of Emesa's third-century Greek prose romance, the *Aethopica*, or *Theagenes and Chariklea*. The first Spanish translation appeared anonymously in Antwerp in 1554. Fernando de Mena, working from a Latin version, produced a second translation in 1587 entitled the *Historia etiópica de los amores de Teágenes y Cariquea* [Ethiopian tale of the love of Theagenes and Chariclea], which was reissued in 1614, 1615, and 1616 (Sacchetti 95–6).

recounts the adventures of a Neapolitan Christian prince held captive by the Sultan of Persia in the mistaken belief that ingesting his heart will cure the sultan of blindness. Ironically, the source of this belief is the sultan's Christian doctor. Threatened with death if he fails to cure his master, the doctor concocts a remedy for the sultan that will take time to procure—hence prolonging his own life. Once the prince of Naples is captured, the task becomes one of tenderizing his heart for the sacrifice. To this end, the sultan sends his daughter Axa to entertain the captive. However, in a plot twist propelled by the transformation of dissimulation into authenticity, the captive prince manages to win Axa's true affections: "la voluntad fingida y de industria disimulada que ella mostraba se convirtió en un amor entrañable y verdadero [her insincere yet well-disguised good will gave way to a true and tender love]" (158).[24]

Modern critics have not widely perceived the thematic consonance between the novella and Gracián Dantisco's courtesy treatise as a whole. For Morreale, "Lugar aparte en la narrativa del *Galateo español*, en cuanto al tema si no al estilo, pertenece la 'Novela del Gran Soldán' [The 'Novella of the Great Sultan' occupies a unique space within the narrative of the *Spanish Gallant*, with respect to theme if not style]" (157). Certainly none of the three folk-motifs that Morreale identifies—"sovereign's illness cured by captive's blood," "youth saved from evil powers with the help of a young maiden with whom he flees," and "marriage union thwarted by spell"—bears any obvious relation to the theme of sociability that the *Galateo español* espouses. But the optic of dissimulation points to another lesson of the novella as a whole: "courtesy could save your life," a lesson that complements the *Galateo español*'s mission of teaching the rewards of sociability in an entertaining manner.

The phrase "insincere yet well-disguised good-will," cited above, marks Axa as a wily schemer. But how did the prince manage to elicit her volte-face? He relies upon dissimulation to save the day. The passage immediately preceding the quotation above hints that he duplicitously charmed Axa for the purpose of winning her allegiance: "Y como él de suyo fuese tan agradable y perfecto galán, supo tan bien agradecer y servir con tanta destreza y gallardía a su nueva señora Axa, que [...] [And since he was such an agreeable and perfect gentleman already, he figured out how to gratify and serve his new mistress Axa with so much skill and gallantry that [...]]" (158). Unlike Axa's initial connivance, the prince's equally contrived gallantry passes without reproof. Indeed, the prince's seductive ploy leads to four positive outcomes. First, the pair manages to escape; second, Axa converts to Christianity (a prized outcome from the Spanish perspective); third, the cowardly Christian doctor repents of having endangered the prince; and fourth, the prince and Axa eventually marry one another.

Two further explicit uses of the word "dissimulation" occur in "La novela del gran soldán." In the first case, the prince, in disguise, finally returns to Naples

---

[24] The motif of the Christian captive winning the heart of a Moslem noblewoman will be familiar to readers of the Romance cycle of the *Infantes de Lara*, Cervantes's Captive's Tale (*Don Quixote* I.39–41), and the *Abencerraje* in its ballad and novelized forms.

to marry Axa. Dissimulation here takes the form of obscuring one's identity: "El príncipe [llegó] muy disimulado por no quererse dar a conocer por entonces [The prince arrived very secretively because he did not yet wish to make himself known]" (160). However, after the prince confesses his identity to one of his captains, he warns him not to show him special deference: "Mas el príncipe le hizo del ojo, y le mandó que disimulase y le tratase como a caballero particular, que no se quería por entonces dar a conocer [But the prince winked at him and told him to dissimulate, and treat him like a lowly courtier, because he did not yet want to make himself known]" (160). The second usage, like the first, involves concealment, but the captain's dissimulation is more active and creative for he is bid to assume a disguise that hides the truth. Once a bishop is called upon to betroth the prince and Axa, the newly-wed groom and the doctor return to Naples, this time dressed as pilgrims. Disguise allows them to mingle with other courtiers while gradually leaking hints that the prince is alive and hidden somewhere at court. This ploy is designed to soften the shock when he finally reveals himself to his parents, who had presumed him to be dead.[25] Christianized, Axa continues to practice dissimulation, actually impersonating herself (wealthy princess visiting Neapolitan court) to win the Prince's parents' approval for her marriage to their son. Her charade works; their wedding is celebrated with universal joy. Ambassadors announce that the impending threat of war has been averted, and peace and prosperity reign. In this manner, the same narrative that had criticized the infidel Axa's scheming, now rewards "wise" Christianized Axa with marriage to her equally dissimulating husband.

"La novela del gran soldán" glamorizes the tedium of civility, making it a matter of urgency and drama rather than merely a wearisome duty or "vana significación de honra y reverencia [an insincere profession of honor and reverence]" (131). In this sense, its message fits perfectly into the overall thematic structure of the *Galateo español*, that of teaching the rewards of amiability. But in order to foreground the struggle between the Persian infidels' cannibalistic barbarism and the Neapolitan Christians' genteel civility, the narrator is forced to apply a double standard that condemns Axa's "insincere yet well-disguised good-will" (158) while painting a more favorable picture of the prince's calculated attentiveness. This ideological bias implies that dissimulation is justifiable when bent toward Christian aims, but not when employed by enemies, a suggestion reminiscent of Thomas Aquinas's indulgence toward "officious" or "helpful" lies.

The Perils of *Privanza*

Gracián Dantisco wrote the *Galateo español* as if to a younger brother. For this reason, the treatise appealed to inexperienced newcomers as well as to elite veterans of court. At the opposite extreme, Francisco de Quevedo (1580–1645) dedicated

---

[25] "[E]ntró en la antecámara, y allí después de haber hecho con los caballeros mil burlas y donaires, con el gozo que tenía se descubrió para que poco a poco dijesen al Rey su padre su venida de suerte que la mucha alegría no le causase alteración" (161).

his short treatise on royal favorites to King Philip III. As noted in Chapter 1, the position of favorite attained quasi-official status under Philip III (r. 1598–1621). In response to the heretofore unheard-of privileges and power that Philip invested in his favorite, the Duke of Lerma, a spate of new handbooks appeared, devoted not to the moral education of the king but to that of his *privado*.[26] Among these was Quevedo's *Discurso de las privanzas*. Believed to have been written early in Quevedo's career, the *Discurso de las privanzas* adapts the Medieval *speculum* or mirror of princes treatise to the moral, political, and civic education of the favorite. Conceptually, Quevedo places the monarch on a higher plane than his ministers. The *privado*'s job is to reflect the king's glory much as the moon reflects the sun's rays. If the king is a first cause, the *privado* for Quevedo serves as an indispensable secondary cause (chapter 3, 204–5). The *Discurso*'s 10 brief chapters define *privanza* and highlight various risks of working closely with the king. In particular Quevedo warns of the paradoxical role that dissimulation played in pleasing and appeasing the monarch.[27]

A principal source of danger facing the king's closest advisor according to Quevedo is the monarch's caprice. Chapter 5 of the *Discurso*, "Cómo ha de haber en las cosas de la fortuna el privado" [How the favorite should act under changing circumstances], offers three strategies for maintaining good relations with the monarch in the face of his changing whims. All three strategies demand some degree of dissimulation. First, Quevedo urges the *privado* to "sufrirlo el enojo y la ira [put up with his anger and his bile]" as well as show gratitude when the sovereign would expect complaint. Dissimulation here is salted with hypocrisy, for in addition to advising the *privado* to exercise the self-control necessary to respond mildly to the king's fits of rage, Quevedo also urges the favorite to act appreciatively in the face of royal piques. His second recommendation, "No refutarle por mala ninguna excusa o razón que diere [Never refute as bad any excuse or reason that he might give]," is accompanied by the admonishment to avoid appearing to be the king's equal. Placed at the service of diplomatic dissuasion, dissimulation requires the *privado* to take the lead while appearing always to follow. In addition, when petitioning the king on behalf of a third party, Quevedo counsels the *privado* to request the boon in light of the supplicant's merits rather than as a personal favor to himself.[28]

---

[26] The following sampling of guides to favorites provides an idea of their scope and aim: Juan Pablo Mártir Rizo's *Historia de la vida de Lucio Anneo, Séneca español* (1625); Vicente Mut's *El prínicpe en la guerra y en la paz* (1640); Salvador de Mallea's *Rey pacífico y gobierno del príncipe* (1646); Jerónimo de Ortega y Robles's *El despertador que avisa a un príncipe católico* (1647); Andrés Mendo's *Príncipe perfecto y ministros* (1657); and Pedro de Navarra y de la Cueva's *Logros de la monarquía* (1669) (see Díaz Martínez 39–40).

[27] Renowned poet, courtier, and satirist Francisco de Quevedo served in high positions in Sicily and at the courts of Philip III and Philip IV. Notorious for his mordant pen, he experienced both the rewards of favor and the pain of falling into disgrace (see Jauralde Pou).

[28] "Si pidiere algo al rey, advierte que lo ha de pedir proponiendo primero de suerte la persona para quien es, que lo pidan antes sus méritos y partes al rey que él" (216).

While the *Discurso* seldom employs the word *disimulación*, each recommendation relies upon an element of omission or concealment. The same chapter carries this endorsement even further by exhorting the *privado* to credit the king for every achievement, "En todo ha de confesarse por hechura suya [He must give credit to the king for all achievements]" (216–17). Furthermore, if the favorite cannot (or chooses not to) avoid perverting justice, he must present unjust actions to the king in a favorable light: "[El privado] ha de procurar hacer todas las cosas con justicia, y las que no pudiere o quisiere, por lo menos que lo parezca a los ojos del príncipe [[The favorite] should try to exercise justice in all cases, and where he cannot or wishes not to, at least he should make the case appear to be just in the eyes of the prince]" (217).

Quevedo only invokes dissimulation explicitly when condemning flatterers, whom he deems to be the favorite's most pernicious foes. Chapter 6, "De cómo diferenciará el privado el amigo del adulador" [On how the favorite shall distinguish friend from flatterer] compares a certain breed of fatuous sycophants to a surgeon who would rather trim his dying patient's hair and nails than amputate his snake-bitten arm. Such cowardly ministers prefer to focus on trivial faults instead of confronting crucial issues: "Pero vamos a la [forma de adulación] que tiene su parte de reprehensión que ya todos los aduladores han dado en disimularse en eso. [But let's move on to the [kind of flattery] that contains a grain of criticism, since these days the flatterers have taken to dissimulating in this way]" (226). Ironically, the behavior that Quevedo condemns in flatterers bears a strong resemblance to the strategy of evasive redirection that the *Discurso* recommends for not contradicting the monarch ("Never contradict him"), cited above. Quevedo's advice becomes more inconsistent in chapter 7, "De cómo se ha de haber con sus enemigos" [How [the favorite] should deal with his enemies]. After warning of rivals who pose as friends in order to inveigle their way into the favorite's confidence (229), the text identifies two classes of enemy: public and private. Yet the advice for dealing with each is the same: treat them as if you do not know them for what they really are: "Ni de unos ni de otros se ha de dar por entendido que lo sabe el privado o el príncipe [In either case, the prince or the *privado* should not let on that he knows]" (233). Suspicion in this scenario unleashes a defensive response: the favorite and/or the king must defy dissimulators by practicing even more dissimulation.

Weapons of Concealment

In general, the *Discurso de las privanzas* takes up a series of issues relevant to the *privado* without presuming to instruct the monarch. The only case in which Quevedo draws a parallel between the two occurs in the example of outmaneuvering enemies who pose as friends, cited above. By contrast, Spanish statesman Diego Saavedra Fajardo's collection of 100 moral-political empresas or devices, the *Idea de un príncipe político cristiano representada en cien empresas* of 1640, applies the same code of conduct to the monarch and his ministers.[29]

---

[29] López Poza, ed., *Empresas políticas* (524n* ed.).

While the *Idea* appears to be a mirror of princes dedicated to the then 10-year-old heir to the Spanish throne, Don Baltasar Carlos, it shares with Quevedo's *Discurso* an acute concern for the instruction of royal ministers and favorites.[30] In this sense, Saavedra Fajardo practices the very virtue of dissimulation that he preaches, for, under cover of a guide to princes, he instructs the men of court, particularly Philip IV's favorite, the Count-Duke of Olivares, whose attempts to reinvigorate the monarchy were widely perceived to have failed by 1640.[31]

Moral-political *empresa* collections like Saavedra Fajardo's *Idea* were well known in Spain by the seventeenth century.[32] The famous theorist of Baroque painting, Antonio Palomino, defined the emblem as "A meaningful metaphor for a moral lesson transmitted through 'iconological' figures—idealized, mythological, or some other ingenious and erudite representation—accompanied by a clear, witty, and clever motto or poem."[33] Palomino's definition provides a solid orientation for approaching *empresas* (devices) and emblems. Both forms confront the reader with an enigma resolved in an accompanying gloss in prose or verse. The erudite representation or *figura* consists of a pseudo-Egyptian hieroglyph or symbolic engraving usually framed within a decorative border or frame that isolates the rarefied field of emblematic signification from the everyday denotative world. This figure, also known as a *pictura* or *imago*,[34] recombines a repertoire of visual icons that relies for intelligibility on its conventionality. The lion's pelt, for example, was associated with Hercules; it usually symbolized royal power. More polysemous icons—a tree, a sailing vessel, a comet—could convey diverse messages depending on their relationship to other icons and words.

Working against each other in creative tension, hieroglyph and text concealed as much meaning as they revealed, creating a quizzical puzzle, or, as Juan de Horozco observed, a charade: "Their first advantage is that emblems are composed of signifying figures such that they speak by means of signs as if they were mute; that is, their inventor speaks through them."[35] As noted above, Saavedra Fajardo dedicated the *Idea* to Philip IV's son, Prince Baltasar Carlos. By electing

---

[30] Don Baltasar Carlos was Philip IV's son and heir by his first wife, Isabel de Borbón. He died of uncertain causes in 1646.

[31] Saavedra Fajardo may have had in mind another royal reader when he dedicated the *Idea de un príncipe político cristiano en cien empresas* to the youthful prince: Baltasar Carlos's father, King Philip IV (r. 1621–65).

[32] González de Zárate lists 130 "classic" European emblem collections published between 1531 and 1638 (33–8).

[33] Antonio Palomino de Castro y Velasco, *Museo pictórico y escala óptica* (Madrid, 1715), 104 (qtd. in González de Zárate 24). The idea that Egyptian hieroglyphs were repositories of hermetic wisdom kept alive by a priestly cult gained prominence during the Renaissance with the discovery in 1419 of Horapollo's fifth-century *Hieroglyphica*. Later Egyptologists questioned the authenticity of the volume (see Gómez 72–3).

[34] Latin, *pictura, icon, imago,* símbolo (see González de Zárate 32).

[35] "La primera conveniencia es, que los Emblemas se hacen de figuras que significan y que siendo como personas mudas hablan por señas, a lo menos habla en ellas la persona que las inventa" (*Emblemas morales* I, ch. 18 (qtd. in González de Zárate 6).

to instruct the prince in the language of signs rather than words alone, Saavedra Fajardo engaged his pupil in a pedagogically motivated game of dissimulation and discovery that only begins to hint at the positive benefits that cloaking the truth could render. In other words, Saavedra Fajardo was teaching the prince that by "speaking mutely" the prince could turn himself into a cipher, a symbol of power, that he would be privileged to gloss as he saw fit.

Above each emblem or empresa's *pictura*, an epigrammatic inscription or motto, known in Spanish as the *mote* or *lema*, appeared, often written in Latin on a scroll or banner.[36] In order for an emblem or empresa to be effective, the relationship between the aphoristic inscription and the hieroglyph had to remain somewhat—but not too—unintelligible. For Paulo Giovio, who published the first collection of empresas, the motto should "not be so obscure as to require calling on the Sybil to understand it, nor so obvious that any common man could understand it."[37] In his study of emblems and Spanish Baroque culture, Bradley Nelson compares the creative tension between image and text to Spanish perspectivist painting, which provokes the viewer into actively synthesizing a totality of meaning out of unintelligible fragments:

> The success of this perspectival construction rests not on a recognition of what is represented, but on a calculated misrecognition. *Like the hieroglyphic sign*, the image in its very opaqueness seems to conceal something more, an empty space into which the spectator projects a desire to reach eternal, universal realities and truths about the optical experience. (171, emphasis added)

In perspectivist painting, the puzzling disjunction between an assemblage of brushstrokes and the promise of wholeness and meaning, like the obscure relationship between the hieroglyph and its motto, excites the viewer or the reader's curiosity beckoning him or her to look more closely for coherence. To this end, the emblem or empresa provides an explicative gloss in verse or prose to elucidate the riddle of the juxtaposed image and text.[38]

The empresa is similar to the emblem: both combine an engraved illustration with a text to convey a message. The empresa traces its roots to Medieval heraldry while the emblem derives from humanist sources. The subsequent confluence of these artistic and philosophical currents made it difficult to maintain a strict separation between the two. Juan de Horozco y Covarrubias, who composed the

---

[36] Latin *inscriptio, titulo, motto, lemma* (see González de Zárate 6). González de Zárate lists seven sources for emblematic material: mythology, classical literature, nature and natural histories, scriptural and Patristic sources, legend and historical narrative, hieroglyphs and prior emblem books, and Medieval and travel literature (11). Not surprisingly, Saavedra Fajardo drew heavily upon these well-worn iconographic and aphoristic repertoires.

[37] "[N]o sea tan oscura que sea menester llamar la sibila para entenderla, ni tan clara que cualquier hombre vulgar la entienda" (trans. Alfonso Ulloa, qtd. in Gómez 190). Paulo Giovio's *Dialogo dell'Impresse* of 1551 was translated into Spanish by Alonso de Ulloa in 1558; engravings were added to the 1561 and 1562 editions (see Gómez 29–108).

[38] Latin *subscriptio, epigramma, declaratio* (see González de Zárate 6).

Fig. 3.2 "Bellum collegit qui discordias seminant," Empresa 75. Diego Saavedra Fajardo, *Idea de un príncipe político christiano*, 1675, Valencia. The Harold and Mary Jean Hanson Rare Books Collection, Special & Area Studies Collections, George A. Smathers Libraries, University of Florida.

first Spanish emblem-book in 1589, attempted to sort out the difference between *emblemas* [emblems], *empresas*, *jeroglíficos* [hieroglyphs], and *divisas* [devices], but in practice the boundaries between these textual-graphic (or "icono-logic") hybrids remained blurred. For example, according to Horozco, the human figure should not appear in an empresa, an abstracting feature which lends empresas their austere and premonitory air.[39] Saavedra Fajardo generally respects this dictum, but he might be accused of breaking it by depicting human hands and other parts of human bodies in 19 of his *Empresas*.[40] Empresa 75, "Bellum collegit qui discordias seminant" [He who sows discord reaps war], might be criticized for breaking

---

[39] *Emblemas morales*, book I, chapter 16, rule 4 (qtd. in González de Zarate 4).

[40] Hands in Saavedra Fajardo's *Idea* are represented as: holding a painter's palette (Empresa 2, 202); holding a rudder and scepter over a globe (Empresa 18, 329); passing a torch to another hand (Empresa 19, 342); pulling an empty net from the sea (Empresa 29, 419); holding a coronet (Empresa 35, 466); taming a pony (Empresa 38, 485); stretching toward another hand with eyes on each finger (Empresa 51, 610); grasping a scepter adorned with three eyes (Empresa 55, 644); writing with one point of a compass (Empresa 56, 658); lighting a torch with the help of another hand (Empresa 58, 674); wearing a glove and armor touching a porcupine (Empresa 59, 685); brandishing a sword and a branch over a globe (Empresa 69, 782); splitting apart a tree with another hand (Empresa 70, 799); blocking the flow of a fountain (Empresa 72, 812); throwing dust at a swarm of bees (Empresa 73, 818); weighing a sword and shield (Empresa 81, 878); holding a stone pierced by a dagger (Empresa 88, 936); grasping a lion pelt (Empresa 97, 1002); and being protected by a shield while holding an olive branch (Empresa 98, 1008).

Fig. 3.3   "Formosa superne," Empresa 78. Diego Saavedra Fajardo, *Idea de un príncipe político christiano*, 1675, Valencia. The Harold and Mary Jean Hanson Rare Books Collection, Special & Area Studies Collections, George A. Smathers Libraries, University of Florida.

Horozco's rule by representing half-bodies. Its *pictura* depicts a "crop" of fighting soldiers who have sprouted from the waist up in a field. In addition, Empresa 78, "Formosa superne" [Beautiful above], portrays a nude female figure submerged from the waist down in the sea with a fish-tail visible among the waves; in other words, a mermaid.

Despite Horozco's best efforts, the distinctions between empresas and emblems would not be enforced, and the term *emblema* became the generic descriptor for many types of didactic word/image combinations.

Saavedra Fajardo composed the explanatory glosses for his *empresas* as mini-treatises. Each essay offers a moral-political lesson that clarifies the opaque connection between the hieroglyph of the empresa and its motto. In this fashion, the act of decoding the empresas becomes a cat-and-mouse chase after hidden meaning; an apprenticeship in the aesthetics of dissimulation. But dissimulation is more than a literary ornament for Saavedra Fajardo. Eleven of his 100 empresas deliver explicit advice on the art of dissimulation to the future monarch Prince Baltasar Carlos (or perhaps his father, the then-reigning Philip IV) and the courtiers who served them.

The first prologue of the *Idea* addresses Prince Baltasar Carlos, but a second prologue confirms that general readers should adopt for themselves his advice to the prince: "I don't spend as much time dealing with grooming the prince and governing his actions because I don't wish to digress from the topic of governing republics—their growth, preservation, and decline—and with molding a minister of state and a forewarned courtier."[41] Saavedra Fajardo reinforces this parallelism in Empresa 33 with the image of a lion regarding himself in a broken mirror.

By convention, the lion symbolized royalty, but in Spain it referred particularly to the León in the united realms of Castile and León. The image of the lion in the mirror links the conduct of the monarch to that of his courtiers. Its gloss explains, "Just as the royal minister must wrap himself in the wisdom of his prince, so must he wear his decorum, courage, and greatness of spirit."[42] The author further develops the mirror conceit by exhorting royal ministers to cultivate the same virtues as the king: "And since the royal councils, tribunals, and ministries are part of this mirror of State, they too ought to exhibit the same qualities, and the same is true for the ministers who represent him."[43] The image of a mirror helps Saavedra Fajardo to recast the king and his ministers as essentially similar rather than dissimilar, as the doctrine of divine right asserted.[44] The metaphor of coinage draws the sovereign even closer to his court officials:

> Una moneda pública es el ministro, en quien está figurado el príncipe, y si no es de buenos quilates y le representa vivamente, será desestimada como falsa. Si la cabeza que gobierna es de oro, de oro sean también las manos que le sirven, como eran las del esposo en las Sagradas Letras.[45]
>
> [The royal minister is a coin upon which the prince's image is stamped, and if it be not made of quality metal, and the likeness vivid, it will be scorned as counterfeit. If the head that governs is made of gold, of gold too shall be the hands that serve him, as were those of the husband in the Holy Writ.] (459)

The *Idea* alternately defends and condemns dissimulating performances. Although the empresas tend overall to favor dissimulating strategies, it is not easy to quantify this impression due to Saavedra's rhetorical style, which revels in paradox and contradiction.[46] Empresa 18, "A deo" [From God], for example, praises the beauty of virtue, whose secret force ["secreta fuerza"] attracts people to venerate her (329).

---

[41] "No me ocupo tanto en la institución y gobierno del príncipe, que no me divierta al de las Repúblicas, a sus crecimientos, conservación y caídas, y a formar un ministro de Estado y un cortesano advertido" (176).

[42] "Así como se ha de vestir el ministro de las máximas de su príncipe, así también de su decoro, valor y grandeza de ánimo" (460).

[43] "Y porque son partes de este espejo los Consejos, los Tribunales y las Chancillerías, también en ellas se han de hallar las mismas calidades y no menos en cada uno de los ministros que le representan" (459).

[44] Guido Colonna's *De regimine principum* (1473, 1517) expounded the doctrine of divine right. For further discussion, see Chapter 1.

[45] Song of Songs 5.11 and 5.14.

[46] Within the 11 empresas that explicitly cite the word *disimulación* [dissimulation] or its variants (Empresas 18, 32, 33, 34, 36, 43, 44, 45, 48, 62, and 78), I estimate that 20 arguments favor practicing dissimulation and seven arguments oppose it.

Fig. 3.4 "Siempre el mismo," Empresa 33. Diego Saavedra Fajardo, *Idea de un príncipe político christiano*, 1675, Valencia. The Harold and Mary Jean Hanson Rare Books Collection, Special & Area Studies Collections, George A. Smathers Libraries, University of Florida.

But within the same empresa, the author also opts for dissimulation over full disclosure: "Hide news of your vices until time can cure them, encouraging good subjects with rewards and correcting bad subjects with punishment, and using other means that teach prudence."[47] If the prince cannot serve as a mirror of virtue to his subjects, he should hide his faults.

Another seeming contradiction occurs in Empresas 33 and 34, which counsel the prince and the courtier to assume a public mask of impartiality that neither flinches at insults nor betrays fear in adversity. When a courtier does not receive the reward he is due, he should not complain; rather, much like Quevedo's *privado*, Saavedra Fajardo's ill-treated courtier "ha de acabar dando gracias a todas sus pláticas con el príncipe [ought to close all of his conversations with the prince with words of gratitude]" (Empresa 33, 458). Empresa 34 alludes to Christopher Columbus. In the face of danger, the man of court should imitate Columbus, who bore uncertainty with sufferance and hope (462–3). On the other hand, on public ceremonial occasions, if the courtier is not properly honored, he should drop all pretenses and grab his rightful place, because "he who hesitates discredits himself. He who feigns indifference invites disrespect. Modesty falls behind, disparaged."[48] These conflicting pronouncements arise from a clash of principles. The overall game-plan of being well liked dictates the necessity of performing

---

[47] "Disimule la noticia de los vicios hasta que pueda remediarlos con el tiempo, animando con el premio a los buenos y corrigiendo con el castigo a los malos, y usando de otros medios que enseña la prudencia" (338).

[48] "Quien duda desconfía de su mérito. Quien disimula confiesa su indignidad. La modestia se queda atrás despreciada" (Empresa 33, 457).

Fig. 3.5   "A deo," Empresa 18. Diego Saavedra Fajardo, *Idea de un príncipe político christiano*, 1675, Valencia. The Harold and Mary Jean Hanson Rare Books Collection, Special & Area Studies Collections, George A. Smathers Libraries, University of Florida.

acts of deference toward superiors. At the same time, a public slight or loss of face could degrade the courtier's social capital, thereby shrinking his field of influence and eroding his likeability.[49] Therefore, the best way to protect against a potential loss of face is to prevent its occurrence.

Empresa 43, "Ut sciat regnare" [For him who knows how to govern], also oscillates between two views on dissimulation. The *pictura* depicts a lion's pelt with serpents on its head, the whole draped under a royal awning or canopy. The motto is a variant of "Qui nescit dissimulare, nescit regnare [He who know not how to dissimulate knows not how to rule]," which serves as the opening epigraph to this chapter. The Medieval French King Louis "The Prudent" XI (r. 1461–83) is believed to have given this advice to his son, Charles VIII. The lion's skin represents a show of royal strength while the serpents symbolize royal artfulness. As Saavedra Fajardo explains, the prince must avail himself of many masks, as circumstance demands:

> No siempre ha de parecer humano. Ocasiones hay en que es menester que se revista de la piel del león, y que sus vasallos y sus enemigos le vean con garras y tan severo, que no se le atreva el engaño con las palabras halagüeñas de que se vale para domesticar el ánimo de los príncipes. Pero, porque alguna vez conviene cubrir la fuerza con la astucia, y la indignación con la benignidad, disimulando y acomodándose al tiempo y a las personas, se corona en esta Empresa la frente del león [...] con las sierpes, símbolo del Imperio y de la majestad prudente y vigilante.

---

[49] For sociologist Pierre Bourdieu, "social capital" measures one's contacts and networks with well-placed individuals (see Grenfell 28).

Fig. 3.6   "Ut sciat regnare," Empresa 43. Diego Saavedra Fajardo, *Idea de un príncipe político christiano*, 1675, Valencia. The Harold and Mary Jean Hanson Rare Books Collection, Special & Area Studies Collections, George A. Smathers Libraries, University of Florida.

[The sovereign needn't always show himself to be human. On some occasions, he must wear a lion's skin and let his vassals and servants see him with claws bared, so terrible that they don't dare deceive him with the flattering words with which princely spirits are tamed. But, since sometimes it is useful to hide strength behind cleverness and indignation behind benignancy, dissimulating and adapting to circumstance and people, the lion's head in this emblem is crowned [...] with serpents, a symbol of Empire, majesty, prudence, and vigilance [...].] (527)

Yet within the same discourse, Saavedra Fajardo acknowledges that dissimulation corrodes public trust. "How long can something exist that is based on deceit and lies?" he asks. "How reliable would contracts be if the prince, who serves as their guarantor, lacked credibility in the eyes of the public? Who would trust him?" Here Saavedra Fajardo coincides with Gracián Dantisco in warning that excessive posturing damages credibility.

Serpents symbolize a different sort of dissimulation in Empresa 44, "Nec a quo nec ad quem" [Neither from whom nor towards whom], which depicts the entwined length of a serpent with its head raised toward the sky. The snake's coils confound the viewer, making it impossible to know if he is coming or going. Analogously, the prince should keep his counsel to himself: "Es ilícito y peligroso obligar al príncipe a que descubra sus pensamientos ocultos [It is improper and dangerous to oblige the prince to reveal his hidden thoughts]" (538). But if an opponent is playing the same game, one should feign innocence, a ruse especially useful for the ministers of excessively shifty sovereigns: "This dissimulation, or feigned simplicity is very necessary to those ministers serving calculating and treacherous

Fig. 3.7   "Nec a quo nec ad quem," Empresa 44. Diego Saavedra Fajardo, *Idea de un príncipe político christiano*, 1675, Valencia. The Harold and Mary Jean Hanson Rare Books Collection, Special & Area Studies Collections, George A. Smathers Libraries, University of Florida.

princes who jealously protect their schemes from being exposed" (538). Saavedra's enthusiasm for feigning innocence recalls Quevedo's advice regarding how the favorite should deal with his enemies: "In either case, the prince or the *privado* should not let on that he knows" (*Discurso* 233).

Empresas 45, 48, 62, and 78 confront issues associated with dissembling princes and ministers. Empresa 45, "Non majestate securus" [Majesty does not guarantee safety], offers perhaps the *Idea*'s most untempered call for engaging in dissimulation—with one caveat. The empresa depicts a recumbent lion whose eyes are half-opened, signifying that, even while appearing to be off-guard, the prince should always remain vigilant. The visual impact of the slit-eyed lion, however, does not inspire trust in the monarch. Therefore, Saavedra reverts to Quevedo's double standard, preferring that the sovereign be trustworthy and the courtiers be dissimulating. The gloss that accompanies the alert lion acknowledges that the arts of dissimulation "are better relegated (when unavoidable) to royal ministers than princes; because the latter have something divine hidden within them that is debased by such concerns."[50]

Empresa 48, "Sub luce lues" [Beneath the light, corruption], evokes a bleak socioscape in which mistrust and dissembling inevitably corrode all social interactions. The engraving depicts a star-studded lizard that represents ministers dissatisfied with their subservience and whose glittering words of praise conceal venomous hatred for the prince.

---

[50]   "[M]ejor están (cuando se pueden excusar) en los ministros que en los príncipes; porque en éstos hay una oculta divinidad que se ofende d[e] este cuidado" (543).

Fig. 3.8   "Non majestate securus," Empresa 45. Diego Saavedra Fajardo, *Idea de un príncipe político christiano*, 1675, Valencia. The Harold and Mary Jean Hanson Rare Books Collection, Special & Area Studies Collections, George A. Smathers Libraries, University of Florida.

Yet within the same empresa Saavedra Fajardo adduces biblical evidence to make the paradoxical claim that dissimulation helps to spread truth. Even God, Saavedra Fajardo reminds his readers, relied on prophets, apostles, signs, and dreams rather than reveal his word directly to his people:

> Aun Dios las manifestó con recato a los príncipes, pues aunque pudo por Josef y por Daniel notificar a Faraón y a Nabucodonosor algunas verdades de calamidades futuras, se las representó por sueños cuando estaban enajenados los sentidos y dormida la majestad. Y aun entonces no claramente sino en figuras y jeroglíficos, para que se interpusiese tiempo en la interpretación, con que previno el inconveniente del susto y sobresalto, y excusó el peligro de aquellos ministros, si se las dijesen sin ser llamados. Conténtese el ministro con que las llegue a conocer el príncipe; y, si pudiere por señas, no use de palabras.

> [Even God revealed his truth to princes with caution, for, although through Joseph and Daniel he could have warned Pharaoh and Nebuchadnezzar of future calamities, instead he represented them to them through dreams while their senses were suspended and their majesty benumbed. And even then, not directly, but rather through figures and hieroglyphics, so that the time it took to understand them would be prolonged, thereby precluding the annoyance of fright and distress, and minimizing the risk to those ministers had they revealed the truth before being summoned. Let the minister be content with letting the message reach the prince, and, if this can be managed with signs, make do without words.] (575)

Fig. 3.9   "Sub luce lues," Empresa 48. Diego Saavedra Fajardo, *Idea de un príncipe político christiano*, 1675, Valencia. The Harold and Mary Jean Hanson Rare Books Collection, Special & Area Studies Collections, George A. Smathers Libraries, University of Florida.

Hebrew Scriptures recount that Joseph succeeded in deciphering the Egyptian Pharaoh's dreams of the cows and the sheaves (Gen. 41.15) and that Daniel succeeded in elucidating the Babylonian king Nebuchadnezzar's dream of the great tree (Dan. 4.2) where other soothsayers had failed. The two monarchs prospered by heeding the advice of these unlikely messengers. But they only called on Joseph and Daniel as a last resort. If those prophets had delivered their prophecies sooner, the monarchs would not have listened. Only when the kings' enigmatic dreams proved insoluble to others were the lowly Hebrews invited to speak. There can be no arguing when God exemplifies the practice of "officious" dissimulation. From these examples, Saavedra Fajardo deduces that dissimulated messages reach the king's ear more effectively than open communication, and that coded speech, especially if the news is bad, reduces the risk inherent in the impulse to "kill the messenger." Nonetheless, Saavedra Fajardo harbors no illusions about the dangers of taking this practice too far. He closes Empresa 48 by blaming sycophantic ministers for corrupting their sovereigns: "Apenas hubiera príncipe malo, si no hubiera ministros lisonjeros [There would scarcely be any bad princes if there were no flattering ministers]" (578).

Empresa 62, "Nulli Patet" [He reveals himself to none], mobilizes the secrecy of bees—whose waxy hive conceals the complexities within—to support the use of dissimulation in matters of statecraft. By contrast, Empresa 78, "Formosa superne" [Beautiful above], cited above, teaches mistrust of superficial appearances. The hieroglyph of a mermaid's torso, whose tail lies hidden under the waves, teaches that ambitious ministers, like sirens, hide their dangerous designs beneath a comely surface (see Figure 3.3). On the other hand, Saavedra Fajardo's gloss adds

Fig. 3.10   "Nulli patet," Empresa 62. Diego Saavedra Fajardo, *Idea de un príncipe político christiano*, 1675, Valencia. The Harold and Mary Jean Hanson Rare Books Collection, Special & Area Studies Collections, George A. Smathers Libraries, University of Florida.

that a good prince should not reveal his end-game, or he risks never achieving it: "Because no rationale obliges him to reveal at all times the object at which he is aiming; to the contrary, unless he feigns at that moment that he is shooting elsewhere, he risks missing the mark."[51]

Conclusion

Dissimulation evinced differing degrees of aversion and enthusiasm from Gracián Dantisco, writing in c. 1586, Quevedo in 1606–08, and Saavedra Fajardo in 1640, yet all three might have agreed with Norbert Elias, for whom excessive self-surveillance carried with it intrinsic dangers: "But a higher degree of rationality and drive inhibition can also, in certain situations, have a debilitating and adverse effect. 'Civilization' can be a very two-edged weapon" (*Power and Civility* 283). It may be said that Gracián Dantisco's *Galateo español*, Quevedo's *Discurso de las privanzas*, and Saavedra Fajardo's *Idea* examine both edges of the weapon of dissimulating speech. While Gracián Dantisco grudgingly makes room for the possibility of dissimulation where public decorum is concerned, Quevedo warms to dissimulation for the good of the state, albeit with misgivings. The *Idea* expresses the most highly developed arguments in favor of engaging in dissimulating conduct, but also echoes Quevedo's reservations about the danger of misreading inherent in the prevailing "culture of secrecy."

---

[51] "Porque no hay razón que le obligue a señalar siempre el blanco adonde tira, antes, no pudiera dar en uno si al mismo tiempo no pareciese que apuntaba a otros" (861).

Gracián Dantisco's narrator in the *Galateo español* grudgingly acquiesces to dissembling as a social lubricant, but he decries concealing the truth for the sake of self-aggrandizement or personal ambition. Looking more closely at the *Galateo español*'s embedded narrative, "La novela del gran soldán," however, a more complex picture emerges, for his novella rewards its protagonist, the prince of Naples, for multiple deft concealments, both verbal and physical. To a certain extent the prince's actions are overdetermined by the conventions of Byzantine romance, which demand that the story's rhythm of loss and recovery be accomplished by means of disguise. But the fact that the *Galateo español* frames these instances of dissimulating behavior within an orientalizing romance is itself significant. The distancing effect created by the novel's exotic settings (Persia and Naples), the extreme, life-threatening circumstances that justify the prince's dissimulations, and the generic expectations that the novella establishes by aligning itself with the vehicle of Byzantine romance create a safely circumscribed space. Like the decorative border that frames the *pictura* of an emblem, setting apart its rarefied play of signification from the world of everyday objects, the imaginative space of Byzantine romance allows Gracián Dantisco to unleash uses of dissimulation that may not yet have gained widespread acceptance in late sixteenth-century Spain. Safely ensconced within their fictional borders, these potentially controversial models of behavior could not contaminate the more orthodox portions of his text with the taint of ethical ambiguity.

The practice of isolating ethically ambiguous advice also characterizes Castiglione's *Book of the Courtier* of 1528 (adapted for Spanish readers in 1534), which similarly brackets certain dissimulating ploys within a separate domain. As JoAnn Cavallo has shown, jokes provide Castiglione the safety zone for experimenting with daring forms of dissimulation:

> When Bibbiena later includes dissimulation as an element of joke-telling (2.72), thus giving a theoretical stamp of approval to the practice he demonstrated earlier, he is explicitly calling attention to an essential courtly "virtue" whose usefulness goes beyond joke-telling to pervade all forms of social interaction. (424)

Cavallo adds that dissimulating would only rise to the status of the courtier's *modus operandi* in Italy with the publication of Torquato Accetto's 1641 treatise *Della dissimulazione onesta* [On honest dissimulation].

Quevedo's *Discurso de las privanzas* registers awareness of the pragmatic benefits that dissimulation affords to those who serve the powerful. Majesty magnifies and complicates the challenges implicit in any patron-client relationship; to disagree with the king is treason; to gain his confidence is to capture power itself. The royal favorite must learn to adapt and accommodate to the sovereign's caprice while at the same time steering him on a prudent course. Two dissimulating strategies that the *Discurso* advises for accomplishing this delicate task are: to guide the king on a prudent path with convincing counter-arguments and then to credit him for adopting them.

Saavedra Fajardo sacrifices internal coherence to the rhetorical principles of *copia* [profusion] and *varietas* [variety] to produce a gratifying exercise in Baroque hermeneutics. Saavedra Fajardo's empresas oscillate between two sides of an argument that seldom mesh. The *Idea*'s chiaroscuro effect of dramatic contrasts yields many aesthetic and conceptual rewards but few fruits in the way of didactic utility. In keeping with the contradictory sources that Saavedra Fajardo reshapes, his discourse pulls in opposite directions. Yet paradox too counts as a dissimulating practice, inviting the reader to return again and again to his enigmatic empresas to pry open their hidden messages. Like Gracián Dantisco, Saavedra Fajardo accepts as a matter of course that the court hierarchy necessitates dissimulation, but the *Idea* envisages its practice on a greatly expanded scale. Whereas Gracián Dantisco deplored and condemned dissimulation for the sake of self-interest and expedience, Saavedra Fajardo accepts the inevitability of dissimulation "por obligación [for the sake of custom]," "por vanidad [for self-promotion]," and "por utilidad [for reasons of expedience]."

Chapter 4
Adaptability

> Fire whirls, Air flies, Water ebbs and flows, the face of the Earth alters her looks, Time stays not; the Color that is most light will take most dyes: so in Men, they that have the most reason are the most alterable in their designs […].
>
> —John Donne, *Juvenilia*, Paradox 1

As we saw in Chapter 3, Lucas Gracián Dantisco criticized "chameleons" at court—those who changed color in accordance to prevailing conditions. However, even during Gracián Dantisco's lifetime the need to respond to change elevated chameleon-like mutability to new heights of respectability. Expecting—and responding capably to—unexpected circumstances became a matter of individual and collective urgency as Spain underwent rapid centralization, economic destabilization, and overseas expansion between 1500 and 1700 (see Chapter 1). These accelerating challenges favored those best able to adapt, as we will see in the case of Philip II's favorite, Ruy Gómez de Silva (1516–73), a contemporary of Gracián Dantisco. Although the term "adaptability" did not yet enjoy widespread usage during the sixteenth and seventeenth centuries, we use the term to embrace a cluster of revalorized courtly strategies that includes adjustment, flexibility, accommodation, adaptation, agility, and mutation in response to new situations.

The Renaissance is often thought of as a period of breaking free from scholastic patterns of thought and received doxa. Mental flexibility for trying novel approaches and for assimilating new information came to the fore, although not without ethical debate hard-fought in both religious and lay circles. Resistance to change came primarily from two quarters: an ecclesiastical hierarchy protective of Church authority and the secular philosophy of Neostoicism, which sought refuge from tumultuous times in contemplation of the inevitability of change. Unhappiness was seen to arise from passionate resistance to change; therefore the only proper response to fortune's whims lay in dispassionate self-control. Neostoic philosophers bore the burden of change with resignation rather than opposing or out-maneuvering it. Indeed, they measured masculine virtue against a yardstick of fortitude or constancy. By contrast, female inconstancy made women untrustworthy, weak, and inferior. Yet as the British metaphysical poet John Donne wryly observed in 1633, "they that have the most reason are the most alterable in their designs" (see epigraph above). Alterability or inconstancy, in addition to intimating lack of resolve, caprice, or fickleness, also make possible the transformative whirl and flow of change both in nature and society.

Donne was joking when he admired women's inconstancy in Paradox 1, but the joke contains a telling element of truth. In order for the Renaissance gender order to assimilate adaptability as a masculine virtue, it was necessary for alterability to shed the stigma of femininity assigned to it by Neostoicism. In this chapter we will examine conduct writings by Lope de Vega, Francisco de Quevedo, Miguel de Cervantes, Baltasar Gracián, and others that work to dislodge inconstancy from the column of so-called negative feminine traits in order to recast it as a new masculine ideal: that of adaptability. The primary texts to be analyzed below are Cervantes's exemplary novel "El coloquio de los perros" [The Dogs' Colloquy] (1613), Lope de Vega's *comedia* [play] *El perro del hortelano* [*The Dog in the Manger*] (1618), and Gabriel de la Gasca's writing manual, the *Manual de avisos para el perfecto cortesano* [Advice manual for the perfect courtier] (1681). However, since those works wrestle with prevailing Neostoic codes of conduct, it will first be useful to review the ethical tenets of Neostoicism as it veered away from classical Stoic precept in the sixteenth century.

Constancy as Neostoic Virtue

To live a virtuous happy life, wrote Belgian philosopher Justus Lipsius (1547–1606) in his *De Constantia* [*On Constancy*] of 1584, one should imitate God by being immovable.[1] For Neostoics like Lipsius and his Spanish avatars, wisdom, or *sapientia*, consisted of harmonizing the classical Stoical values of self-control, constancy, and non-striving with the Christian imperative to feel compassion for others. The unwise individual, or *apáthes*, according to the Neostoic view, is one who falls victim to desire and its attendant dissatisfactions.[2] Lipsius taught that the well-being of empires—and Spain then had the largest empire in the world—rested upon the public service of virtuous subjects on behalf of the republic. As long as royal ministers subscribed to what Theodore Corbett has called the "cult of Lipsius," they policed their own actions and devoted themselves to public service (151–2). Lipsius presents a finely tuned system that integrates Christian and classical values into a coherent whole, which "[m]ore clearly perhaps than any classical Stoic […] conveys the need for constancy in a world of continual change where nothing is stable except the rocklike strength of the human mind," according to Geoffrey Miles, who brings Neostoic philosophy to bear on his reading of Shakespeare (75). López Poza, in her analysis of the Neostoic concept

---

[1] Lipsius's *De Constantia* underwent 49 reprintings in Latin, and was extensively translated, including a slightly expurgated Spanish edition that came out in 1616. By 1600 it had reached Mexico and the Spanish colonies of the New World (López Poza 148–9). Lipsius maintained correspondences with Spanish humanists such as Francisco de Quevedo and Benito Arias Montano, and he dedicated the 1604 Spanish translation of his six-volume *Políticas* not only to Philip III, but to all those members of the Spanish nobility unable to read Latin.

[2] Kenneth Krabbenhoft, who discerns in Neostoic philosophy an important heuristic for reading Spanish Golden Age masterpieces, explains that "El *apáthes* o anti-*sapiens* vive sujeto a los impulsos del cuerpo, los juicios temerarios, la codicia y la ambición [The *apáthes* or unwise man lives enslaved to bodily impulses, rash judgements, greed and ambition]" (30).

of the wise man, remarks that even political philosophers such as Baltasar Gracián, Diego Saavedra Fajardo, Álamos de Barriento, and Juan de Vera, who suspected Lipsius of writing from an anti-Hapsburg perspective, paid homage to his teachings (López Poza 150). An important school of Neostoicism in Seville influenced Philip IV's favorite, the Count-Duke of Olivares, to adopt policies of "authority, moderation, constancy, discipline, and prudence rooted in pragmatism" (Oestreich 275). Francisco de Quevedo's anti-Machiavellian political treatise, the *Política de Dios y gobierno de Cristo* (1617–26), placed responsibility for the welfare of the state in the hands of disciplined ministers and servants.[3] As long as Spanish subjects devoted themselves to public service, the sovereign need not coerce them with fear and force.

The Neostoic program of ethical self-surveillance finds expression in many literary works of the period, although not always convincingly. Pedro Calderón de la Barca's martyr drama, *El príncipe constante* [*The Constant Prince*] (1629), apotheosizes the ordeal of the so-called "Saint Prince" Ferdinand of Portugal (1402–43). The King of Morocco held Prince Ferdinand hostage for many years in order to pressure Portugal to return the North African outpost of Ceuta to Moroccan control. Several Portuguese military expeditions failed to free the prince, and Ferdinand died in captivity in Fez. Later, he was declared a Christian martyr and beatified in 1470. Yet the Portuguese gained little by sacrificing their prince because the tiny peninsula fell into Spanish hands in 1580.[4] But despite history's hindsighted rebuke to old paradigms of heroic resistance, Calderón's play devalues the option of applying a more flexible policy to Portugal's diplomatic impasse with Morocco, and instead exalts Ferdinand's Neostoic steadfastness.

The vicissitudes of Lipsius's career also called into question the ongoing utility of Neostoic constancy. Caught between Catholic and Protestant patrons during a period of intense religious rivalry, Lipsius was obliged to flee academic posts and switch allegiances frequently throughout his lifetime. He began his career serving as Philip II's Latin secretary in Catholic Rome, later teaching for 12 years at the new Calvinist University of Leiden. So egregious was the disconnect in Lipsius's life between his theoretical embrace of constancy and his flitting allegiances to patrons of clashing faiths that the British bishop and moralist Joseph Hall (1574–1656) attacked Lipsius's hypocrisy in a satire called *Heaven on Earth and Characters of Vertue* (Kirks 48, qtd. in Miles 50).

The two examples cited above—Portugal's loss of Ceuta despite Prince Ferdinand's steadfastness, and the divergence between Lipsius's mercurial religious positions and his credo of immovability—illustrate anecdotally the practical limits of Neostoic constancy as a course of individual or collective action. In response to the need for more effective strategies for confronting shifting circumstances,

---

[3] On Neostoic thought in the seventeenth century, see also Octavio Paz, especially ch. 4. For an alternative non-Neostoic reading of Calderón's *El príncipe constante*, see Stroud 202–24.

[4] Even after Portugal wrested independence from Spain in 1640, the subjects of Ceuta sided with Spain and against the restored Portuguese monarchy.

it is instructive to observe that social and cultural institutions during this period began experimenting with more flexible approaches than the Neostoic doctrine of resoluteness would allow. Transatlantic navigation, global missionary outreach, dramaturgy, and the unofficial office of *privado* [royal favorite] were five realms of cultural activity that found virtue in adaptability rather than constancy, thereby ratifying the sagacity of Donne's ironic wit.

Adaptability in Action

Transatlantic sea-pilots struggled to reconcile Medieval assumptions concerning the movements of the sun and stars with their on-deck observations. Although sixteenth-century navigators may have wished to cling to Ptolemaic cosmography, empirical evidence forced them to admit that a discrepancy between true and magnetic North was interfering with their calculations. In response to this dawning realization the pilots became adept at coupling received knowledge with independent observation. The collaborations between Portuguese *converso* mathematician Pedro Nunes (1502–78) and his student, João de Castro (1500–1548), yielded new declension charts (charts for measuring the height of the North Star or other heavenly objects) for calculating latitude. De Castro, a naval officer and future viceroy of Brazil, spent much time on military expeditions to India, Africa, and the New World. He brought with him his teacher's "nonius" or "shadow instrument" in order to compare its measurements to existing sea-charts. Together, teacher and student helped the commander of the Portuguese fleet bound for Brazil in 1530 to discern defects in the existing quadrate marine maps. For Onésimo Almeida, the collaboration between land-bound Nunes and his seafaring student João de Castro marks a departure from the Medieval mindset of unwavering faith in received authority and represents a significant step toward adapting received knowledge to systematic observation:

> All of these were incipient phases of the modernity that was gradually establishing itself. Pedro Nunes and João de Castro, the first with a more theoretical and abstract vocation, the second with more practical inclinations, though profoundly dedicated to careful observation, are both pioneers of a scientific approach that is characterized by attention to the real, by a preoccupation with rigor and exactness in measurements, by the collection of data (even that which contradicts theory), and by experimentation, questioning, and a clearly formed notion of the unknown world being immense and immersed in the secrets of Apollo for a long time to come. (92)

Nunes and De Castro's work illustrates that, as early as the sixteenth century, stalwart faith in received knowledge had begun to lose ground to an empirical epistemology that accommodated new discoveries and observations.

A slightly different situation confronted the Jesuit missionaries who fanned out from Castile to the East and West to spread Roman Catholicism. They could not fail to observe that the best way to optimize their credibility among distant peoples was to shed their Western attire and adopt local customs. While they did not practice the kind of epistemological adaptability exemplified by Nunes and De Castro, they developed a doctrine of cultural accommodation that allowed them to exercise what sociolinguist Erving Goffman terms "impression management." In the interest of gaining favor and influence, the Jesuits in the Far East sought to identify and adopt the semiotic status markers of the target culture. Thus, in Japan, they found it expedient to wear Buddhist robes, while in China, once they discerned that Buddhists were not as highly respected as scholars, they instead styled themselves after the prestigious Confucian intelligentsia (Standaert 356). By relinquishing their own customs, learning local languages, and managing their appearance, the missionaries reduced many barriers between themselves and their intended audience. This flexibility in the realm of self-fashioning contributed to their effectiveness as evangelizers and teachers.

Lope de Vega's *Arte nuevo de hacer comedias en este tiempo* [New art of composing drama in our times] (1609) represents a third instance of daring empirical logic, that is, adaptability to observed conditions. Lope noted that ticket sales rose when he ignored classical theatrical conventions, concentrating instead on giving the audience a good time. Conversely, they fell when he clung to precept rather than indulge local taste. In light of this observation, Lope abjured the rote parroting of classical dramaturgy in favor of adapting his plays to the changing taste of *el vulgo*, the "common throng":

> It is true, at times, that I have written according to that art that few still know. Yet, observing elsewhere that throngs and women mob the theaters to watch monstrosities laden with special-effects, I too return to barbaric practices, seeing that the public canonizes these pathetic spectacles. In fact, when I am about to write a play I lock up classical precepts under six keys. I toss out the works of Terence and of Plautus so they can't scold me (since truth gives cry in silent texts), and I write for the sake of an art that those who crave applause invented. After all, if it's the idiot crowds that pay, it is only fair to humor them by sinking down to their level.[5]

In the prose translation above, I have tried to evoke the self-irony that dances between the lines of Lope's ostensibly grave and pompous discourse. Even granted the risks inherent in over-freighting a self-ironizing text with too much meaning, it is clear from Lope's creative trajectory that he practiced what he preached. Known as the "monstruo de la naturaleza" [prodigy of nature] for his copious and varied literary production, Lope's prodigiousness also extends to the bold liberties he

---

[5] "Verdad es que yo he escrito algunas veces / siguiendo el arte que conocen pocos, / mas luego que salir por otra parte / veo los monstruos de apariencias llenos / adonde acude el vulgo y las mujeres / que este triste ejercicio canonizan, / a aquel hábito bárbaro me vuelvo, / y cuando he de escribir una comedia, / encierro los preceptos con seis llaves, / saco a Terencio y Plauto de mi estudio / para que no me den voces, que suele / dar gritos la verdad en libros mudos, / y escribo por el arte que inventaron / los que el vulgar aplauso pretendieron / porque como las paga el vulgo, es justo / hablarle en necio para darle gusto" (lines 33–48, 133).

took with theatrical dicta.⁶ His *Arte nuevo* might be characterized as polymetrically perverse for, along with exploiting Spanish prosody, it also abandoned classical theater's three unities of time, place, and action, reduced the number of acts in a full-length play to three, and dissolved Aristotle's rigid boundaries separating comedy from tragedy. By adapting public theater to local taste rather than worshipping at the altar of tradition, Lope created a theater for the masses that attracted patronage from the aristocracy of his time and that is still performed today.

A fourth institution that improvised boldly in response to new conditions was the Spanish court itself. Historian Fernando Bouza praises the administrative flexibility of the Spanish court between 1548 and 1590, which was subjected to major reorganizations both by the Burgundian King Charles I and his son and successor in Spain, Philip II. For Bouza, the court "had more than proven its adaptability by assimilating both the change to Burgundian protocols of 1548 and the restructuring of the royal office imposed by Philip II" (186). Another departure from tradition carried out during this period, although with unhappier consequences, was the Crown's decision to resort to venality—the granting of titles of nobility in exchange for large gifts or loans of money. Philip II had taken to selling increasing numbers of municipal positions from 1557 through the 1570s (Fortea Pérez 242). The selling of titles of nobility increased dramatically under the reign of the latter Hapsburgs. From 28 marquis and dukes in 1530, the number rose to 113 dukes and 334 marquis by 1700 (Asch 16). This trend was not matched by a parallel increase in population.

Francisco de Quevedo's *Discurso de las privanzas* [Discourse on favorites] discussed at length in Chapter 3, points to another feature of the Spanish court: the royal favorite or *privado*. The ascent of Philip II's first *privado*, Gómez de Silva (1516–73), serves as a dramatic final illustration that adaptability was shedding its stigma and gaining adherents, in practice if not yet in theory. The son of an unremarkable Portuguese noble family, Gómez de Silva succeeded in penetrating and dominating the innermost circles of power at the royal court by virtue of his skill as a consummate courtier. He has been characterized by historian James M. Boyden as "a self-made man in the style of his time and place; that is, he knew how to manipulate his superiors into clearing an ascending path for him" (151). Once he gained the king's favor his middling origins gave way to enviable privileges and power. To fortify Gómez de Silva's relatively feeble credentials, Philip II created for him the title of Prince of Éboli, further honoring him with the hand in marriage of the Duchess of Pastrana, Ana de Mendoza y de la Cerda. These favors rendered Gómez de Silva extremely sensitive to the king's wishes. In Boyden's words, "the maintenance of his intimacy with Philip became Ruy Gómez's principal study and occupation" (151). What was Gómez de Silva's secret for winning over the king in the first place? Historian Richard Kagan attributes the *privado*'s ascent to his "oily

---

⁶ Melveena McKendrick calculates his dramatic output at approximately 800 plays (76). However, Lope set the number at 1,500 (see Morley and Bruerton, "How Many Plays […]?").

affability" coupled with adept social skills and his uncanny knack for second-guessing the monarch's wants and needs.[7]

Much has been written about the courtly art of sociability, especially the unaffected grace that Castiglione called *sprezzatura*, translated by Charles Singleton as "nonchalance." According to Castiglione, *sprezzatura* aimed "to conceal all art and make whatever is done and said appear without effort and almost without any thought about it" (*The Book of the Courtier* I, 32). Juan Boscán rendered the term *sprezzatura* into Spanish in 1534 as *descuido* [carelessness] or *desprecio* [disdain] (59). However, the "techniques, aspirations and mentality" that Kagan observes in the ascent of Gómez de Silva have less to do with the minister's air of insouciance than with his "uncanny knack" for accommodating to the wishes of the monarch. Undoubtedly, the king's wishes fluctuated; otherwise no knack would have been called for to anticipate them. Ruy Gómez's genius consisted in the capacity to act in consonance with those fluctuations so that he always appeared to support—even foresee—Philip's desires. This maneuverability might well be called an "oily affability" since, like a well-lubricated ball-joint, it permitted Ruy Gómez to change directions without a squeak or hitch.

A willingness to switch direction, accommodate to new circumstances, and improvise new solutions was modernizing the way that navigation, missionary outreach, dramaturgy, court administration, and the office of *privado* achieved their respective goals in early modern Spain. Furthermore, as we saw in chapters 2 and 3 above, shifting attitudes toward fame and secrecy testify that adaptability was becoming as deeply embedded in institutional practice as constancy was ingrained in Neostoic theory. From this gap between theory and praxis sprang the search for an exit from the gender bind that assigned men the increasingly onerous role of heroic resistance to change, while deriding women for their alterability.

Adapt: A Belated Word

A curious problem arises when seeking the right word for denoting this attribute of alterability in early modern Spain. Just as *sprezzatura* failed to find an adequate English or Spanish equivalent, it seems that Spanish also lacked a ready designation for agile responsiveness to changing circumstances. For the purposes of this volume, I have chosen the English verb "adapt," along with its Spanish cognate *adaptar* to convey the strategic accommodation adopted by missionaries, practiced by sea-pilots, and personified by Gómez de Silva's rise to power. Unlike the proximate word-pairs accommodate/*acomodar* or adjust/*ajustar*, adapt/*adaptar* gestures toward the idea of fitting in, while also conveying a more active sense of maneuverability. In reality, it must be pointed out that the word *adaptar* had only begun to circulate during the sixteenth and seventeenth centuries. In English, as in its Romance cognates, the word "adapt" derives from the Latin *adapto*, itself a compound made up of *ad*, meaning in or toward, and *apto*. "To

---

[7] See book jacket review by R. Kagan of Boyden's biography of Ruy Gómez de Silva, *The Courtier and the King*.

adapt or modify; (w. dat.) to fit into" (*Oxford Latin Dictionary*).[8] The *Diccionario de Autoridades* of 1726 echoes the Latin sense of "fitting into": "To accommodate, calibrate one thing with another. For the most part, it is used metaphorically, as in to adapt or accommodate a principle to the case at hand or an example to the principle at hand."[9]

Autoridades attests to scattered sixteenth-century usages of *adaptar* and its derivations, including one attributed to noted humanist Diego Gracián. In his translation from Greek into Spanish of Plutarch's *Moralia* (1548) Diego Gracián writes, "Thus it is well that we leave to the philosophers the task of adapting our medicine to us."[10] This usage recognizes that transferring something from one sphere to make it useful in another requires a specialized skill. This usage is significant for its possible impact on Diego's son, Lucas Gracián Dantisco, whose *Galateo español* [*The Spanish Gallant*] (c. 1583) was discussed in Chapter 3.

The baby Seneca anecdote from the preface to Gracián Dantisco's *Galateo español*, cited in Chapter 3, illustrates that different circumstances demand different behaviors. It was right for Seneca to play with toy soldiers when he was a boy; each age must adhere to its own standards of comportment. For this reason, the *Galateo español* does not dictate universal precepts for good or bad behavior, but rather insists that social actors adapt their conduct in keeping with the circumstance of the moment:

> Por esto nadie debe dudar que quien se dispone a vivir [...] en las ciudades y cortes entre las gentes, que no les sea utilísima cosa el saber ser en sus costumbres gracioso y agradable, y de suerte que *temple su conversación y trato* no tanto a su albedrío y voluntad, cuanto al contento y agrado de aquellos con quien trata.
>
> [Therefore no one should deny that, for anyone who plans to live [...] in cities and courts, among other people, that it can be an extremely useful thing for him to know how to be gracious and pleasing in his manner so as to *modulate his conversation and salutations*, not according to his own will and whim, but according to the contentment and pleasure of those with whom he is in contact.] (105–6, emphasis added)

Although Gracián Dantisco makes use of the Spanish verb *templar* [to temper; to modulate] rather than the verb *adaptar* for summoning the idea of fine-tuning one's public conduct to please others, this notion seems to echo his father Diego's reference to the verb *adaptar*.

---

[8] The *O.L.D.* lists five definitions for *adapto*: (1) put in position, fit, put on (armor, ornament) oneself, to don (2) bring to bear, apply, to position for use, employ, apply (3) fit together, join (4) to ready, prepare (5) modify so as to suit; adapt mentally, to bring into suitable frame of mind, attune.

[9] "Adaptar. Acomodar, igualar una cosa con otra. Por la mayor parte se usa en sentido metafórico, como adaptar, acomodar, una doctrina al caso propuesto, o un ejemplo a la doctrina que se propone."

[10] "Y así es bien que dejemos a los filósofos, que nos adapten la medicina" (Folio 266, qtd. in *Autoridades*).

Autoridades also registers the derivative noun form *adaptado*: "el que es hábil y dispuesto para alguna cosa [he who is able and well-equipped for some task]." This usage is rooted in the Latin adjectival or participial form, *aptus, -a, -um*, specifically when applied to a person. *Aptus, -a*, like its English cognate, "apt," describes a person who is ready for or well-suited to a task. The *Oxford Latin Dictionary* offers several examples of this acceptation: "(5) Prepared or equipped, ready (b) ready for use, handy, convenient. (c) (of persons) adapted or adaptable (to) [...] (7) (Of persons or agents) Efficient or good (at doing something), fitted (for), able (to)." In 1511, Diego Rodríguez de Almela's popular *Valerio de las historias* [Sayings and stories of Valerio Maximus] disseminated the word *adaptados* with reference to those precocious children who show an unusual penchant or talent for certain tasks: "But often it is observed that children show proclivities from an early age. And if they continue to cultivate them, they become better at those than at others for which they showed no such promise."[11]

Just as significant as the presence of these lexical traces, however, is their relative scarcity. Nebrija's *Vocabulario* [Vocabulary] (1492) along with its later appended *Léxico de derecho civil* [Lexicon of civil law] (c. 1506) as well as Sebastián de Covarrubias's *Tesoro de la lengua castellana* [Treasury of the Castilian language] (1611) yield no entries for *adaptar* or related words.[12] If discourse is seen to be "a system which structures the way that we perceive reality" (Mills 55), then one explanation for the presence of adaptability as an idea prior to its widespread lexicalization could be that it had only partially penetrated the cultural imaginary by mid-seventeenth century. The compounding of the Latin *ad* with *aptus* and the assimilation of the resulting compound neologism into the Romance languages during a period of active borrowing conforms to normal processes of word formation (Brinton and Traugott 32–61). A corresponding recent example of such word-formation processes can be seen in the 2012 *Merriam-Webster Collegiate Dictionary*, which added the words "life-coach," "mash-up," and "man-cave" in response to cultural practices that had inspired new terminology.[13]

---

[11] "[P]ero muchas veces es visto que los niños desde su juventud demuestran sus habilidades. Y si aquellas a que son adaptados usan y continúan, más hábiles son a ellas que no a las otras que de sí no demuestran" (79). *Autoridades* cites only the second sentence up to the word *ellas*. Almela's *Valerio* was republished more than 10 times between 1511 and 1587.

[12] A survey of the concordances of Cervantes's *Don Quixote*, Góngora's *Fábula de Polifemo*, and *Soledades*, and the *Vocabulario completo de Lope de Vega* likewise comes up empty-handed.

[13] "A Sample of New Dictionary Words for 2012." Merriam-Webster Online. Alex Gibney and Alison Elwood's documentary provides an analogous instance of delayed lexical reification. Gibney and Elwood document the cross-country odyssey of Ken Kesey, Neal Cassidy, and their "Merry Band of Pranksters" during the summer of 1964 using real footage that Kesey shot during the trip. Apparently, in 1964, the negatively laced terms "hippie" and "drug freak" had not yet overshadowed the more positive "flower-children" or "merry pranksters." As a result, the counter-cultural youth bus elicited a joyful welcome wherever it stopped. As a narrative voice-over in the film explains, "People didn't think we were hippies or that we were drug freaks because it hadn't gotten into the media yet."

Similarly belated word formations can be observed in the development of many academic disciplines. The modern field of economics, for example, is commonly acknowledged to have arisen following the publication of Adam Smith's *Wealth of Nations* in 1776. Nonetheless, during the sixteenth century Francisco de Vitoria, Domingo de Soto, Martín de Azpilcueta, and other University of Salamanca jurists were already articulating questions of supply and demand, risk calculation, and the commercial value of time—under the rubric of moral philosophy (see Grice-Hutchinson). That is to say, the concept of economics was being imagined and theorized before it had solidified into a recognizable modern discipline. Literary history likewise often tags movements, generations, or genres long after their practices have come into being. *Lazarillo de Tormes*, the anonymous prose satire (1554), to cite a well-known case, did not become associated with the picaresque novel until after the publication of Mateo Aleman's multi-volume *Guzmán de Alfarache* in 1599 and 1604, after which the *Lazarillo* was consecrated as the founding text of that genre.

In effect, *adaptar* assimilated slowly and belatedly into Spanish. Perhaps for this reason, Valencian humanist Juan Lorenzo Palmireno (1524–79) found it expedient to coin the neologism *agibilia* to convey a sense of adaptability to his pupils. In his Latin primer, *El estudiante cortesano* [The student courtier] (1573), Palmireno encouraged his pupils not only to memorize passages of classical Latin, but to engage in creative and original Latin speech. *Agibilia* for Palmireno referred to the capacity for free unscripted speech, but he extended its meaning to include performances outside the classroom as well. Homer's epic hero Ulysses, Palmireno taught, exercised *agibilia* to come out ahead no matter what the circumstance (Gallego 40). For the Valencian humanist,

> [*Agibilia*] llama el vulgo la desenvoltura que el hombre tiene en ganar un real, en saberlo conservar y multiplicar, en saberse bien asentar sobre su cuerpo la ropa, tratarse limpio, buscar su descanso, ganar las voluntades y favores, conservar su salud, no dejarse engañar cuando algo compra, y regirse de modo que no puedan decir: "Este hombre sacado del libro, es un grande asno." (Qtd. in Gallego 41).

> [[*Agibilia*] is what commonfolk call the confidence it takes to make a buck, to conserve and invest it, to dress to best advantage, be polished, take one's leisure, influence others and win favor, maintain good health, not fall for scams, and govern one's self in such a manner that no one is tempted to say: "This rube, he is nothing but a big ass."] (*EC* Folio A vi, v)

Like Erasmus, whose *De civilitate morum puerilium* [On the education of young boys] Norbert Elias considered to be the founding guidebook on Renaissance manners for children, Palmireno sought to produce "a cultured young man, the opposite of brutish and filthy, for one can find educated men who please everyone with their pen, but whose incivility makes them flee" (*De civilitate*, qtd. in Varela 90). If *agibilia* evened the playing field for Ulysses, Palmireno saw that it could do the same for his pupils. Regardless of rank or title, young boys could avoid appearing to be a "big ass" by adapting their actions to the unfolding situation at hand.

The neologism *agibilia* fits in well with Neostoic teachings on self-control. It also avoids the negative implications of inconstancy by aligning itself with the positive trait of self-confidence as well as the desirable reward of winning favor. These features of *agibilia* allow Palmireno to sidestep any moral quibbles that might arise from challenging the Neostoic virtue of constancy. *Agibilia* signified a willingness to modulate speech and behavior rather than adhere to a fixed paradigm; to navigate via observed coordinates rather than obey received orthodoxies. Indeed, as noted in the Introduction, Gabriel de la Gasca employed nautical metaphors in his *Manual de avisos para el perfecto cortesano* [Advice manual for the perfect courtier] in much the same manner: to point an approving finger toward acts of pragmatic adaptability that might otherwise have raised the specter of Machiavellianism.

Palmireno chose Ulysses as his patron saint of *agibilia* due to that hero's famed ingenuity when facing novel circumstances. To cite just two well-known examples, the Trojan horse was Odysseus's idea, and he led his crew to safety from the Cyclops by tying his men to the underbelly of the blinded monster's sheep. Yet Odysseus's dissimulating ways had been condemned during the Middle Ages. In Canto 26 of the *Inferno*, Dante placed Ulysses in the eighth ring of hell in punishment for his duplicity.[14] Petrarch inaugurated a rehabilitation of Odysseus, which reached its fullest expression in the Renaissance (Montiglio 150–51).[15]

Social transactions at the Spanish court demanded that courtiers practice Odyssean adaptability, so as not to make "asses" of themselves. Baltasar Gracián's multi-volume allegorical novel, *El criticón* [*The Critic*], reprises Palmireno's positive valuation of this adaptive virtue. Near the end of the first volume, Critilo and his protégé Andrenio struggle to make their way through the *golfo* [deep] of the royal court. Critilo asks a bookseller for an *aguja de marear* [mariner's needle] to help them negotiate the social perils that confront them there. Once the merchant penetrates Critilo's allegorical meaning he realizes that his customer seeks a courtly conduct guide and offers to lend him Gracián Dantisco's *Galateo español* (964–5). But a querulous onlooker dismisses not only the *Galateo español*, but also the more recent conduct guide of Juan de Silva, the *Comentarios* [Commentaries].[16] For this veteran of the court, Homer's *Odyssey* surpasses any other model for courtly conduct:

---

[14] Dante, it should be noted, only knew the *Odyssey* by hearsay.

[15] Perhaps the most famous Renaissance testimonial to Ulysses's renewed prestige was Luis de Camões's epic poem *Os Lusíadas* [*The Lusiad*] (1572), which credits Ulysses with founding the city of Lisbon.

[16] As noted in Chapter 2, the *Comentarios* were composed by Juan de Silva, Count of Portalegre, in 1592. They comment upon an earlier conduct guide, the *Instrucciones* [Instructions], written in 1549 by the then-Viceroy of Sicily, Juan de Vega. Juan de Silva's *Comentarios* are reproduced in Fernando Bouza, *Imagen y propaganda* (219–34).

Digo que el libro que habéis de buscar y de leerlo de cabo a cabo es la célebre *Ulisíada* de Homero. ¡Aguarda. No os admiréis hasta que me declare! ¿Qué pensáis, que el peligroso golfo que él describe es aquél de Sicilia [...]? Sabed que el peligroso mar es la corte, con la Cila de sus engaños y la Caribdis de sus mentiras [...]. Este libro os digo que repaséis, que él os ha de encaminar, para que, como Ulises, escapéis de tanto escollo como os espera y de tanto monstruo como os amenaza.

[I tell you that the book you must find and read from end to end is Homer's celebrated *Odyssey*. Wait! Let me explain before you react. What did you think? That the perilous deep that he describes is the one near Sicily [...]? Know rather that the treacherous sea is the court, with the Scylla of its deceptions and the Charybdis of its lies [...]. I tell you to study it because it will set you on the right track so that, like Ulysses, you evade all of the menacing shoals and lurking monsters that await you.] (972)

Gracián places this ironic tribute to Ulysses in the mouth of an onlooker, but Critilo and Andrenio heed his advice and prosper on their journey by practicing Ulyssean adaptability (972–3).[17]

Tropelía

Novelistic aspirations notwithstanding, Gracián's allegorical novel, *El criticón*, remained too encumbered by its own erudition to transcend the precincts of the didactic conduct treatise. But the virtue of adaptability found a more popular outlet in prose-fiction and drama. Such works pit their quick-witted protagonists against Homeric odds. Both Cervantes's *novela ejemplar* [Exemplary novella] "El coloquio de los perros" [The Dogs' Colloquy] and Lope de Vega's *comedia* [play] *El perro del hortelano* [*The Dog in the Manger*] fit this description. Both of these works reward adaptable protagonists rather than inflexible ones. Cervantes and Lope expose the limits of constancy and steer their respective readers and spectators toward a more protean and mercurial ideal of manly conduct. "El casamiento engañoso" [The deceptive marriage] and "El coloquio de los perros" form a cohesive narrative unit within the collection of short stories that comprise Cervantes's *Novelas ejemplares* of 1613. Their respective protagonists take a remarkably flexible approach to that which they can and cannot change. They face the challenges of impermanence and transformation with adaptability rather than constancy, and they exercise agency rather than accepting misfortune.

Both *novelas* mobilize a remarkable number of deictic figures that point to processes of change and the attendant need to make adjustments to flux.

---

[17] Note that Gracián puns by referring to the *Odyssey* not by its standard Spanish title, the *Odisea*, but as the *Ulisíada,* which is phonetically similar to Camões's epic poem, *Os Lusíadas* [*The Lusiads*] (1572). Ironically, Gracián condemns auditory punning, or paronomasia, as an "infelicitous" form of wit in the *Agudeza y arte de ingenio* (1642, 1648) (598).

These deictic markers include the motifs of recuperation from illness, alchemy, sorcery, and rootlessness. By itself, this attention to impermanent phenomena would not qualify Cervantes's *novelas* as anti-Neostoic. As noted above, acceptance of impermanence represented a cornerstone of Stoic and Neostoic thought. The Greek sage Epictetus (55–135 CE) proclaimed the vanity of ambition: "Not in our hand lie the body, wealth, worldly honor, titles and positions (equally enviable and tiresome), and finally, all things that one might desire yet which do not originate in who we are."[18] Neostoic philosophers divided the world into two kinds of objects: those that lie within our hands to control and those that do not lie within our hands, the former being desirable and the latter being undesirable. Honor, prosperity, and bodily condition, which are subject to natural and social forces beyond the individual's control, were classified as *apaxía* or bad things. Good things, or *axía*, were those that do lie "within our hands" or that can be chosen by reason, such as moral intention, manual skills, intellectual development, health, beauty, and strength. In this regard, Quevedo warns, "Should you discern something that isn't in your hands and that lies beyond your control, your only concern should be to avoid it."[19] Yet, as we shall see, Campuzano, the protagonist of "El casamiento engañoso," and Berganza of "El coloquio de los perros" take an exceptionally expansive approach to human (or canine) agency in the face of change, pushing the boundaries of *axía* to include honor, prosperity, and bodily condition.

"Casamiento" opens with the pathetic sight of its protagonist, Campuzano, tottering weakly up the street in Valladolid, as witnessed by his old friend Peralta. The *novela* then proceeds to backfill that astonishing scene by means of retrospective narrative. A soldier recently returned from Flanders, Campuzano had hoped to parlay his military allure into conning a wealthy woman into marriage. However, as he tells his friend, the first "lady" that falls into his trap turns out to be considerably less refined than she first appeared. Doña Estefanía ends up cheating Campuzano, leaving him only a bad case of syphilis as a bitter souvenir. "Coloquio" departs from the point at which "Casamiento" leaves off, recounting a dialogue between two guard dogs that Campuzano claims to have overheard while treating his illness at the Hospital of the Resurrection in Valladolid.

The paired *novelas* chronicle numerous transformational processes. The first is Campuzano's recovery from syphilis at the hospital called Resurrection. What kind of new life will Campuzano have after his illness? Cervantes's narrative suggests that Campuzano exchanges the life of dishonor that Estefanía's betrayal portended for the honorable life of a writer, recounting his adventure of disenchantment (with Estefanía) and enchantment (with the dogs' colloquy he claims to overhear during his recovery). Campuzano seems to have been fated to cross paths with Estefanía,

---

[18] "No están en nuestra mano, / el cuerpo, la hacienda, ni el profano / honor, las dignidades y puestos / (igualmente envidados y molestos), / y al fin, todas las cosas / que apetecer se pueden / si de nosotros mismos no proceden" (Epictetus I, 369; qtd. in Krabbenhoft 20).

[19] "[L]o que no está en tu mano y está fuera de tu poder, sólo te toca, si lo previenes, evitarlo" (*La cuna y la sepultura* 1341b, qtd in Krabbenhoft 21).

to lose everything in his attempt to win her, and to merit the consuming case of syphilis that this liaison produced. Yet his response to these reversals of fortune veers away from Neostoic fatalism and resignation. For example, he describes the onset of the disease to Peralta merely as a change: "Within a few days, I changed lodgings and I changed hair style, because my eyebrows and eyelashes started peeling off, and pretty soon my hair abandoned me, and I became unseasonably bald. I had caught a disease called *lupicia*, also known by the more descriptive name of *the haircut*."[20]

Campuzano recognizes that he, not Fortune, had caused the disease: "I clearly see that I tried to deceive but was myself deceived: I was vanquished by my own weapons. Still and all, I am not so impartial that I can resist the temptation to rebuke myself."[21] Since Campuzano blames himself rather than Providence, he also concludes that he can pull himself out of his misfortune. Instead of stiffening his resolve to suffer in silence, he views his illnes as *axía* rather than *apaxía*:

> Fue la enfermedad caminando al paso de mi necesidad, y, como la pobreza atropella a la honra, y a unos lleva a la horca y a otros al hospital, y a otros les hace entrar por las puertas de sus enemigos con ruegos y sumisiones (que es una de las mayores miserias que puede suceder a un desdichado), por no gastar en curarme los vestidos que me habían de cubrir y honrar en salud, llegado el tiempo en que se dan los sudores en el Hospital de la Resurrección, me entré en él, donde he tomado cuarenta sudores. Dicen que quedaré sano si me guardo: espada tengo, lo demás Dios lo remedie.
>
> [The disease was advancing as fast as my resources were running out. Considering how poverty tramples honor, leading some of its victims to the noose and others to the hospital, and still others it obliges to enter the gates of their enemies with appeals and supplications (one of the greatest miseries that can befall an unfortunate person), I decided against selling off the clothes that would cover and honor me once I got well just to underwrite the cost of my cure. So when the time came for the Hospital of the Resurrection to offer its sweat treatment, I went in and took forty rounds. They say I'm cured as long as I take care of myself; I have my sword; the rest I leave to God.] (534)

If Campuzano sounds resigned ("The rest I leave to God"), consider what would have happened to him had he taken the more obvious course of action and sold his sword and finery for a more respectable cure. Had he not adapted with alacrity to

---

[20] "Mudé posada y mudé el pelo dentro de pocos días, porque comenzaron a pelárseme las cejas y las pestañas, y poco a poco me dejaron los cabellos, y antes de edad me hice calvo, dándome una enfermedad que llaman *lupicia*, y por otro nombre más claro, la *pelarela*" (534). It may be conjectured that the modern-day confusion as to whether lupus is or is not a venereal disease arises from the popular pronunciation of *alopecia* [loss of hair] as *lopecia*, as registered here by Cervantes.

[21] "Bien veo que quise engañar y fui engañado, porque me hirieron por mis propios filos; pero no puedo tener tan a raya el sentimiento que no me queje de mí mismo" (533).

his predicament, he might have regained his health, but his friend Peralta would not have recognized him out of uniform as the ensign and comrade-in-arms that he once was. Instead, he chooses for himself how to face his new circumstances. By saving his distinguishing credentials (his sword and his military regalia) and taking the common man's cure at the hospital, Campuzano maintains the means by which to reconnect to his own social cohort, the first step toward reintegration into society. In addition, he reclaims his autonomy amidst these changes by writing down what his delirium tells him he heard at the hospital. Interpreting his bodily dissolution as a case of *axía*, something that lay within his hands, rather than of *apaxía* or something beyond his control, Campuzano retains the agency necessary to self-"resurrect"—as a comrade and writer.

Campuzano's recovery and subsequent discovery of his potential to become a writer exemplify adaptability without prejudice to Campuzano's masculinity. However, this overarching positive model finds its counterpoint in several negative depictions of transformational processes embedded within Campuzano's tale. The word *alquimia* [alchemy] that appears with respect to the ensign's phony gold chains suggests that processes of transmutation lead to fraud: "[All] that glitters is not gold. The chains, rings, jewels, and sequins were satisfied with merely aping the real thing. They were so carefully crafted that only touch or trial by fire could prove the counterfeit."[22]

This mistrust of transformational processes extends to the dark portrait of Cañizares and two other crones who appear in the central episode of "El coloquio de los perros." Berganza, the guard dog whose life-story Campuzano "transcribes" during his convalescence at the hospital, narrates his encounter with an old witch named Cañizares. This hag seems to recognize Berganza from the distant past and offers to tell him about the bizarre circumstances of his birth. According to Cañizares's story, Berganza's mother, Montiela, was to have given birth to human twins, but another powerful sorceress named La Camacha, who served as her midwife, betrayed her, claiming that the newborns had been turned into dogs.[23] As part of her malediction on the newborns, La Camacha prophesied that the pups could only regain human form after certain cosmic conditions came to pass.

---

[22] "[No] es todo oro lo que reluce, las cadenas, cintillos, joyas y brincos, con sólo ser de alquimia se contentaron; pero estaban tan bien hechas, que sólo el toque o el fuego podía descubrir su malicia" (532).

[23] Cárdenas-Rotunno notes that Cervantes avoids affirming definitively that La Camacha actually performed an act of sorcery. Either she merely claimed they were turned to dogs, or she exchanged them for dogs, or, possibly, she transformed them herself. However, since both Cañizares and La Camacha are unreliable narrators, and since Cervantes presents La Camacha's affirmation in indirect rather than direct discourse, even this claim must be greeted with skepticism. The text declares, "Cuando la comadre recibe las criaturas de la madre, dice que son perros [When the midwife catches the babes, she declares them to be dogs]" (qtd. in Cárdenas-Rotunno 307). By casting these doubts on the truth-status of La Camacha's declaration and Cañizares's subsequent account of it, Cervantes evades inquisitorial censure.

Berganza relates the details of his encounter with Cañizares to his canine interlocutor, Cipión. His narrative evinces disgust not only for Montiela's repellent features and moral depravity (i.e., she consorts with the Devil), but also for the metamorphoses associated with her craft. In the course of describing La Camacha's powers, as Cañizares had enumerated them to him, Berganza affirms,

> Ella *congelaba* las nubes cuando quería, cubriendo con ellas la faz del sol, y cuando se le antojaba *volvía* sereno el más turbado cielo; *traía* los hombres en un instante de lejas tierras, *remediaba* maravillosamente las doncellas que habían tenido algún descuido en guardar su entereza, *cubría* a las viudas de modo que con honestidad fuesen deshonestas, *descasaba* las casadas y *casaba* las que ella quería [...]. Tuvo fama que *convertía* los hombres en animales [...]. Pero en ti, hijo mío, la experiencia me muestra lo contrario: que sé que eres persona racional y te veo en semejanza de perro, si ya no es que esto se hace con aquella ciencia que llaman *tropelía*, que hace parecer una cosa por otra.

> [She *stilled* the clouds at will, covering the face of the sun with them, and whenever she pleased, *calmed* the stormiest sky; she instantly *transported* men from distant lands and did a fantastic job of *repairing* young ladies who had been careless with their most precious possession, and *veiled* widows, so they could carry on their sordid affairs with decorum. She *unmarried* spouses and *married* whomever she chose [...]. She was known for *turning* the men who served her into beasts [...]. But in you, my son, experience shows me the opposite. I know that you are a rational being, yet I see you in the shape of a dog. I'm thinking this was done with that science called *tropelía* that makes one thing appear to be another.] (591–2, emphasis added)

For Rogelio Miñana, the implications of the word *tropelía* extend beyond the black arts: "That science of *tropelía* can cover apparently supernatural phenomena produced by natural causes, or even just deceit" (10). According to *Autoridades*, the term *tropelía* is also associated with any kind of disorganized movement, such as the "*tropelía* de las tribunales [tumult of the courts]" (367). This broader interpretation also describes Berganza and Campuzano, whose linked narratives chronicle provisional identities morphing peripatetically in response to unstable circumstances. Berganza's distaste for the adaptive power of *tropelía* rings false in light of his own checkered picaresque past, for he, like the ensign Campuzano, applies the science of "making one thing appear to be another" to satisfy a motley parade of different masters.

As Berganza tells Cipión, he served as a butcher's assistant, shepherd, pet, police-dog, circus performer, and watch-dog, switching *habitus* or style of self-presentation in accordance with the demands of each subsequent protector. Campuzano mirrors Berganza's disorderly progress. He begins as a soldier, then becomes a suitor, husband, patient, and finally, writer. By disavowing constancy and practicing the science of adapting their outward appearances, first in one way and then another, Berganza and Campuzano move forward in a disorderly fashion in search of their place in the world. The concept of *tropelía* encapsulates the turbulent life-trajectories related by Berganza and Campuzano, and thematically conjoins their interlocking tales. Their assiduous practice of adaptability to change marks them, if not as outright anti-Neostoics, then at least as characters who broaden the definition of *axía*, things that lie within one's power to change. Conversely, the protagonists' life-narratives legitimize the proscribed practice of *tropelía*. As far as Cañizares was concerned, *tropelía* belonged to the domain of magic, transgression, and depravity. Yet Cervantes rescues the transformative powers of *tropelía* from the *aquelarre*, the "witch's coven," and unleashes them to help a soldier to restyle himself as a writer in civilian society.

The textual or verbal emblems of *tropelía* scrawled across the pages of "El casamiento engañoso" and "El coloquio de los perros" coupled with the *novelas*' seemingly haphazard paratactic structure, suggest that an operating mode alien to Neostoic fortitude has won the day for Campuzano and Berganza. Just as self-transformation, or what Stephen Greenblatt calls "self-fashioning," served as Gómez de Silva's magic wand for success at court, the capacity for *tropelía* that would come to be known as adaptability grants Cervantes's paired ensign and dog a new lease—or leash—on life.

Agibilia

Lope de Vega's palatine *comedia*, *El perro del hortelano*, also affirms the pragmatic benefits of adaptability. Like a courtesy manual, it sets forth the pros and cons of flexible conduct in the face of change, but it also lights an amorous fuse under these deliberations. In typical Lopean fashion, the drama is set to verse, and servants play a decisive role in the resolution of conflict. *El perro del hortelano* is thought to have been written around 1613, but was not published until 1618. The fictional Condesa [countess] Diana de Belflor's reluctance to wed any of her less-than-appealing suitors provides the play's dramatic tension. Diana is the *comedia*'s "perro del hortelano que no come ni deja comer [farm dog who won't steal the fruit yet guards against poachers]," in the words of a popular Spanish saying. Her sense of duty to marry within her station conflicts with the unexpected surge of attraction she feels toward her secretary, Teodoro. Diana also struggles with jealousy toward Teodoro's *belle*—her own lady-in-waiting, Marcela. Torn between incommensurate desires—honor versus passion—the Countess neither frees Teodoro to pursue Marcela nor claims him for herself. Her mixed messages throw Teodoro into the dangerous game of second-guessing the Countess's affections. Unsure of where he stands with her, he must adapt to her changing whims.

Diana's and Teodoro's names subtly reinforce the anti-Neostoic discourse of Lope's play. Diana's name links her with the eponymous Roman huntress goddess Diana. Like the Countess at the outset of Lope's *comedia*, Diana retreated from men, preferring the rustic pleasures of the hunt. Lope reinforces this connection by placing the Countess in charge of the pastoral-sounding land of Belflor [Beautiful Flower]. Diana is also considered the Roman equivalent of the Greek goddess

Artemis, daughter of Zeus and twin sister of Apollo, born on the Greek island of Delos. In Classical Greek cosmology, Apollo governed the sun god, while Artemis/Diana ruled over the changing phases of the moon. The fluctuations of the moon evoked by Diana's name call to mind her fluctuating feelings for Teodoro. Thus, Countess Diana represents *ataxía*—an object of desire to be avoided because her capriciousness lies beyond Teodoro's control.

Teodoro is a Greek name given to many Eastern Orthodox saints. In Greek, it means "gift of the gods," but to the Spanish ear the second half of the name forms a contraction of the preposition *de* [of] and *oro* [gold]. Together, the Greek–Spanish compound Teo-*doro* or Teo-*d'oro* could be interpreted to mean god of gold. Onomastically, Diana's secretary's name slyly foreshadows his attraction to the Countess's wealth. Furthermore, both names, Diana and Teodoro, call to mind the Mediterranean basin of antiquity; a region visited by gods and populated by seafaring heroes such as Odysseus. Already an Odyssean note was struck by Diana's suitors, whose impatience for Diana to decide whom to wed recalls Penelope's predicament during Odysseus's prolonged absence from Ithaca. As we shall see, Lope's text continues to develop these early allusions to the Ulysses whom Juan Lorenzo Palmireno so admired for his *agibilia*.

It is not surprising that Teodoro should initially seek to remain faithful to Marcela rather than wax and wane in his loyalties like the phases of the moon that Diana personifies. In Act 1, after Diana's romantic innuendos toward him become too obvious to ignore, Teodoro remains ambivalent as to whether or not to reciprocate the Countess's overtures because he prefers not to be inconstant to Marcela. Although he rejects the comical advice of the play's *gracioso* [clown, or buffoon] Tristán, to dwell on Marcela's defects in order to justify leaving her, Teodoro finds the Countess's fickleness exasperating:

> Well, Tristán, you just missed her, that capricious sunflower; that weathervane; that brittle glass; that river by the sea that flows backwards despite being a river! That Diana, that moon; that woman, that incantation; that transmogrifying monster that tries to shake me off if only to make a mockery of my subjugation![24]

By linking womanhood—"That Diana, that moon; that woman"—with mutability, Teodoro takes refuge in an essentialist distinction between the inconstancy of women and the constancy of men. Teodoro's tirade implies that, as a man, he will rise above caprice and remain Neostoically steadfast. But in the face of Diana's phase changes, Teodoro too finds he must alter his course. When Diana announces that she plans to wed the tiresome Marquis Ricardo—whose overwrought *octavas reales* critics have likened to a parody of Góngora's *Soledad primera*—Teodoro

---

[24] "Pues, Tristán, ahora vino / ese tornasol mudable, / esa veleta, ese vidrio, / ese río junto al mar, / que vuelve atrás, aunque es río; / esa Dïana, esa luna, / esa mujer, ese hechizo, / ese monstruo de mudanzas, / que sólo perderme quiso / por afrentar sus vitorias" (lines 1751–66, 116).

responds by returning to Marcela.[25] In his zeal to regain Marcela's shaken confidence in him, Teodoro compares his devotion to her to the popular Neostoic image of a firm rock that withstands the ocean's fury: "No es tan firme / ninguna roca en el mar [No rock in the sea is as firm]" (lines 1944–5, 123).[26]

Teodoro's unpredictable changes of heart infuriate Marcela, but Tristán reassures her that Teodoro is merely undergoing "una mudancita / que a las mujeres imita / Teodoro [a little change, since Teodoro is imitating women]" (lines 1489–91, 105). While appearing to comfort Marcela, Tristán is actually justifying an adaptive course of action from which he stands to benefit, for if his master marries the Countess, he will likewise rise in station. Thus, Tristán minimizes Marcela's concern that Teodoro is behaving inconstantly by using the diminuitive form *mudancita* [little change] instead of *mudanza* [change]. Soon Tristán's nudging begins to pay off. As Teodoro's sonnet at the close of Act 1 reveals, the secretary is starting to makes peace with his inner chameleon:[27] "What will I do?" he wonders, with respect to the question of whether to pursue the Countess or remain faithful to Marcela,

> What shall I do? Shall I—despite the uncertainty of this venture—turn my back on fear and enlist courage in pursuit of my good fortune? But, is it fair to leave Marcela in the lurch? After all, women should not expect our word of honor to yield such suffering. Yet, if they drop us on a whim for anyone new or exciting, let them die just as we men also die![28]

---

[25] An *octava real* is a hendecasyllabic eight-verse stanza with rich rhyme popularized in Renaissance epic poetry. By having the Marquis speak in *octavas reales*, Lope implies, on the one hand, the idea that he is a pompous bore, and on the other, that anyone who composes *octavas reales* (such as Góngora) is equally bombastic. M. Artigas's claim that Góngora's *Soledad primera* [*First Solitude*], which was written in *octavas reales*, had begun circulating in manuscript form in Madrid between May and June of 1613 allows speculation that Lope composed the play not long thereafter (see Armiño 14).

[26] For example, the polyglot emblem book *Devises et emblèmes anciennes et modernes* published in Amsterdam in 1691 depicts a gull perched atop a rock at sea while the epigram explains, "I rust on constancie [I rest on constancy]" (De la Feuille and Offelen 35). For a detailed analysis of the land-sea isotope, see Marie-Eugènie Kaufmant. Kaufmant, too, identifies Teodoro with Ulysses. However, she associates Marcela in Lope's play with faithful Penelope rather than noting the parallelism that the play establishes between Diana and Penelope beset by suitors. For this reason, she cannot justify Teodoro's refusal of Marcela (155–6).

[27] *El perro del hortelano* offers an exceptional display of sonnets—nine in all. Two are coded love letters that broach the taboo subject of a *mésalliance* between Diana and her secretary. The remaining seven serve the purpose of slowing the break-neck speed of farcical romantic reversals unleashed by the specter of a deviation from the social contract. The sonnets create space for the principals to reflect on events as they unfold.

[28] "¿Qué haré? Seguir mi suerte venturosa; / si bien, por ser la empresa tan dudosa, / niego al temor lo que al valor concedo. // Mas dejar a Marcela es caso injusto; / que las mujeres no es razón que esperen / de nuestra obligación tanto disgusto. // Pero si ellas nos dejan cuando quieren / por cualquiera interés o nuevo gusto, / mueran también como los hombres mueren" (lines 1178–86, 90–91).

Teodoro closes his soliloquy by overturning Petrarchan convention: if men suffer unto death for the love of their ladies, then it is only fair to give women a taste of their own medicine by treating them with equal fickleness. Despite pressure to remain firm and steadfast, Teodoro opts for mutability. His *mudancita*, as Tristán calls it, represents an early attempt to pry inconstancy from the jurisdiction of women; to reconsecrate alterability as adaptability and caprice as prudence.

Ultimately, it is Tristán whose adaptability catalyzes Teodoro's emancipation from the Neostoic code of constancy. Lope lards the hilarious play-within-a-play that Tristán stages to win Diana's hand for Teodoro with allusions to Homer's epic hero. Disguised as a Mediterranean merchant and wearing a turban, Tristán approaches one of Diana's suitors, the aging Duke Ludovico, whose son and only heir, coincidentally also named Teodoro, had been lost to pirates some twenty years earlier. Fortifying himself with Greek wine to loosen his tongue, Tristán improvises a zany Byzantine romance embellished by pseudo-Greek jargon, to convince the Duke that Diana's secretary is actually his long-lost son.

Tristán crams his adventure tale with suffering lovers separated by shipwreck, corsairs and captivity, disguise, miraculous rescue, and dramatic reunions, in accordance with literary conventions established by prose love epics introduced into Spain in the sixteenth century (see Chapter 3). For added effect, he peppers his narrative with Mediterranean toponyms, both real and imaginary—Constantinople, Cyprus, Venice, Azteclias, Greece, Malta, Chafalonia, Tepecas, Armenia—and ridiculous macaronic names such as Serpalitonia, Catiborrato, Terimaconio, and Mercaponios (lines 2755–72, 158–63). Duke Ludovico succumbs to Tristán's yarn for two reasons. First, Tristán has played upon his deepest desire: the return of his missing son. Second, Tristán exploits the generic conventions of the Byzantine romance, which almost invariably ends with the happy reunion of the separated parties, precisely in order to lull the Duke into expecting a jubilant denouement. Tristán's burlesque mastery of these techniques produces the desired effect: Ludovico rejoices at the return of his missing "son," declaring Diana's secretary to be his long-lost heir, and blessing Teodoro's marriage to the Countess.

Lope takes pains to associate Tristán's success with Ulysses. We already noted that Diana's impatient suitors call to mind Penelope's unruly houseguests in the *Odyssey*. In Act 2, Teodoro also makes explicit his own identification with Ulysses by comparing his susceptibility to Diana's charms to Ulysses's propensity for falling under sorceresses' spells: "But, is it so extraordinary that those eyes deceive me if they could have deceived even Ulysses?"[29] Finally, Teodoro compares Tristán's resourcefulness to that of Ulysses: "Que a ti se te pasa / a Ulises el espíritu [You could outfox Ulysses himself!]" (lines 2543–4, 150).

Even after Teodoro confesses to Diana the genealogical hoax that Tristán had perpetrated on Count Ludovico, the Countess remains satisfied with the outcome, assuring him that "satisfaction does not arise from titles, but from adjusting one's

---

[29] "Pero, ¿es mucho que me engañen / aquellos ojos a mí / si pudieran ser bastantes / a hacer engañar a Ulises?" (lines 1701–4, 114).

soul to the object of desire. I am determined to be your wife."[30] Like Homer's vagrant mariner, Tristán and Teodoro improvise novel solutions rather than accept their supposed fates with Neostoic fortitude. By deploying a more supple approach to courtship, both master and servant succeed at achieving their interlinked goals. Tristán helps Teodoro to win Diana's hand in marriage so that Count Teodoro might then promote Tristán to the post that he had formerly occupied, that of secretary. Diana, however, proves to be less forgiving of Tristán than of Teodoro, for he too knows the secret of Teodoro's trumped-up lineage. To silence him, she proposes to Teodoro that they entomb the lackey's body in a well (line 3317, 181). Diana's bid to bury Tristán sounds a dissonant note in Lope's otherwise joyous denouement. Tristán's existence reminds Diana that a denizen of the margins, the lower strata of society, had breathed new life into stagnant seigniorial practices. Tristán was no Odysseus; his epic was a joke, a heist, a fraud. If anything, the servant evokes the *pícaro*, whose resourcefulness seventeenth-century readers tolerated as entertainment or counterexample, but not as an alternative to Neostoic *gravitas*. Until Teodoro saves him, Tristán hovers perilously between the underworld of ne'er-do-well ruffians and the respectable role of secretary to Count Teodoro. For a brief moment he becomes "Santayana's *stranger*, Deleuze and Guattari's *nomad*, Stonequist's *marginal man* who 'leaves one social group or culture without making a satisfactory adjustment to another [and] finds himself on the margin of each but a member of neither'" (Trigo 104). Yet Lope's play does not permit Tristán, nor the cultural memory that he embodies, to die; the lackey is saved from Diana's wrath and even favored with the ultimate seventeenth-century token of social stability: a wife. By these acts, *El perro del hortelano* not only dramatizes the triumph of a new mode of seigniorial conduct—that of adaptability—but it also acknowledges its decidedly non-aristocratic origins.

Kenneth Krabbenhoft takes issue with a number of critics (including Américo Castro and Juan Bautista Avalle-Arce) who restrict the impact of Neostoic thought in Spain to the domains of moral and political philosophy.[31] For Krabbenhoft, the Neostoic influence extends to many works of literature, including *Lazarillo de Tormes* and *Don Quixote*. I concur that a better understanding of Neostoic codes of conduct can serve to illuminate Golden Age letters, but I do not think that those codes went uncontested. Both Cervantes and Lope disengage the success of their protagonists from Neostoic platitudes. Cervantes's novellas tackle the picaresque conundrum of achieving happiness in a world of continual change. Dogs, as Berganza and Cipión remind us early in "El coloquio de los perros," symbolize

---

[30] "[El] gusto no está en grandezas / sino en ajustarse al alma / aquello que se desea. / Yo me he de casar contigo" (lines 3309–12, 180).

[31] "[El] acercamiento neostoico vierte luz sobre la expresión de valores sociales y morales en comedias tan aparentemente disimilares como lo son *Peribáñez y el Comendador de Ocaña* de Lope de Vega y *La verdad sospechosa* de Ruiz de Alarcón [Neostoicism sheds light on the expression of social and moral values in theatrical works as disparate as *Peribáñez y el Comendador de Ocaña* by Lope de Vega and *La verdad sospechosa* by Ruiz de Alarcón]" (Krabbenhoft 160).

marital fidelity and unbreakable bonds of friendship: in short, constancy (542–3). With a dog rather than a boy as its putative picaresque *mozo de muchos amos* [servant of many masters], the narrative effectively contrasts that animal's fabled constancy with the unstable circumstances that propel his narrative forward. By responding to those circumstances with the agility of a circus dog, Berganza manages to escape the horrific slaughterhouse of Seville and take refuge in the restorative patio of the Hospital of the Resurrection. In the same pair of *novelas*, the ensign Campuzano dreams of a social *tropelía* that would transform his ersatz jewelry into a stable place in society. But Estefanía's marital inconstancy causes a much more interesting *tropelía* to take its place, for, as Campuzano hands his manuscript to his friend, the Licenciate Peralta, the former man of arms becomes a man of letters. Teodoro and Tristán undergo a parallel metamorphosis in *El perro del hortelano*. As soon as Teodoro becomes Count Teodoro de Belflor by marrying Diana, his ascent floats Tristan's boat as well. No longer lackey to a secretary, Tristan will now become, in his words, "el secretario del secretario [secretary of the secretary]" (line 2424, 145). Berganza, Campuzano, Tristán, and Teodoro prevail, not by firmly resisting adversity, but by practicing *tropelía*, the science of manipulating surface appearances for the sake of adapting to change.

Lope's *Perro del hortelano* and Cervantes's "El casamiento engañoso" and "El coloquio de los perros" were not unique in contesting Neostoic ideals of masculine virtue in early modern Spain. In fact, if we look closely, many familiar dramatic and fictional works expose the gulf between Neostoic beliefs and the pragmatic challenges of both courtship and courtiership. In 1620, Lope would create the figure of Don Alonso Manrique, the protagonist knight of *El caballero de Olmedo*. Critics have long looked upon Don Alonso as the perfect embodiment of masculine virtue: valiant, discreet, and constant in his affections for his lady, Doña Inés (Valdés García 204). Don Alonso's death at the end of the play is therefore traditionally viewed as tragic. However, reframing Lope's play within the discourse on adaptability casts the knight in a less heroic light.

Comedy's principal trope is exaggeration; tragedy's is noble blindness. Yet *El caballero de Olmedo* provides no compellingly noble justification for Don Alonso's blindness to the need to adapt his conduct to real and present danger. Don Alonso travels from his home in Olmedo to the town of Medina, where he bests his rivals at a tournament. He lingers in Medina after dark to profess his love to Inés at her *reja* [grill-enclosed window]. As they part, the knight debates whether to remain in Medina until daybreak or to set out for Olmedo immediately in order to relieve his parents' concern over the outcome of the tournament. Foreboding floods Inés's thoughts, angry rivals lurk, yet the knight insists on going home. As one premonitory figure after another urges Alonso to turn back, the knight's common sense loses out to his pride: "¿Qué han de decir si me vuelvo? [What will they say if I turn back?]" (line 2426, 148). Only after his rivals ignobly ambush and shoot him down does Don Alonso admit that hewing to a chivalric code of valor had subverted its own end-game—that of winning Doña Inés's hand in marriage. In his final hour, Don Alonso confesses, "Valor propio me ha engañado [My own pride has betrayed me]" (line 2467, 150).

Don Alonso's obsession with preserving his honor marks him as a dramatic caricature or *figurón* rather than a tragically flawed hero. Absent a stronger motive for jeopardizing his own safety, Don Alonso's dogged constancy in the face of the play's exaggerated omens begs for a more humorous, mocking treatment than modern theatrical productions of the play conventionally receive. Like Don Quixote, the Knight of Olmedo represents a risible throwback, comfortable within the confines of an archaic tournament, but unable to adapt to life outside the jousting field. Indeed, a half-century later, the foolish knight who insisted on trotting home on a black night thick with portent would reappear in Francisco Antonio de Monteser's 1651 burlesque comedy of the same name—this time unequivocally wearing the mask of Democritus (see Valdés García).

The Secretary's Needle

A contemporary of Monteser's, Jesuit theologian and social critic Baltasar Gracián, grants adaptability rather than constancy a place of honor among the manly virtues. Returning to maritime imagery, he advises his discreet man of court to follow the example of the sea-pilot: "Vivir a la occasión [... El] sabio sabe que el norte de la prudencia consiste en portarse a la ocasión [To exploit present circumstances [... the] wise man knows that the pole-star for coming out ahead consists of adapting to prevailing conditions]" (*Oráculo manual*, Aphorism 288; 298). However, as noted in the Introduction, a small manual published in 1681, while maintaining Gracián's seafaring imagery, carries his endorsement of adaptability one step further. Gabriel de la Gasca y Espinosa's *Manual de avisos para el perfecto cortesano* [Advice manual for the perfect courtier] extends courtesy codes beyond face-to-face interactions and into the realm of written correspondences. De la Gasca, who served as secretary at the court of Charles II (r. 1665–1700), dedicated the *Manual* to Felipe Antonio Spínola, the Duke of Sexto, who was only 15 years old at the time.[32] As a member of the highest nobility, young Felipe Antonio had no need for a writing handbook, but, as De la Gasca's title ("Advice manual for the perfect courtier") suggests, all courtiers could extrapolate from the specific concerns of royal secretaries to their own situation at court. De la Gasca's double-voiced discourse recalls that of Diego Saavedra Fajardo's *Idea de un príncipe político cristiano* as seen in Chapter 3, which directed its advice to Prince Baltasar Carlos while also instructing his ministers.

The *Manual* is divided into four parts. A lengthy prologue praises the attainments of Carlos Felipe and his forebears and states the purpose of the *Manual*.[33] Part I

---

[32] Carlos Felipe Antonio Spínola y Colona (1665–after 1721), fourth Marquis of the Balbases (Burgos). In his censura [censor page], royal chronicler Alonso Nuñez de Castro cleared De la Gasca's *Manual* for publication in 1679. It would appear that two years passed before the book actually went to press.

[33] The young Duke of Sexto's father, Pablo Spínola y Doria (1628–99), had served as Governor of Milan under Philip IV as well as Plenipotentiary Ambassador charged with arranging Charles II's marriage to María Luisa de Orleans.

delineates the formal parts of a royal missive and defends the art of eloquence. In Part II, De la Gasca expounds his own classification system of 10 types of royal correspondence.[34] Part III contains explicative notes, etymologies, definitions, and an alphabetical grid to illustrate how to compose and decipher secret messages (82). De la Gasca warns court secretaries against following the fixed precepts for letter-writing that other handbooks prescribe. They are all inadequate, he argues, because "Nor could anyone assert, regarding the writing of letters, that the same treatment applies equally to everyone at all times."[35] Courtesy for De la Gasca consists of keying one's conduct to each person's unique status and ephemeral condition.[36] Therefore, before even dipping his quill in the inkwell to write a reply, the royal secretary must parse the current status of each addressee, also bearing in mind his or her potentially changed circumstances. Petitioners' circumstances fall into one of three categories for De la Gasca: prosperity, adversity, or neutrality. Once the secretary locates his addressee along the axes of status and fortune, then he can select the appropriate heading, salutation, and closing compliments for his letter. In addition, he must be attentive to tone, for royal correspondence may be "discursive," "consultative," "decisive," "light," "important," "very grave," or "juridical" (*Manual de avisos*, Index).

As noted in the Introduction, De la Gasca compares the royal secretary's discernment to the now-familiar figure of the sea-captain who must adjust his course at every turn:

> Con [la aguja de marear] se surcan los mares, se siguen con rectitud las derrotas, y los sabios pilotos mediante los vientos, y el conocimiento de ellos, huyendo los escollos, y peligrosos bajos, conducen los bajeles a salvamiento, tomando el Puerto deseado, no de otra manera los cortesanos, que engolfados en el piélago inmenso de la corte siguen las derrotas de sus pretensiones, para no fluctuar en su progreso, combatidos de las furiosas olas de las emulaciones y envidias que levantan tempestades crueles, en que peligran y zozobran los que más presumen de diestros [...].

---

[34] Ten kinds of letters reach the royal secretary: 1) government policy briefs; 2) petitions; 3) follow-up reports and inquiries; 4) documents requiring royal approval; 5) dispatches from chancelleries and tribunals; 6) demands for results; 7) concessions; 8) ensuing advice; 9) mixed letters that inform and advise; 10) reports. De la Gasca 37–9.

[35] "Ni habrá nadie que pueda asegurar que en la correspondencia el trato será siempre igual, ni permanente en ellas" (86).

[36] "Cortesía: Es estimación discreta, de correspondencia entre los hombres, con que según los grados, estados, y calidades de las personas; se contrata con distinción, no acortando un punto lo que de justicia le toca a cada cual. Cuesta poco, y vale mucho [Courtesy: It is discreet calculation of the relationships between men, so that according to people's status, condition, and qualities they treat one another differentially, not departing one iota from that which each one rightly deserves. It costs little and it is worth a great deal]" (De la Gasca 54).

[With [the mariner's needle] waves are furrowed and voyages sailed. The seasoned pilot, using the winds and his knowledge of them, skirts shoals and dangerous shallows to guide his ship to safety and reach the desired port. Just so, courtiers, engulfed in the briny deep of court, fix their sights on their ambitions so as not to stray off course. They combat furious waves of rivalries and jealousies that whip up cruel storms that threaten to capsize even those most proud of their skills [...]]. (Prologue)

De la Gasca compares the seemingly infinite permutations of circumstance that the royal secretary must negotiate when composing royal missives to raging ocean waves rising up to capsize his best intentions. To guide the man of court safely through these dangers, the *Manual* features a fold-out folio bound into the prologue. The extra page bears the illustration of a wind rose, or what we today refer to as a compass face. This graphic is composed of six concentric circles intersected at regular intervals by 16 rays that extend outward from the innermost circle, creating the likeness of a compass dial (see Figure I.1). The inner circle is labeled "Justice" and the rays emanating from it represent "parts or virtues appropriate for the adornment of a good courtier [partes o virtudes que son a propósito para el adorno del buen cortesano]" (Prologue). Since certain virtues such as "Clemency" and "Severity" contradict one another, they point in opposite directions on the dial. Rather than recommend any fixed course of action to courtiers or secretaries for contending with all of the variables of court, De la Gasca offers his *Manual* as an *aguja de navegar* [compass needle] that swings freely to allow for 360 degrees of flexibility at any juncture. No rules of propriety, no matter how minute, can anticipate all of the demands of social grace because each encounter or correspondence springs from a unique calculus of rank, fortune, and circumstance.

Conclusion

De la Gasca required of his secretary the nimbleness of a Ulysses and the adaptability of Philip II's favorite, Gómez de Silva. To succeed at court, he would need to follow the examples of Berganza, Cervantes's talking dog of "El coloquio de los perros," who taught himself new tricks to suit each new master, and of Teodoro, the court secretary of Lope de Vega's *El perro del hortelano*, who adopts an operating mode of inconstancy to win the Countess's hand in marriage. These fluctuations, transformations, and nautical self-corrections spring from critical observation of prevailing circumstances rather than blind adherence to received assumptions. Ten years after De la Gasca's compass lent a positive face to the manly practice of adaptability, Henry Offelen and Danielle de la Feuille would turn to the image of a different kind of dial to defend inconstancy. In their polyglot emblem collection, the *Devises et emblèmes anciennes et modernes* (Amsterdam, 1691), Offelen and de la Feuille recast the sun, not as the stable counterpart to a wavering moon, but rather as a proud symbol of changeability in its own right. As if to destroy once and for all the gender antinomy that opposed constant, solar men to inconstant, lunar women, the motto "Somos inconstantes [We are inconstant]"—in the words of the Spanish version—accompanies the simple image of a sundial (44). As noted in Chapter 3, Norbert Elias calls the degree of distance from present risks necessary to adapt to changing environs "detachment." By adjusting their conduct in accordance with circumstance, Lope's Teodoro and Cervantes's Campuzano and Berganza achieve the critical distance necessary to improve their circumstances. Adaptability, previously viewed with suspicion as a threat to the ethical order, thus begins to take hold as a masculine virtue.

Epilogue

Nostalgia is not what it used to be.[1]

"Men are not born; they are made," assert Michael Kimmel and Michael Messner in their edited collection of essays on masculinity, *Men's Lives* (2010), "[and] men make themselves, actively constructing their masculinities within a social and historical context" (xvii). The dual pillars of historicity and self-fashioning that ground Kimmel and Messner's understanding of gender also provide the foundation for this book. Similarly, I have presented masculinity not as a fixed or static code but *"en obras,"* as an ongoing construction project (see Introduction). However, as any city councilwoman can attest, whenever new buildings are zoned for old neighborhoods, opposition will follow. Changes to the prevailing gender order in early modern Spain provoked vociferous opposition, but that resistance does not signify that a crisis occurred, nor does it prove that the new constructions tottered or collapsed. Many critics nonetheless have issued citations against early modern Spanish masculinity for its crisis, its failure, or its degeneracy. Elizabeth Lehfeldt's otherwise thorough and penetrating essay, "Ideal Men: Masculinity and Decline in Seventeenth-Century Spain," for example, arrives at the conclusion that the great minds of seventeenth-century Spain foundered in their search for a masculine ideal equipped to redefine their nation's place among its more successful rivals. Blinded by nostalgia for past military glories and stymied by a "lack of creativity," Spain's reformers and moralists could only decry new codes of courtly sociability and urge men to return to the "virtuous rusticity" (464) of their Medieval forebears. Rather than cultivate other options, Lehfeldt finds that these thinkers "had instead nostalgically fashioned idealized men whose existence would remain illusory" (491).

In this book I have sought to counter the notion that the discourse on masculinity in seventeenth-century Spain produced no viable ideations of manly conduct. The key to my approach, following John Snyder, has been to assemble a corpus of texts that mobilize their figurative resources to incite readers to think about courtesy (see Chapter 1). This broadened scope allows genres as diverse as emblem books, poetry, drama, courtesy treatises, and prose-fiction to join the polemic on courtly conduct. Chapters 2, 3, and 4 foreground three vectors of contestation that energize this diverse corpus. The first area is fame. The word fame has variously signified good reputation, self-reliance, renown, transient celebrity, and historical memory. Fame for Rodrígo Díaz de Vivar, champion knight of the Medieval epic poem the *Cantar del mio Cid*, means clearing his family's name of any taint of dishonor. For

---

[1] French film star Simone Signoret used this popular quip as the title of her 1976 autobiography, *La Nostalgie n'est plus ce qu'elle était*.

Jorge Manrique fame acquires the sense of remembrance after death. Manrique praises his family's lineage, but he also exalts his father's good deeds, independent of high birth. This sense of fame would gain stature in the anonymous picaresque novel *Lazarillo de Tormes*. Lázaro's low birth does not hold the promise of fame, but the reformed rogue hopes that the autobiographical narrative of his rise from poverty will earn him greater renown than the exploits of those who were born with the social advantages that he lacks. Cultivating a good reputation becomes an obsessive theme for many early modern writers who seek fame yet fear religious injunctions against pride and vanity. Cervantes's Don Quixote exhibits a disproportionate concern for his reputation that appears alternately clownish and vain. By contrast, Baltasar Gracián tries to allay ambivalence towards striving for fame. Eminence and immortality in human memory are not only ennobling and laudable in Gracián's view; they represent the apex of courtly aspiration.

Chapter 3 examines another morally dubious practice: that of dissimulation. As noted in Chapter 1, the royal court in Madrid became a locus of power, a seat of patronage, and a theater of self-display. To win allies, the courtier had to hide his flaws and advertise his merits, conceal his ambitions and publicize his affability. Lucas Gracián Dantisco concedes in his Spanish adaptation of Giovanni della Casa's *Il galateo*, *El galateo español*, that survival at court necessitates the exercise of hypocrisy. Novelistically, in "La novela del gran soldán," Gracián Dantisco transforms this necessary evil into an exciting adventure replete with perils and rewards. Francisco de Quevedo and Diego Saavedra Fajardo scrutinize dissimulation as it might affect the security of the polis, the decisions of the monarch, and the strategies of communication deployed by those closest to the prince: his counselors and *privado*. Although they denounce Machiavelli and abjure outright lying, these theorists manage to insert a measure of pragmatic realism into their interpretation of Catholic doctrine.

Chapter 4 traces a third vector of change in masculine conduct codes, that of adaptability. While the word "adapt" did not gain widespread use in early modern Spain, contemporary writers exploited the linguistic and rhetorical resources available to them to confront issues associated with mutability and accommodation. Cervantes, in "El casamiento engañoso" and "El coloquio de los perros," deploys the figures of illness, alchemy, witchcraft, and rootlessness to recast adaptability as a social good. Lope de Vega wrestles inconstancy away from the domain of feminine weakness to place it at the disposal of two socially disadvantaged men in his palatine *comedia*, *El perro del hortelano*. By practicing Odyssean adaptiveness, the play's *gracioso*, Tristán, manages to ennoble himself and his master, Teodoro. Like Tristán, Gabriel de la Gasca, who served as secretary to King Charles II of Spain, eschews fixed rules in favor of an improvisational model of virtue in his *Manual de avisos para el perfecto cortesano*. To accommodate the unique requirements of each royal missive, De la Gasca urges royal secretaries to avail themselves of the 360 degrees of choice demarcated on the face of his graphic wind rose or compass. By extension, he exhorts all courtiers to adapt their conduct to the situation at hand rather than falling back on received precepts that lack ongoing relevance.

Cultivating fame, practicing dissimulation, and adapting to new situations require what Norbert Elias calls "detachment." Elias's theory of "involvement and detachment" is less well known than the overarching trajectory of his "processes of civilization," but it sheds light on Spanish writers' success in generating new models of masculine virtue.[2] For Elias, the earliest human societies did not enjoy the luxury of separating themselves from the barrage of hostile forces to which they were subject. In consequence, they relied on modes of shamanistic or magical thinking to confront inexplicable threats. However, as states assumed more responsibility for the safety of their citizens, a process Elias refers to as "internal pacification," survival anxiety decreased, making way for a regime of greater critical distance or "detachment." During the Renaissance, the process of internal pacification accelerated. Less absorbed with the ordeal of defense against immediate danger, Renaissance subjects began to contemplate their surroundings with greater curiosity and impartiality. Not coincidentally, new ways of perceiving the world proliferated, nourishing the rise of scientific thought. In Stephen Mennell's words:

> If it proves possible for people to observe the relations of elements in the process with a measure of detachment, relatively unimpeded by emotional fantasies and in a realistic manner, they may be able to form a symbolic representation—a "theory," a "model"—of their situation and, by means of action based on that representation, change the situation. (*Norbert Elias* 164)

Elias points to Velázquez's symbolic representation of his position within the royal household on the canvas of *Las Meninas* as a paradigmatic instance of detachment (see Chapter 2). In that painting, Velázquez represents himself within the domestic precincts of the royal apartments, not as an underling, but as an honored household member.[3]

In like fashion, I would argue that the discourse on detachment offers insight into the successes and failures of many of the literary figures that appear in chapters 2 through 4. Cervantes's dogs and Lope's ingenious *gracioso*, Tristán, take a realistic, detached approach to the task of repositioning themselves in society. The figure of a wind rose or compass inserted into the pages of Gabriel de la Gasca's conduct manual performs a similar function. The compass reminds court secretaries to allow empirical observation of the unique circumstances of each letter to govern their compositional choices. For example, some missives

---

[2] See also Ogborn 66–8. Elias published "Involvement and Detachment" in 1956 in the *British Journal of Sociology*. It was subsequently issued by Blackwell as *Involvement and Detachment* (1987). Excerpts from *Involvement and Detachment* also appear in Mennell and Goudsblom's *Norbert Elias: On Civilization, Power, and Knowledge* (217–48).

[3] By associating detachment with early modern masculine virtue I do not mean to impose a positivist valuation on this process. As noted in Chapter 1, processes of civilization do not necessarily improve the world. For an overview of various feminist and post-colonial implications of detachment see Ogborn 75.

demand severity; others clemency. No single set of formulae can predict every situation that will arise. Therefore the secretary must imitate the sea-captain and steer in accordance with reality. This proto-scientific approach to letter-writing certainly represents an innovative model of masculine virtue for its time. It beckons in the direction of proto-Enlightenment scientists or *novatores* such as Juan de Cabriada (1665–1714) whose 1687 manifesto, the *Carta filosófica*, called for abandoning scholastic medicine in favor of anatomical observation and chemical experimentation (see Hill, López-Piñero, and Deacon).

Sixteenth- and seventeenth-century reflections upon new habits of seigniorial action in the realms of fame, dissimulation, and adaptability did not necessarily evolve diachronically towards consensus. I do not claim that aristocratic conduct resolved itself into a coherent triad of virtues at a given point in time or within a given text, or that the three spheres of courtly action that I have selected for this study exhaust the field. The protagonist of this book is the literature of masculine conduct itself, in all of its fractious exuberance. Spain's experiment in centralized governance unfolds in real time and in its own words on the pages of conduct guides published between 1500 and 1700. Like the ancient deities in the creation stories of the *Popol Vuh*, writings on seigniorial decorum fashion, discard, and refashion their heroes, who prove to be all too flawed and ephemeral. Still, this storied genealogy does not bespeak a "crisis of masculinity" in early modern Spain. Rather, it invites further reappraisal of the conduct literature corpus, broadens our understanding of the history of gender in Spain, and restores a salutary prequel to Norbert Elias's account of processes of civilization in France.

Bibliography

Adams, Rachel and David Savran, eds. *The Masculinity Studies Reader*. Malden, MA: Blackwell, 2004. Print.
Alabrús, Rosa. "El final de la dinastía." García Cárcel 379–429.
Albaladejo, Pablo Fernández. *La crisis de la Monarquía*. Barcelona: Crítica; Madrid: Marcial Pons, 2009. Print.
Alborg, Juan Luis. *Historia de la literatura española*. Madrid: Gredos, 1974. 4 vols. Print.
Alciati, Andrea. *Emblemas*. Trans. Bernardino Daza. Ed. Manuel Montero and Mario Soria. Madrid: Editora Nacional, 1975. Print.
Alciati, Andrea and Claude Mignault. *V.C. Emblemata*. 4th ed. Leiden: Plantiniana, 1591. Print.
Alemán, Mateo. *Guzmán de Alfarache*. Ed. Benito Brancaforte. Torrejón de Ardoz, Madrid: Akal, 1996. Print.
Alighieri, Dante. *Inferno*. Ed. Michael Palma. NY: Norton, 2002. Print.
Allen, Prudence. *The Concept of Woman: The Aristotelian Revolution, 750 BC–AD 1250*. Grand Rapids, MI: W.B. Eerdmans, 1997. Print.
Almeida, Onésimo T. "Science During the Portuguese Maritime Discoveries: A Telling Case of Interaction between Experimenters and Theoreticians." *Science in the Spanish and Portuguese Empires: 1500–1800*. Ed. Daniela Bleichmar, Paula de Vos, et al. Stanford: Stanford UP, 2009. 78–92. Print.
American Heritage Dictionary of the English Language. Boston: Houghton, 1981. Print.
Aquinas, Thomas. "The Second Part of the Second Part, Treatise on Prudence and Justice, Question 110: "Of the Vices Opposed to Truth, and First of Lying." *St. Thomas Aquinas: The Summa Theologica*. Trans. Fathers of the English Dominican Province. NY: Benziger Bros, 1947. Web. August 5, 2014.
Arditi, Jorge. *A Genealogy of Manners: Transformations of Social Relations in France and England from the Fourteenth to the Eighteenth Century*. Chicago: U of Chicago P, 1998. Print.
Arellano, Ignacio and Marc Vitse, eds. *Modelos de vida en la España del Siglo de Oro*. Madrid: Iberoamericana, 2004. Print.
Aristotle. *Poetics*. Ed. Malcolm Heath. London: Penguin, 1996. Print.
Ariza Canales, Manuel. *Retratos del príncipe cristiano de Erasmo a Quevedo*. Córdoba: U de Córdoba P, 1995. Print.
Armiño, Mauro. Introduction. *El perro del hortelano*. By Lope de Vega. Madrid: Cátedra, 2003. Print.
Armon, Shifra. "The Dancing of an Attitude: Inconstancy as Masculine Virtue in Lope de Vega's *El perro del hortelano*." *Comedia Performance* 10 (2013): 93–118. Print.

———. "(Des)cifrando voluntades: Códigos de la masculinidad en la corte austríaca española." *Sociabilidad y literatura en el Siglo de Oro.* Ed. Mechthild Albert. Biblioteca Áurea Hispánica 84. Madrid: Iberoamericana; Frankfurt: Vervuert, 2013. 203–17. Print.

———. "Gracián Dantisco and the Culture of Secrecy in Hapsburg Spain." *Ingenium: Revista Electrónica de Pensamiento Moderno y Metodología en Historia de las Ideas* 5 (2011): 55–75. Web. August 5, 2014.

———. "The Paper Key: Money as Text in Cervantes's *El celoso extremeño* and José de Camerino's *El pícaro amante.*" *Bulletin of the Cervantes Society of America* 18.1 (1998): 96–114. Print.

———. *Picking Wedlock: Women and the Courtship Novel in Spain.* Lanham, MD: Rowman and Littlefield, 2002. Print.

Arnot, Chris. "Protestant v. Catholic: Which Countries are More Successful?" *The Guardian* October 31, 2011. Web. August 5, 2014.

Artigas, Miguel. *Don Luis de Góngora y Argote.* Madrid: "Revista de Archivos," 1925. Print.

Asch, Ronald. *Nobilities in Transition 1550–1700: Courtiers and Rebels in Britain and Europe.* London: Arnold; NY: Oxford, 2003. Print.

Avalle-Arce, Juan Bautista. *Nuevos deslindes cervantinos.* Barcelona: Ariel, 1975. Print.

Baranda, Nieves. "La literatura del didacticismo." *Criticón* 58 (1993): 25–34. Print.

———. "Los nobles toman cartas en la educación de sus vástagos." *Actas del IV Congreso de la Asociación Internacional Siglo de Oro (AISO).* Ed. M. Cruz García de Enterría and A. Cordón de Mesa. Vol. 1. Alcalá de Henares, Spain: University of Alcalá de Henares, 1998. 215–23. Print.

Bataillon, Marcel. *Erasmo y el erasmismo.* Ed. Francisco Rico. Barcelona: Crítica, 1977.

Bates, Catherine. *The Rhetoric of Courtship in Elizabethan England.* Cambridge, UK: Cambridge UP, 1992. Print.

Becker, Ernst. *Escape from Evil.* NY: Free Press, 1975. Print.

Bennassar, Bartolomé. *La España del Siglo de Oro.* Barcelona: Crítica, 1990. Print.

———. "Patterns of the Inquisitorial Mind as the Basis for a Pedagogy of Fear." *The Spanish Inquisition and the Inquisitorial Mind.* Ed. Ángel Alcalá. Boulder: Social Science Monographs, 1987. 177–84. Print.

Berger, Harry, Jr. "Sprezzatura and the Absence of Grace." Javitch 295–307.

Blanco, Mercedes. "Le Discours sur le Savoir-Vivre dans l'Espagne du Siècle d'Or." *Pour une histoire de savoir-vivre.* Clermont-Ferrand, France: Université Blaise Pascal, 1995. 111–49. Print.

Blanco-González, Bernardo. *Del cortesano al discreto: Examen de una "decadencia."* Madrid: Gredos, 1962. Print.

Borja, Francisco de. *Las obras en verso de Don Francisco de Borja.* Antwerp: Balthasar Moreto, 1654. Print.

Bourdieu, Pierre. *La distinción: Criterio y bases sociales del gusto.* Trans. María del Carmen Ruiz de Elvira. Madrid: Taurus, 1979. Print.

Bouza, Fernando. *Imagen y propaganda: capítulos de historia cultural del reinado de Felipe II*. Madrid: Akal, 1998. Print.
Bowman, Jeffrey. "Infamy and Proof in Medieval Spain." *Fama: The Politics of Talk and Reputation in Medieval Europe*. Ed. Thelma Fenster and Daniel Lord Smail. Ithaca: Cornell UP, 2003. 95–117. Print.
Boyden, J.M. *The Courtier and the King: Ruy Gomez de Silva, Phillip II and the Court of Spain*. Berkeley: U of California P, 1995. Print.
Braudy, Leo. *The Frenzy of Renown*. New York and Oxford: Oxford UP, 1986. Print.
Brinton, Laurel and Elizabeth Traugott. *Lexicalization and Language Change*. Cambridge, UK: Cambridge UP, 2005. Print.
Brown, Jonathan and John Elliott. *A Palace for a King: The* Buen Retiro *and the Court of Philip IV*. New Haven: Yale UP, 1980. Print.
Bryson, Anna. *From Courtesy to Civility: Changing Codes of Conduct in Early Modern England*. Oxford: Clarendon, 1998. Print.
Burke, Peter. *The Fortunes of the Courtier: The European Reception of Castiglione's Cortegiano*. University Park, PA: Pennsylvania State UP, 1995. Print.
Butler, Judith. *Bodies that Matter: On the Discursive Limits of "Sex."* NY: Routledge, 1993. Print.
———. *Gender Trouble: Feminism and the Subversion of Identity*. NY: Routledge, 1990. Print.
Calderón de la Barca, Pedro. *El gran teatro del mundo*. Ed. Eugenio Frutos Cortés. Madrid: Cátedra, 1976. Print.
———. *El príncipe constante*. Ed. Enrica Cancelliere. Madrid: Biblioteca Nueva, 2000. Print.
Camões, Luís. *Os Lusíadas*. Ed. Frank Pierce. Oxford: Clarendon, 1973. Print.
Cárdenas-Rotunno, Anthony J. "Bestialidad y la palabra: El parto perruno en el 'Coloquio de los perros'." *Hispania* 91.2 (2008): 301–9. Print.
Carrasco Martínez, Adolfo. "La construcción problemática del yo nobiliario en el siglo XVII: Una aproximación." *Dramaturgia festiva y cultura nobiliaria en el Siglo de Oro*. Ed. Bernardo J. García and María Luisa Lobato. Madrid: Iberoamericana; Frankfurt: Verveurt, 2007. 21–44. Print.
Cartagena, Alonso de. *Doctrinal de los cavalleros*. Ed. José María Viñas Liste. Santiago de Compostela: U of Santiago de Compostela P, 1995. Print.
Cartagena Calderón, José. *Masculinidad en obras: el drama de la hombría en la España imperial*. Newark, DE: Juan de la Cuesta, 2008. Print.
Carvajal, Mariana de. *Navidades de Madrid y noches entretenidas*. Ed. Catherine Soriano. Madrid: Comunidad de Madrid, 1993. Print.
Carvajal, Miguel de and Luis Hurtado de Toledo. *The Conquest on Trial: Carvajal's Complaint of the Indians in the Court of Death*. Ed. Carlos Jáuregui. University Park, PA: Pennsylvania State UP, 2008. Print.
Cascales, Francisco. *Tablas poéticas*. Ed. Benito Brancaforte. Madrid: Espasa Calpe, 1975. Print.

Castiglione, Baldesar. *The Book of the Courtier*. Trans. Charles Singleton. Ed. Daniel Javitch. NY: Norton, 2002. Print.

———. *El Cortesano*. Trans. Juan Boscán. Ed. Marcelino Menéndez Pelayo. Madrid: CSIC, 1942. Print.

Castro, Américo. "Algunas observaciones acerca del concepto del honor en los siglos XVI y XVII." *Revista de Filología Española* 3 (1916): 1–50; 375–86. Print.

———. *De la edad conflictiva*. Madrid: Taurus, 1961. Print.

———. *El pensamiento de Cervantes*. Barcelona: Crítica, 1987. Print.

———. *La realidad histórica de España*. Mexico City, Mexico: Porrúa, 1966. Print.

Cavallo, JoAnn. "Joking Matters: Politics and Dissimulation in Castiglione's *Book of the Courtier*." *Renaissance Quarterly* 53 (2000): 402–24. Print.

Certeau, Michel de. *The Writing of History*. Trans. Tom Conley. NY: Columbia UP, 1988. Print.

Cervantes Saavedra, Miguel de. *Don Quijote de la Mancha*. Ed. Francisco Rico. Barcelona: Crítica, 1998. Print.

———. *Don Quixote*. Trans. Edith Grossman. NY: Ecco, 2003. Print.

———. *Novelas Ejemplares*. Ed. López J. García. Barcelona: Crítica, 2001. Print.

Chandler, Richard and Kessel Schwartz. *A New History of Spanish Literature*. Baton Rouge: Louisiana State UP, 1974. Print.

Chartier, Roger, ed. *Passions of the Renaissance*. Cambridge: Belknap-Harvard UP, 1989. Print.

Checa, Jorge. "Didactic Prose, History, Politics, Life-Writing, Convent Writing, Crónicas de Indias." Gies 283–90.

Corbett, Theodore. "The Cult of Lipsius: A Leading Source of Early Modern Spanish Statecraft." *Journal of the History of Ideas* 36.1 (1975): 139–52. Print.

Correll, Barbara. *The End of Conduct: Grobianus and the Renaissance Text of the Subject*. Ithaca: Cornell UP, 1996. Print.

Covarrubias, Sebastián de. *Tesoro de la lengua castellana o española*. Ed. Martín de Riquer. Barcelona: Horta, 1943. Print.

Crow, John A., ed. *An Anthology of Spanish Poetry: From the Beginnings to the Present Day, Including Both Spain and Spanish America*. Baton Rouge: Louisiana State UP, 1979. Print.

Cruickshank, Donald. "Literature and the Book Trade in Golden-Age Spain." *Modern Language Review* 73 (1978): 799–824. Print.

Curtius, Ernst Robert. *European Literature and the Latin Middle Ages*. Bollinger Series 36. Princeton: Princeton UP, 1990. Print.

Dante, Alighieri. *Inferno*. Trans. Stanley Lombardo. Indianapolis: Hackett, 2009. Print.

Davetian, Benet. *Civility: A Cultural History*. Toronto: U of Toronto P, 2009. Print.

Davis, Charles. "Baltasar Álamos de Barrientos and the Nature of Spanish Tacitism." *Culture and Society in Habsburg Spain*. Ed. Nigel Griffin. London: Tamesis, 2001. 57–78. Print.

Deacon, Philip. "Early Enlightenment and the Spanish World." *Eighteenth Century Studies* 37 (2003): 129–40. Print.

De Armas, Frederick. "'En dos pechos repartido': Felipe IV y su valido en *Cómo ha de ser el privado.*" *Hispanófila* 140 (2004): 9–21. Print.
De la Feuille, Daniel and Henry Offelen. *Devises et emblèmes anciennes et modernes.* Amsterdam, 1691. Print.
De la Gasca y Espinosa, Juseph Gabriel. *Manual de avisos para el perfecto cortesano.* Madrid, 1681. Print.
Del Río, Ángel. *Historia de la literatura española.* 2 vols. NY: Holt, 1963. Print.
Deyermond, Alan. "Pleberio's Lost Investment: The Worldly Perspective of *Celestina,* Act 21." *Modern Language Notes* 105.2 (1990): 169–79. Print.
Díaz Martínez, Eva María. Introduction. *Discurso de las privanzas.* By Francisco de Quevedo. Pamplona, Spain: EUNSA, 2000. Print.
Díaz-Plaja, Fernando. *Historia de España en sus documentos: Siglo XVII.* Madrid: Cátedra, 1987. Print.
Díaz-Plaja, Guillermo. *A History of Spanish Literature.* Trans. Hugh Hunter. NY: New York UP, 1971. Print.
Diccionario de Autoridades. Madrid: Gredos, 1976. Print.
Díez-Borque, José María. "Bibliotecas y novela en el Siglo de Oro." *Hispanic Review* 75 (2007): 181–203. Print.
Donne, John. *Paradoxes and Problems.* Ed. Helen Peters. Oxford: Clarendon, 1980. Print.
Donnell, Sidney. *Feminizing the Enemy: Imperial Spain, Transvestite Drama, and the Crisis of Masculinity.* Lewisburg, PA: Bucknell UP, 2003. Print.
"Dubai Rape Dispute Points to Wider Islamic Rules." *USA Today* July 25, 2013. Web. August 11, 2014.
Duindam, Jeroen. *Myths of Power: Norbert Elias and the Early Modern European Court.* Amsterdam: Amsterdam UP, 1994. Print.
Dutch, Dorata. *Feminist Discourse in Roman Comedy: Echoes and Voices.* Oxford: Oxford UP, 2008. Print.
Egginton, William. "Gracián and the Emergence of the Modern Subject." *Rhetoric and Politics: Baltasar Gracián and the New World Order.* Ed. Nicholas Spadaccini and Jenaro Talens. Minneapolis: U of Minnesota P, 1997. 151–69. Print.
Egido, Aurora. "Los manuales de escribientes desde el Siglo de Oro (Apuntes para la teoría de la escritura)." *Bulletin Hispanique* 97.1 (1995): 67–94. Print.
Elena y María (Disputa del clérigo y del caballero). Ed. Ramón Menéndez Pidal. Madrid: Sucesores de Hernando, 1914. Print.
Elias, Norbert. *The Civilizing Process.* Trans. Edmund Jephcott. NY: Urizen, 1978. Print.
———. *The Civilizing Process: Sociogenetic and Psychogenetic Investigations.* Ed. Eric Dunning, Johan Goudsblom, et al. Oxford: Blackwell, 2000. Print.
———. *The Court Society.* Oxford: Blackwell, 1983. Print.
———. *Involvement and Detachment.* Ed. Michael Schröter. Oxford: Blackwell, 1987. Print.
———. *Norbert Elias: On Civilization, Power, and Knowledge.* Ed. Stephen Mennell and Johan Goudsblom. Chicago and London: U of Chicago P, 1998. Print.

———. *On the Process of Civilisation*. Ed. Stephen Mennell, Eric Dunning, et al. Dublin: UCD Press, 2012. Print.

———. *Power and Civility*. Trans. Edmund Jephcott. NY: Pantheon, 1982. Print.

Elliott, John H. *The Count-Duke of Olivares: The Statesman in an Age of Decline*. New Haven: Yale UP, 1986.

———. *España y su mundo (1500–1700)*. Trans. Ángel Rivero Rodríguez and Xavier Gil Pujol. Madrid: Taurus, 2007. Print.

———. *Lengua e imperio en la España de Felipe IV*. Salamanca: U of Salamanca P, 1994. Print.

———. "'Máquina insigne': La monarquía hispana en el reinado de Felipe II." Feros and Gelabert 41–60.

Epictetus. *The Discourses as Reported by Arrian: The Manual and Fragments*. Ed. William A. Oldfather. Cambridge: Harvard UP, 1989. Print.

Erasmus, Desiderius. *De la urbanidad en las maneras de los niños*. Trans. Agustín García Calvo. Ed. Julia Varela. Madrid: Ministerio de Educación y Ciencia, 2006. Print.

Fenster, Thelma and Daniel Lord Smail, eds. *Fama: The Politics of Talk and Reputation in Medieval Europe*. Ithaca: Cornell UP, 2003. Print.

Fernández Gómez, Carlos. *Vocabulario completo de Lope de Vega*. Madrid: Real Academia Española, 1971. 3 vols. Print.

Fernández-Luzón, Antonio. "El legado cultural." García Cárcel 511–87.

Fernández-Santamaría, J.A., ed. *La formación de la sociedad y el origen del Estado: ensayos sobre el pensamiento político español en el Siglo de Oro*. Madrid: Centro de Estudios Constitucionales, 1997.

———. *Kingship and Favoritism in the Spain of Philip III, 1598–1621*. Cambridge, UK: Cambridge UP, 2000. Print.

———. *The State, War and Peace: Spanish Political Thought in the Renaissance 1516–1559*. Cambridge, UK: Cambridge UP, 1977. Print.

Feros, Antonio. "'Por Dios, por la patria y el rey': El mundo político en tiempos de Cervantes." Feros and Gelabert 61–96.

Feros, Antonio and Juan Gelabert, eds. *España en tiempos del "Quijote."* Madrid: Taurus, 2004. Print.

Flor, Fernando R. de la. *Pasiones frías: secreto y disimulación en el barroco hispano*. Madrid: Marcial Pons, 2005. Print.

Fortea Pérez, José Ignacio. "Las ciudades, las oligarquías y el gobierno del Reino." Feros and Gelabert 235–78.

Foucault, Michel. *The History of Sexuality Vol. 1*. Trans. Robert Hurley. NY: Pantheon, 1978. Print.

———. *The Order of Things: An Archaeology of the Human Sciences*. NY: Pantheon Books, 1971. Print.

Frye, Northrop. "Specific Continuous Forms: Prose Fiction." *Theory of the Novel: A Historical Approach*. Ed. Michael McKeon. Baltimore: Johns Hopkins UP, 2000. 5–13. Print.

Gallego, André "Santo, latino y ladino, o el modelo de sabio propuesto por Juan Lorenzo Palmireno en las aulas de gramática." Arellano and Vitse 31–48.

García Cárcel, Ricardo, ed. *Historia de España Siglos XVI y XVII: La España de los Austrias*. Madrid: Cátedra, 2003. Print.

García Marín, José María. *Teoría política y gobierno en la monarquía hispánica*. Madrid: Centro de Estudios Políticos y Constitucionales, 1998. Print.

Garza Carvajal, Federico. *Butterflies Will Burn: Prosecuting Sodomites in Early Modern Spain and Mexico*. Austin: U of Texas P, 2003. Print.

Gelabert, Juan. "La restauración de la república." Feros and Gelabert 197–234.

Gerber, Jane S. *The Jews of Spain: A History of the Sephardic Experience*. NY: Free Press, 1992. Print.

Gerli, E. Michael. *Refiguring Authority: Reading, Writing and Rewriting in Cervantes*. Lexington, KY: U of Kentucky P, 1995. Print.

Gibney, Alex and Alison Elwood, screenplay. *Magic Trip: Ken Kesey's Search for a Kool Place*. Magnolia Films, 2011. Documentary.

Gies, David, ed. *Cambridge History of Spanish Literature*. Cambridge, UK: Cambridge UP, 2004. Print.

Goffman, Erving. *The Presentation of Self in Everyday Life*. NY: Overlook Press, 1973. Print.

Goldsmith, Elizabeth. *"Exclusive Conversations": The Art of Interaction in Seventeenth-Century France*. Philadelphia: U of Pennsylvania P, 1988. Print.

Gómez, Jesús. Introduction. *Diálogo de las empresas militares y amorosas*. By Paulo Jovio. Madrid: Polifemo, 2012. Print.

Góngora, Luis de. *Selected Poems. A Bilingual Edition*. Ed. and trans. John Dent-Young. Chicago: U of Chicago P, 2007. Print.

González de Zárate, Jesús María. Introduction. *Emblemas regio-políticos*. By Juan de Solórzano Pereira. Madrid: Tuero, 1987. Print.

Gossy, Mary. *The Untold Story: Women and Theory in Golden Age Texts*. Ann Arbor: U of Michigan P, 1990. Print.

Gracián, Baltasar. *Obras Completas*. Ed. Luis Sánchez Laílla. Madrid: Biblioteca de Literatura Universal-Espasa, 2001. Print.

Gracián Dantisco, Lucas. *Galateo español*. Ed. Margherita Morreale. Madrid: CSIC–Clásicos Hispánicos, 1968. Print.

Greenblatt, Stephen. *Renaissance Self-Fashioning: From More to Shakespeare*. Chicago: U of Chicago P, 1988. Print.

Grenfell, Michael. *Pierre Bourdieu: Agent Provocateur*. London and NY: Continuum, 2004. Print.

Grice-Hutchinson, Marjorie. *The School of Salamanca: Readings in Spanish Monetary Theory, 1544–1605*. Oxford: Clarendon Press, 1952. Print.

Grice-Hutchinson, Marjorie, Laurence Moss, et al., eds. *Economic Thought in Spain: Selected Essays*. Aldershot, UK: Edward Elgar Press, 1993. Print.

Gronow, Jukka. *The Sociology of Taste*. London: Tamesis, 1997. Print.

Guellouz, Suzanne. "Gracián en la Francia del siglo XVII." *Anthropos*, Supplement 37 (1993): 93–104. Print.

Guevara, Antonio. *Relox de príncipes*. Ed. Emilio Blanco. Madrid: ABL; CONFRES, 1994. Print.

———. *Le Réveille-matin des courtisans ou moyens légitimes pour parvenir à la faveur et pour s'y mantenir*. Edition bilingue. Trans. and ed. Nathalie Peyrebonne. Paris: Honoré Champion, 1999. Print.

Guevara, María de. *Warnings to the Kings and Advice on Restoring Spain*. Trans. and ed. Nieves Romero-Díaz. Chicago: U of Chicago P, 2007. Print.

Hamilton, Earl J. *American Treasure and the Price Revolution in Spain, 1501–1650*. NY: Octagon Books, 1970. Print.

Hamilton, Rita, ed. *The Poem of the Cid*. Trans. Janet Perry. NY: Penguin, 1984. Print.

Hazard, Paul. "El héroe según Gracián." Trans. Alfonso Moraleja. *Gracián hoy: La intemporalidad de un clásico*. Ed. Alfonso Moraleja. Cuadernos Gris 1. Madrid: Universidad Autónoma de Madrid, 2002. 50–53. Print.

Heliodorus of Emesa. *Ethiopian Story*. Ed. J.R. Morgan. Trans. Sir Walter Lamb. London: Dent; Rutland, VT: Tuttle, 1997. Print.

Hill, Ruth. *Sceptres and Sciences in the Spains: Four Humanists and the New Philosophy (ca. 1680–1740)*. Liverpool: Liverpool UP, 2000. Print.

Homer. *The Odyssey*. Trans. and ed. Robert Fagles and Bernard Knox. NY: Viking, 1996. Print.

Horace. *Odes*. Trans. Franklin P. Adams. Web. August 8, 2014.

Horozco y Covarrubias, Sebastián. *Emblemas Morales*. Ed. Carmen Bravo-Villasante. Madrid: Fundación Universitaria Española, 1978. Print.

Huizinga, J. *Homo Ludens*. Trans. R.F.C. Hull. London: Routledge, 1949. Print.

Jauralde Pou, Pablo. *Francisco de Quevedo: (1580–1645)*. Madrid: Castalia, 1998. Print.

Javitch, Daniel, ed. *The Book of the Courtier*. By Baldesar Castiglione. Trans. Charles Singleton. NY: Norton, 2002. Print.

Jones, R.O. *Golden Age Poetry and Prose*. London: Ernest Benn, 1971. Print.

Jovio, Paulo. *Diálogo de las empresas militares y amorosas*. Ed. Jesús Gómez. Madrid: Polifemo, 2012. Print.

Kamen, Henry. "The Decline of Spain: A Historical Myth?" *Past and Present* 81 (1978): 24–50. Print.

———. *Spain: 1469–1714: A Society in Conflict*. Harlow, UK: Pearson-Longman, 2005. Print.

Kaufmant, Marie-Eugènie. "*El perro del hortelano* et autres traversées dramatiques: l'imaginaire marin dans la *comedia nueva* à travers la métaphore maritime." *L'Imaginaire des Espace Aquatiques en Espagne et au Portugal*. Ed. François Delpech. Paris: Presse Sorbonne Nouvelle, 2009. 147–68. Print.

Kegan Gardiner, Judith, ed. *Masculinity Studies and Feminist Theory: New Directions*. NY: Columbia UP, 2002. Print.

Kelly, Joan Gadol. "Did Women Have a Renaissance?" *Women, History, and Theory*. Ed. Joan Kelly. London and Chicago: The U of Chicago P, 1984. 19–50. Print.

Kennedy, Kristin. "Fame, Memory, and Literary Legacy: Jorge Manrique and the 'Coplas por la muerte de su padre'." *Negotiating Heritage: Memories of the Middle Ages*. Turnhout, Belgium: Brepols, 2008. 103–16. Print.

Kennedy, William. "'Voice' and 'Address' in Literary Theory." *Oral Tradition* 2.1 (1987): 214–30. Print.
Kimmel, Michael and Michael Messner, eds. *Men's Lives*. Boston: Pearson, 2010. Print.
Krabbenhoft, Kenneth. *Neoestoicismo y género popular*. Salamanca: U of Salamanca P, 2001. Print.
Las Casas, Bartolomé. *Brevísima relación de la destrucción de las Indias*. Ed. Olga Camps. Mexico City, Mexico: Fontamara, 2001. Print.
Lazarillo de Tormes. Ed. Francisco Rico. Barcelona: Planeta, 1976. Print.
Lehfeldt, Elizabeth. "Ideal Men: Masculinity and Decline in Seventeenth-Century Spain." *Renaissance Quarterly* 61 (2008): 463–94. Print.
Lemke, J.L. "Notes on Masculinity and Academic Discourse." City University of New York. Web. August 6, 2014.
Liñán y Verduga, Antonio. *Guía y aviso de forasteros que vienen a la Corte*. Barcelona: Biblioteca Clásica Española, 1885. Print.
Llull, Ramón. *Libro de la Orden de Caballería*. Web. August 6, 2014.
López-Piñero, J.M. *La introducción de la ciencia moderna en España*. Barcelona: Ariel, 1969. Print.
López Poza, Sagrario. "El concepto neostoico del 'sabio' y su difusión en la emblemática: el *Theatro moral* de Vaenius." Arellano and Vitse 147–90.
Mades, Leonard. *The Armor and the Brocade: A Study of* Don Quixote *and the* Courtier. NY: Las Américas, 1968. Print.
Manrique, Jorge. *Coplas a la muerte de su padre*. Ed. Carmen Díaz Castañón. Madrid: Castalia, 1984. Print.
Manuel, Don Juan. *El Conde Lucanor*. Ed. Alfonso Sotelo. Madrid: Cátedra, 1990. Print.
Marañón, Gregorio. Preface. *Lazarillo de Tormes*. Madrid: Austral, 1973. Print.
Maravall, José Antonio. *Poder, honor y élites en el siglo XVII*. Madrid: Siglo Veintiuno, 1979. Print.
———. "La sociedad estamental castellana y la obra de Don Juan Manuel." *Cuadernos Hispanoamericanos* 67 (1966): 751–68. Print.
———. *Teoría del estado en España en el siglo XVII*. Madrid: Centro de Estudios Constitucionales, 1997. Print.
Martinengro, Alessandro. "Gracián ante Quevedo: La ambigua frontera de los Pirineos." *Ínsula* (July–August 2001): 31–3. Print.
Martínez Torrejón, José Miguel. "'Todo palabras sin verdad': Censura renacentista de la cortesía." *Les Traités de savoir-vivre en Espagne et au Portugal du Moyen Âge à nos jours*. Ed. Rosa Duroux. Clermont-Ferrand, France: Association des Publications de la Faculté des Lettres et Sciences Humaines de Clermont-Ferrand, 1995. 93–106. Print.
Mártir Rizo, Juan Pablo. *"Norte de Príncipes" y "Vida de Rómulo."* Ed. Antonio Maravall. Madrid: Instituto de Estudios Políticos, 1945. Print.
McKendrick, Melveena. *El teatro en España (1490–1700)*. Palma de Mallorca: José J. de Olañeta, 1994. Print.

Mendo, Andrés. *Príncipe perfecto y ministros ajustados*. Lyon, 1662. Print.
Menéndez Peláez, Jesús and Ignacio Arrellano Ayuso. *Historia de la literatura española*. Vol. 2. León, Spain: Everest, 1999. Print.
Mennell, Stephen. *Norbert Elias: Civilization and the Human Self-Image*. Oxford: Basil Blackwell, 1989. Print.
Mennell, Stephen. "On the Civilizing of Appetite." *Theory, Culture and Society* 4: 3 (1987): 373-403. Print.
―――― and Johan Goudsblom, Introduction. *Norbert Elias: On Civilization, Power, and Knowledge*. By Norbert Elias. Ed. Stephen Mennell and Johan Goudsblom. Chicago and London: U of Chicago P, 1998. Print.
Miles, Geoffrey. *Shakespeare and the Constant Romans*. Oxford: Clarendon, 1996.
Miller, J. Hillis. *Literature as Conduct: Speech Acts in Henry James*. NY: Fordham UP, 2005. Print.
Mills, Sara. *Michel Foucault*. NY: Routledge, 2003. Print.
Miñana, Rogelio. "Metaficción y monstruosidad en 'El coloquio de los perros' de Cervantes." *Vanderbilt E-Journal of Luso-Hispanic Studies* 2 (2005). Web. August 6, 2014.
Molina, Tirso de. *El burlador de Sevilla*. Ed. Alfredo Rodriguez López-Vázquez. Madrid: Cátedra, 1995. Print.
Montiglio, Silvia. *From Villain to Hero: Odysseus in Ancient Thought*. Ann Arbor: U of Michigan P, 2011. Print.
Morley, S. Griswald and Courtney Bruerton. "How Many *Comedias* Did Lope de Vega Write?" *Hispania* 19.2 (1936): 217–34. Print.
Morreale, Margherita. *Castiglione y Boscán: El ideal cortesano en el Renacimiento español*. 2 vols. Anejos del *Boletín de la Real Academia* 1. Madrid: Real Academia Española, 1959. Print.
Nebrija, Antonio. *Léxico de derecho civil*. Ed. Carlos H. Núñez. Madrid: CSIC; Instituto "Francisco de Vitoria," 1944. Print.
――――. *Vocabulario Español-Latino*. Madrid: Real Academia Española, 1951. Print.
Nelson, Bradley. "Emblematic Representation and Guided Culture in Baroque Spain: Juan de Horozco y Covarrubias." *Culture and State in Spain, 1550–1850*. Ed. Tom Lewis and Francisco J. Sánchez. NY: Garland, 1999. 157–95. Print.
Núñez Cáceres, Javier, R. Foulché-Delbosc, et al., eds. *Concordancias lexicográficas de la obra poética de don Luis de Góngora*. Madison: Hispanic Seminary of Medieval Studies, 1994. Print.
Núñez de Castro, Alonso. *Libro histórico político, sólo Madrid es corte, y el cortesano en Madrid*. Valencia: Librería "Paris-Valencia," 1996. Print.
Obama, Barack. "Text of President Obama's Remarks at Newtown Prayer Vigil." Minnesota Public Radio Online News. December 16, 2012. Web. August 6, 2014.
Oestreich, Gerhard. *Neostoicism and the Early Modern State*. Trans. David McLintock. Cambridge, UK: Cambridge UP, 1982. Print.
Ogborn, Miles. "Knowing the Individual: Michel Foucault and Norbert Elias on *Las Meninas* and the Modern Subject." Pile and Thrift 57–76.

Oxford Latin Dictionary. Oxford: Clarendon Press, 1996. Print.
Panizza, Emilietta. "*El pasagero* de Suárez de Figueroa entre *Il Cortegiano* y *El discreto*." *Criticón* 39 (1987): 5–62. Print.
Paz, Octavio. *Sor Juana Inés de la Cruz, o las trampas de la fe*. Mexico City, Mexico: Fondo de Cultura Económica, 1998. Print.
Peña, Manuel. "La búsqueda de la paz y el 'remedio general.'" García Cárcel 247–98.
Pile, Steve, and N.J. Thrift. *Mapping the Subject: Geographies of Cultural Transformation*. London: Routledge, 1995. Print.
Plato, *Republic*. Trans. Benjamin Jowett. NY: Vintage, 1991. Print.
Posner, David. *The Performance of Nobility in Early Modern European Literature*. Cambridge, UK: Cambridge UP, 1999. Print.
Quevedo y Villegas, Francisco de. *Discurso de las privanzas*. Ed. Eva María Díaz Martínez. Pamplona, Spain: EUNSA, 2000. Print.
———. *Un heráclito cristiano, Canta sola a Lisi y otros poemas*. Ed. Lía Schwartz Lerner and Ignacio Arellano. Barcelona: Crítica–Biblioteca Clásica, 1998. Print.
———. *Obras en prosa*. Ed. Felicidad Buendia. Madrid: Aguilar, 1981. Print.
———. *Poesía original completa*. Ed. José M. Blecua. Barcelona: Planeta, 1990. Print.
———. *Política de Dios, govierno de Christo*. Ed. James O. Crosby. Madrid: Castalia, 1966. Print.
Quintero, María Cristina. *Gendering the Crown in the Spanish Baroque Comedia*. Farnham, UK; Burlington, VT: Ashgate, 2012. Print.
Quondam, Amedeo. "On the Genesis of the Book of the Courtier." Javitch 283–95.
Redondo, Augustín. *La Formation de l'enfant en Espagne aux XVIe et XVIIe siècles: Colloque International, Sorbonne et Collège d'Espagne, 25–27 Septembre 1995*. Paris: Publications de la Sorbonne, 1996. Print.
Revel, Jacques. "The Uses of Civility." Chartier 167–205.
Rico, Francisco, ed. *Lazarillo de Tormes*. Barcelona: Planeta, 1976. Print.
———. *Tiempos del "Quijote."* Barcelona: Acantilado, 2012. Print.
Riley, E.C. "La singularidad de la fama de *Don Quijote*." *Bulletin of the Cervantes Society of América* 22.1 (2002): 27–41. Print.
Rivas Hernández, Ascensión. *De la poética a la teoría de la literatura*. Salamanca: University of Salamanca Press, 2005.
Robbins, Jeremy. *Arts of Perception: The Epistemological Mentality of the Spanish Baroque, 1580–1720*. Abingdon: Routledge, 2007. Print.
———. *The Challenges of Uncertainty: An Introduction to Seventeenth-Century Spanish Literature*. Lanham, MD: Rowman and Littlefield, 1998. Print.
———. "Renaissance and Baroque: Continuity and Transformation in Early Modern Spain." Gies 137–48.
———. "Scepticism and Stoicism in Spain: Antonio López de Vega's *Heráclito y Demócrito de nuestro siglo*." *Culture and Society in Habsburg Spain*. Ed. Nigel Griffin et al. London: Tamesis, 2001. 137–51. Print.

Rodríguez de Almela, Diego. *Valerio de las historias escolásticas.* Madrid: Don Blas Román, 1793. Print.
Rojas, Fernando de. *La Celestina: tragicomedia de Calixto y Melibea.* Ed. F. Lobera, G. Serrés, et al. Barcelona: Crítica, 2000. Print.
Ruiz, Fornells E. *Las concordancias de* El ingenioso hidalgo Don Quijote de la Mancha. Madrid: Ediciones Cultura Hispánica, 1976. Print.
Saavedra Fajardo, Diego. *Empresas políticas.* Ed. Sagrario López Poza. Madrid: Cátedra, 1999. Print.
———. *Idea de un príncipe político christiano: representada en cien empresas.* Valencia: Francisco Ciprés, 1675. Print.
Sacchetti, Maria A. *Cervantes' "Los Trabajos de Persiles y Sigismunda": A Study of Genre.* Woodbridge, Suffolk, UK; Rochester, NY: Tamesis, 2001. Print.
Salas Barbadillo, Alonso Gerónimo de. *El caballero perfecto.* Ed. Pauline Marshall. Boulder: U of Colorado P, 1949. Print.
"A Sample of New Words for 2012." Merriam-Webster Online. August 14, 2012. Web. August 6, 2014.
Sánchez del Barrio. "Diego Rodríguez de Almela: *Valerio de las historias escolásticas.*" Pieza del mes. Biblioteca de Castilla y León. May 2007. Web. August 6, 2014.
Scaglione, Aldo. *Knights at Court: Courtliness, Chivalry and Courtesy from Ottonian Germany to the Italian Renaissance.* Berkeley: U of California P, 1991. Print.
Scott, Joan Wallach. "Gender: A Useful Category of Historical Analysis." *American Historical Review.* 91.5 (1986): 1053–75. Print.
Sedgwick, Eve K. *Epistemology of the Closet.* Berkeley: U of California P, 1990. Print.
Serra Muñoz, Inés. "Apuntes sobre la recepción del *Oráculo Manual y arte de prudencia* en Francia: de la 'sociedad cortesana' a la 'sociedad del espectáculo'." Ínsula 655–6 (2001): 53–5. Print.
Signoret, Simone. *La Nostalgie n'est plus ce qu'elle était.* Paris: Seuil, 1976. Print.
Smith, Adam. *An Inquiry into the Nature and Causes of the Wealth of Nations.* Ed. R.H. Campbell and Andrew S. Skinner. Oxford: Clarendon, 1976. Print.
Smith, Colin, ed. *Poema del Mío Cid.* Madrid: Cátedra, 1972. Print.
Snyder, John. *Prospects of Power: Tragedy, Satire, the Essay and the Theory of Genre.* Lexington, KY: UP of Kentucky, 1991. Print.
Snyder, Jon R. *Dissimulation and the Culture of Secrecy in Early Modern Europe.* Berkeley: U of California P, 2009. Print.
Soll, Jacob. "Amelot de la Houssaye (1634–1706) Annotates Tacitus." *Journal of the History of Ideas* 61.2 (2000): 167–87. Print.
Solórzano Pereira, Juan de. *Emblemata centum regio política.* Madrid: García Morrás, 1653. Print.
Sönser Breen, Margaret and Warren J. Blumenfeld, eds. *Butler Matters: Judith Butler's Impact on Feminist and Queer Studies.* Aldershot, UK: Ashgate, 2005. Print.

Soria, Enrique. "La sociedad de los siglos XVI y XVII." García Cárcel 433–65.
Sotelo, Alfonso, ed. *El Conde Lucanor*. By Don Juan Manuel. Madrid: Cátedra, 1990. Print.
Standaert, Nicolas. "Jesuit Corporate Culture as Shaped by the Chinese." *The Jesuits: Cultures, Sciences and the Arts 1540–1773*. Ed. John O'Malley, Gauvin A. Bailey, et al. Toronto: U of Toronto P, 1999. 352–63. Print.
Stanton, Domna. *The Aristocrat as Art*. NY: Columbia UP, 1980. Print.
Stonequist, Everett. *The Marginal Man: A Study in Personality and Cultural Conflict*. NY: Russell and Russell, 1961. Print.
Stroud, Matthew. *Plot Twists and Critical Turns: Queer Approaches to Early Modern Spanish Theater*. Lewisburg, PA: Bucknell UP, 2007. Print.
Suárez de Figueroa, Cristóbal. *El Pasajero*. Barcelona: Promociones y Publicaciones Universitarias, 1988. Print.
Taylor, Diane. *The Archive and the Repertoire: Performing Cultural Memory in the Americas*. Durham, NC: Duke UP, 2003. Print.
Ticknor, George. *History of Spanish Literature*. Vol. 2. Boston: Houghton, 1863. Print.
Trigo, Abril. "Shifting Paradigms: From Transculturation to Hybridity: A Theoretical Critique." *Unforseeable Americas: Questioning Cultural Hybridity in the Americas*. Ed. Rita De Grandis and Zilà Bernd. Amsterdam, Atlanta: Rodopi, 2000. 85–111. Web. August 6, 2014.
Urbina, Eduardo. "Lecturas del *Quijote*: Segunda Parte. Capítulo XIIII. Donde se prosigue la aventura del Caballero del Bosque." *Don Quijote de la Mancha*. By Miguel de Cervantes. Volumen Complementario. Ed. Francisco Rico. Barcelona: Crítica, 1998. 137–8. Print.
Valdés García, Celsa Carmen. *De la tragicomedia a la comedia burlesca:* El caballero de Olmedo *de Lope de Vega y F. Monteser*. Pamplona: U of Navarra P, 1991. Print.
Van Anrooj, Wim. "España, los Países Bajos y la tradición de los 'Nueve de la Fama'." *España y Holanda: ponencias leídas durante el Quinto Coloquio Hispanoholandés de Historiadores*. Ed. Jan Lechner and Harm den Boer. Amsterdam and Atlanta: Rodopi, 1995. 11–26. Print.
Varela, Julia. Introduction. *De la urbanidad en las maneras de los niños*. By Desiderius Erasmus. Trans. Agustín García Calvo. Madrid: Ministerio de Educación y Ciencia, 2006. Print.
Vega, Juan de and Juan de Silva. *Instrucciones a su hijo, Hernando, comentados por Juan de Silva*. Bouza 219–33.
Vega Carpio, Lope de. *Arte nuevo de hacer comedias*. Ed. Enrique García Santo-Tomás. Madrid: Cátedra, 2006. Print.
———. *El caballero de Olmedo*. Ed. Francisco Rico. Barcelona: Ave Fénix Clásicos, 1998. Print.
———. *El perro del hortelano*. Ed. Mauro Armiño. Madrid: Cátedra, 2003. Print.
Velasco, Sherry M. *The Lieutenant Nun: Transgenderism, Lesbian Desire, and Catalina de Erauso*. Austin: U of Texas P, 2000. Print.

———. *Male Delivery: Reproduction, Effeminacy, and Pregnant Men in Early Modern Spain*. Nashville: Vanderbilt UP, 2006. Print.

———. "Marimachos, Hombrunas, Barbudas: The Masculine Woman in Cervantes." *Cervantes: The Bulletin of the Cervantes Society of America* 20.1 (2000): 69–78. Print.

Vicens Vives, Jaime. "Estructura administrativa estatal en los siglos XVI y XVII." *Clásicos de historia social de España: una selección crítica*. Ed. Jesús Izquierdo Martín and Pablo Sánchez León. Valencia: UNED; Fundación Instituto Historia Social, 2000. 117–52. Print.

Villacañas Berlanga, José Luis. "Infante don Juan Manuel: *Libro de los estados*." *Biblioteca Saavedra Fajardo de Pensamiento Político Hispánico* (2004): 1–6. Web. August 10, 2014.

Von Ehrenkrook, Jason. "Effeminacy in the Shadow of Empire: The Politics of Transgressive Gender in Josephus's *Bellum Judaicum*." *The Jewish Quarterly Review* 101.2 (2011): 145–63. Print.

Weber, Max. *The Protestant Ethic and the Spirit of Capitalism*, London: Routledge, 2001. Print.

Weigman, Robyn. *American Anatomies: Theorizing Race and Gender*. Durham, NC: Duke UP, 1995. Print.

Weinberg, Bernard. *A History of Literary Criticism in the Renaissance*. Chicago: U of Chicago P, 1961. Print.

Weissberger, Barbara. *Isabel Rules: Constructing Queenship; Wielding Power*. Minneapolis: U of Minnesota P, 2003. Print.

Whigham, Frank. *Ambition and Privilege: The Social Trope of Elizabethan Courtesy Theory*. Berkeley: U of California P, 1984. Print.

———. "Interpretation at Court: Courtesy and the Performer-Audience Dialectic." *New Literary History* 14 (1983): 623–39. Print.

Zuckerman, Edward. "They Won't Call Back." *The New York Times Magazine* December 16, 2012: 62. Print.

Index

Accetto, Torquato 92
adaptability
   in Carvajal 15–16
   examples of 98–101, 122
   femininity and 95–6
   in Gracián Dantisco 75
   lexicography of 101–6
adaptados 103
adaptar 101–4
Age of Decline 23–4
agibilia 104–5, 111–17
Agudeza y arte de ingenio (Gracián) 7, 62
Álamos de Barrientos, Baltasar 1–2
Alciati, Andrea 66, 67*fig*
Aleman, Mateo 104
Alfonso X 46
Allen, Sister Prudence 10
Almeida, Onésimo 98
Amelot de la Houssaye, Nicolas-Abraham 18, 63
apaxía 107–9
Arditi, Jorge 31
Aristotle 6–7
Armas, Frederick de 60
Arte nuevo de hacer comedias en este tiempo (Vega) 7, 99–100
Artemis 111–12
artifice 37
Asch, Ronald 40*n*40
Aviso de privados y despertador de cortesanos (Guevara) 27, 36, 57–8
axía 107–9, 111

Bacon, Francis 25
Baltasar Carlos 80–81, 83
Barrionuevo 2n4
Bataillon, Marcel 25
Becerro, Domingo 72
Becker, Ernst 45
Bennassar, Bartolomé 67
Blanco, Mercedes 57–8
Blanco-González, Bernardo 11

blindness 116
Book of the Courtier (Castiglione) 72, 92
Borja, Francisco de 70–71
Boscán, Juan 101
Bourdieu, Pierre 36n31, 37
Bouza, Fernando 100
Boyden, James M. 100
Braudy, Leo 43, 50–51, 63–4
Brevísima relación de la destrucción de las Indias (de las Casas) 24
Brown, Jonathan 9, 33
Bryson, Anna 26
Burke, Peter 66
Butler, Judith 5–6, 7, 10–11, 14

caballero de Olmedo, El (Lope de Vega) 116–17
caballero perfecto, El (Barbadillo) 15, 27, 58–9
Cabriada, Juan de 124
Calderón de la Barca, Pedro 1, 7–8, 11–12, 16, 60, 97
cantar del mío Cid, El 44–5, 50, 121
Cárdenas-Rotunno, Anthony J. 109n23
Carta filosófica (Cabriada) 124
Cartagena Calderón, José 12–13, 14
Carvajal, Mariana de 15, 16
Carvajal, Miguel de 24
"casamiento engañoso, El" (Cervantes) 107–9, 110–11, 116, 122
Casas, Bartolomé de las 24, 33
Cascales, Francisco 6
Castiglione, Baltasar 14, 27, 28, 34, 72, 92, 101
Castrillo, Alonso de 33
Castro, Américo 43
Catholicism 53
Cavallo, JoAnn 92
censorship 26
Certeau, Michel de 29
Cervantes Saavedra, Miguel de 106–9, 111, 115, 122, 123

change, resistance to 95
Charles V 30, 34, 57, 100
Charles VIII 86
Civility: A Cultural History (Davetian) 18
civilizing processes, theory of 17–18, 20, 36, 123, 124
Colonna, Guido 32
"coloquio de las perros, El" (Cervantes) 106–7, 109–11, 115–16, 122
colorido style 51
Columbus, Christopher 85
Comentarios (de Silva) 59–60, 105
Conde Lucanor (Manuel) 46–7, 48
conduct literature
   description of 26–9
   gestures and 6
   prevalence of 4
   role of 21
   social change and 17–19
constancy, Neostoic 96–8, 105
Coplas por la muerte de su padre (Manrique) 48–50
Corbett, Theodore 96
Council of Trent 7
Count-Duke of Olivares, The (Elliott) 23
court
   description of 29–34
   views of 22–4
court secretaries, decisions of 2–4
courtesy, excessive 72–3, 74–5
Covarrubia, Sebastián de 68, 103
criticón, El (Gracián) 8–9, 62–3, 65, 66, 105, 106
cultural accommodation 99

Dante, Alighieri 43–4, 105
Davetian, Benet 18
de Castro, João 98
De civilitate morum puerilium (Erasmus) 26–7, 104
De Constantia (Lipsius) 96
De regimine principum (Colonna) 32
de Silva, Juan 59–60
Del cortesano al discreto (Blanco-González) 11
Della Casa, Giovanni 72
Della dissimulazione onesta (Accetto) 92
Democritus 2n4
detachment 64, 65, 120, 123

Devises et emblèmes anciennes et modernes 119
Deyermond, Alan 52
Diana 111–15
Díaz de Vivar, Rodrigo 44
Diccionario de autoridades 68–9, 70, 102, 103, 110
Díez-Borque, José María 28
dignitas hominis 25
discovery, period of 24–5
Discurso de las privanzas (Quevedo) 68, 71, 77–9, 91, 92, 100
dissimulation
   in Carvajal 15–16
   definitions of 68–9, 71
   in Gracián 71–7
   in Quevedo 77–9
   role of 67, 122
   in Saavedra Fajardo 79–91
   simulation and 66–71
Divine Comedy (Dante) 43, 105
dogs, symbol of 115–16
Don Quixote (Cervantes) 10, 24, 41–3, 57, 115, 122
Donne, John 95
Donnell, Sidney 10, 11

Elena y María 13
Elias, Norbert 17–18, 20, 36, 64, 65, 91, 104, 120, 123, 124
Elliott, John 1n3, 9, 23, 25–6, 33
Emblemata centum regio politica (Solórzano) 39, 40*fig*
emblems 80, 81–3; *see also Idea de un príncipe politico cristiano en cien empresas* (Saavedra Fajardo)
eminence 59–63
empresas 80, 81–3; *see also Idea de un príncipe politico cristiano en cien empresas* (Saavedra Fajardo)
Epictetus 107
Erasmus 26–7, 40n40, 104
estudiante cortesano, El (Palmireno) 104–5
Examen de ingenios para las ciencias (Huarte de San Juan) 10

"Fábula de Píramo y Tisbe" (Góngora) 69, 70
Fama: The Politics of Talk and Reputation in Medieval Europe (Fenster) 43

fame/*fama*
   in Carvajal 15–16
   in *Don Quixote* 41–3
   early modern 50–59
   in *El cantar del mío Cid* 44–5
   Medieval 44–50
   semantics of 43, 57
   signification of 121
fashion 37
Feminizing the Enemy (Donnell) 10, 11
Fenster, Thelma 43
Ferdinand of Portugal, Prince 97
Fernández-Luzón, Antonio 26
Fernández-Santamaría, J.A. 33
Feros, Antonio 37
Feuille, Danielle de la 119
flattery 79
Flor, Fernando R. de la 66
Foucault, Michel 11, 64
Frye, Northrop 28

Galateo, Il (Della Casa) 72
galateo español, El (Gracián Dantisco) 15, 27, 28, 68, 71–7, 91–2, 102, 105, 122
Galen 10
García Cárcel, Ricardo 28
Gasca y Espinosa, Gabriel de la 1–4, 20, 105, 117–19, 122, 123
gender
   deviancy and 13–14
   fluidity of 10–11
   power and 12
   structures of 10
Gender Trouble (Butler) 5–6, 10–11
genre 28–9
gestures 6
Giovio, Paulo 81
Goffman, Erving 37, 99
Gómez de Silva, Ruy 60, 95, 100–101
Góngora, Luis de 7, 69, 70
good deeds 7–8
Gracián, Baltasar 7–9, 14, 16, 18–20, 61–3, 65, 102, 105–6, 117, 122
Gracián Dantisco, Lucas 15, 27, 28, 68, 71–7, 91–2, 102, 122
gran teatro del mundo, El (Calderón de la Barca) 7–8, 16
Granada, Luis de 26n7
Greenblatt, Stephen 65n3, 111

Guevara, Antonio de 14–15, 27, 31, 36, 57–8
Guevara, María de 28n9
Guía de pecadores (Granada) 26n7
Guía y aviso de forasteros que vienen a la corte (Liñan y Verdugo) 27
gunpowder 35
Guzmán, Gaspar de 60
Guzmán de Alfarache (Aleman) 104

Hall, Joseph 97
hands 82
Hapsburg Dynasty 23, 33
Heaven on Earth and Characters of Vertue (Hall) 97
héroe, El (Gracián) 61
heterosexuality 14
Homer 105–6
Homme de cour, L' (Amelot de la Houssaye) 18, 63
homo agens, use of term 6, 7
honnêteté 19
Horozco y Covarrubias, Juan de 80, 81–3
Huarte de San Juan 10
humanists 25, 44

Idea de un príncipe politico cristiano en cien empresas (Saavedra Fajardo) 27, 38, 39*fig*, 68, 71, 79–91, 82*fig*, 83*fig*, 85–91*fig*, 93, 117
identity, good deeds and 7–8
impression management 99
"In Aulicos" (Alciati) 66, 67*fig*
individuality 47
infamia 45, 46
Inferno (Dante) 105
information explosion 24–6
Instrucciones (de Vega) 59
internal pacification 123

Javitch, Daniel 36, 66
Jesuit missionaries 98–9
jokes 92
Jones, R.O. 28

Kagan, Richard 100–101
Kaiserchronik 13
Kamen, Henry 24
Kegan Gardiner, Judith 5, 19–20
Kelly, Joan Gadol 9

Kennedy, Kristin 50
Kennedy, William 70
Kimmel, Michael 10, 121
king's favor, importance of 17; *see also* monarchy; obedience to sovereign
knights 35–6
Knights at Court (Scaglione) 32
Kosofsky Sedgwick, Eve 14
Krabbenhoft, Kenneth 96n2, 115

Labrador-Arroyo, Félix 9
Lacan, Jacques 11
Lazarillo de Tormes 104, 115, 122
Lehfeldt, Elizabeth 11, 20, 121
Lemke, Jay 19
Lesbians in Early Modern Spain (Velasco) 10
letrados 21, 35
Léxico de derecho civil (Nebrija) 103
Libro de contemplación (Llull) 45
Libro de la Orden de Caballeria (Llull) 45
Libro de los estados (Manuel) 47, 48
Libro de oración y meditación (Granada) 26n7
libro del Cortegiano, Il (Castiglione) 27, 28, 34
lies/liars 68, 73–4, 77
Lieutenant Nun, The (Velasco) 10
Liñán y Verdugo, Antonio de 27
lion symbol 84, 85*fig*, 88, 89*fig*
Lipsius, Justus 96
Literature as Conduct (Miller) 15
Llull, Ramón 45, 50
López de Vega, Antonio 2
Louis "The Prudent" XI 86
Louis XIV 63

Machiavelli, Niccolò 32
Male Delivery (Velasco) 10
Manrique, Jorge 48–50, 122
Manual de avisos para el perfecto cortesano (de la Gasca) 1–4, 20, 105, 117–19, 122
Manuel, Don Juan 46–8, 50, 75
Maranón, Gregorio 56
Maravall, Antonio 8, 33
Mariana, Juan de 33
mariner's needle 2, 3*fig*
Marique de Lara, Rodrigo 48–50
Marshall, Pauline 58n31
Martínez, Carrasco 48, 49

Masculinidad en obras (Cartagena Calderón) 12, 14
masculinity
 crisis of 10–14, 121–2
 as social performance 5–10
McKendrick, Melveena 100n6
médico de su honra, El (Calderón de la Barca) 11–12
Memorial de la [...] restauración (Cellorigo) 23
Mendo, Andrés 38
Meninas, Las (Velázquez) 51, 64, 65, 123
Menippean satire 28
Mennell, Stephen 18, 37, 123
Menosprecio de corte y alabanza de aldea (Guevara) 57
Men's Lives (Kimmel and Messner) 121
merchants and non-nobles 21
Messner, Michael 10, 121
Miles, Geoffrey 96
Miller, J. Hillis 15, 16
Miñana, Rogelio 110
monarchy 29–34, 39–40, 78–9, 92, 101
Montano, Arias 33
Monteser, Francisco Antonio de 117
Morreale, Margherita 71n14, 72, 76
Muñoz, Inés Serra 19

Navidades de Madrid y noches entretenidas 15, 16
Nebrija, Antonio 103
Nelson, Bradley 81
Neostoicism 95–8, 105, 107, 115
Neubauer, Hans-Joaquim 57
New Christians 48
New World, discovery of 25–6
nobility 21, 48, 100
"novela del gran soldán, La" (Gracián) 75–7, 92
Novum Organum (Bacon) 25
Nunes, Pedro 98

obedience to sovereign 8, 57–8; *see also* king's favor, importance of; monarchy
octava real 113n25
Odysseus 105–6, 112
Odyssey (Homer) 105–6, 114
Offelen, Henry 119

Olivares, Count-Duke of 80, 97
Oráculo manual (Gracián) 16, 18–19, 61–2

Pacheco, Francisco de 51
painting 9
Palmireno, Juan Lorenzo 104–5, 112
Palomino, Antonio 80
Pasiones frias (Flor) 66
Paul V, Pope 60
perro del hortelano, El (Lope de Vega) 106–7, 111–16, 122
perspectivist painting 81
Philip II 22, 30–32, 33, 100–101
Philip III 22, 60, 78
Philip IV 23, 33–4, 60, 71
Picking Wedlock (Armon) 9
Plato 2
plurality 5–6
Poetics (Aristotle) 6–7
Política de Dios y gobierno de Cristo (Quevedo) 97
político don Fernando el Católico, El (Gracián) 61
positive face 72
Power and Civility (Elias) 18
Poza, López 96–7
principe constante, El (Calderón de la Barca) 97
privados 60, 78–9, 100–101
privanza 38, 60
Protestantism 53
Pyrenees, Peace of 1n3

Quevedo y Villegas, Francisco de 23, 38, 68, 71, 77–9, 91, 92, 97, 100, 107, 122
Quintero, María Cristina 11–12

Rank, Otto 52
Reconquista 44
Reloj de príncipes (Guevara) 14–15, 57
renown 46–7, 50–51
Republic, The (Plato) 2
reputation 46
Revel, Jacques 6
Riaño Gamboa, Diego de 35
Riley, E.C. 42n4
Rivadeneira, Pedro de 32, 54
Rizo, Juan Pablo Mártir 69–70

Robbins, Jeremy 2n4, 24, 26
Rodríguez de Almela, Diego 103
Rojas, Fernando de 51
Rumour, The (Neubauer) 57
Russell, Peter 52

Saavedra Fajardo, Diego 27, 34, 38, 39*fig*, 68, 71, 79–91, 82*fig*, 83*fig*, 85–91*fig*, 93, 117, 122
sacrifice trope 12
Salas Barbadillo, Alonso Gerónimo de 15, 27, 58
Sandoval y Rojas, Francisco Gómez 60
Santa María, Fray Juan de 60
Scaglione, Aldo 32, 36
Scena XIX (Carvajal) 24
Scott, Joan 12
sea-pilots 2, 98, 101, 117, 118–19
self-concealment 67
self-control 67
self-surveillance 18, 91
Seneca, anecdote of baby 74, 102
serpents 87, 88*fig*
Shail, Robert 14
Siete partidas 30, 46
Silva, Juan de 105
Singleton, Charles 101
Sixtus IV, Pope 31
Smith, Adam 104
Smith, Colin 44
Snyder, John 28, 29, 67, 121
sociability 8, 101
social ascent 35–40
sodomy 13
Solórzano, Juan de 39, 40*fig*
Spain, political decline of 1, 11, 12
Spanish Golden Age 22–3
Spínola, Felipe Antonio 117
sprezzatura 101
Stanton, Domna 36
status/social mobility 17–18
Summa Theologica (Thomas Aquinas) 68
sun/sundial 119–20

Teodoro 111–12, 114–15, 116, 122
Tesoro de la lengua (Covarrubia) 68, 103
theater 12–14
Thomas Aquinas 32, 68, 77
Toledo, Luis Hurtado de 24

tragicomedia de Calixto y Melibea, La (Rojas) 51–3
transculturation 22, 39, 73
Tratado de la religión (Rivadeneira) 32, 54
tres mayores prodigios, Los (Calderón) 60
Tristán 112–15, 116, 122, 123
tropelía 106–11, 116

Über den Prozess der Zivilisation (Elias) 18
Ulysses 104–6, 112, 114

Valerio de las historias (Rodríguez de Almela) 103
Vega, Garcilaso de la 28
Vega, Juan de 59
Vega Carpio, Lope de 7, 12, 99–100, 106–7, 111–17, 122, 123

Velasco, Sherry M. 10
Velázquez, Diego 51, 63–4, 65, 123
venality 100
vida de Lazarillo de Tormes y de sus fortunas y adersidades, La 53–7
Villacañas Berlanga, José Luis 47
Vocabulario (Nebrija) 103
von Ehrenkrook, Jason 13–14

Wealth of Nations (Smith) 104
Westphalia, Peace of 1n3
Whigham, Frank 37
Wiegman, Robyn 20
wind rose/compass face 119, 122, 123
women, conduct of 9; *see also* gender
written correspondence 117–19, 123–4